Freshwater Fishing Secrets

Freshwater Fishing Secrets

Complete Angler's Library™
North American Fishing Club
Minneapolis, Minnesota

Freshwater Fishing Secrets

Copyright © 1990, North American Fishing Club

All rights reserved.

Library of Congress Catalog Card Number 90-61559
ISBN 0-914697-30-7

Printed in U.S.A.
10 11 12 13 14 15 16 17 18 19

Contents

Acknowledgments

T wenty years ago it would have been impossible to compile this book because fishing equipment and methods had yet to undergo the revolution they have in the years since. Today, new equipment has been accompanied by new skills, and experts like those featured in this book have taken the science of freshwater fishing into a new age. Some of their techniques are little known. Others are popular only locally, or regionally. A few of the experts employ long-proven methods, but do so with a refinement not shared by those who have come to imitate the same techniques.

I'd like to thank these experts for helping us all become better anglers. Some of the experts are guides, some are tournament anglers and some are just plain dedicated and innovative fishermen. On the water, they are lifelong students. When in company, they become teachers. They are unusual for their willingness to help others learn. To them, there really are no "secrets" to anything they do. But it is a fact they do it better than 95 percent of all anglers.

Special thanks to the staff members of the North American Fishing Club: Editor and Publisher Mark LaBarbera for his leadership and sense of humor (at all the right times), Managing Editor Steve Pennaz for his constant enthusiasm for the sport of fishing, Associate Editor Kurt Beckstrom for his at-the-ready style, Editorial Assistant Amy Mattson for her attention to details so many of us would otherwise miss and Layout Artist Dean Peters for his patience in listening to the preferences of others. Thanks also to Vice President of Product Marketing Mike Vail, Marketing Manager Linda Kalinowski and Marketing Project Coordinator Laura Resnik. And finally, thanks to the 31 contributors to this book who know a good fisherman when they see one.

Jay Michael Strangis
Managing Editor
Complete Angler's Library

Art And Photo Credits

Illustrations in *Freshwater Fishing Secrets* were created by David Rottinghaus. Wildlife artist Virgil Beck created the cover art. The authors provided most of the photos in this book. Additional photos were contributed by Paul DeMarchi, "Uncle" Homer Circle, Soc Clay, our friends at *In-Fisherman* magazine, Bill Vaznis, Jim Vincent and Jack Wollitz. We would also like to thank the experts featured in this book for their assistance with photos and for sharing their fishing "secrets" with NAFC members.

Betty Hartman with a 52-pound, 1-ounce muskie.

Dedication

Like any other sport, fishing has its heroes—remarkable anglers who perform seemingly magical feats when they take to the water. It seems appropriate in a fishing book of this scope to dedicate its pages to a legend.

In her career as a muskie angler and guide, Betty Hartman caught more than 1,500 muskies, including three weighing more than 60 pounds. She landed her largest, a 64-pound, 4-ounce monster, while fishing alone, without net or gaff.

The wife of noted muskie angler Len Hartman, she traveled to all the great muskie waters in North America. In 1986 she was elected to the National Fresh Water Fishing Hall of Fame.

Betty Hartman died late in 1990 following a determined battle with cancer. She was an inspiration to anglers across North America. The NAFC salutes her.

Foreword

W hen I was a kid a "big stick" was the thing my mom grabbed when I got out of line. (She started out with a paddle, but it broke by the time I was five.)

Today, "big stick" is used to describe those anglers who, for some annoying reason or another, consistently seem to catch fish when no one else can. I'm sure you have seen or met at least one big stick during your years on the water. Generally, they show up about an hour after you decide the fish aren't biting and your thoughts begin to center on the hammock you left on shore. They usually anchor within casting distance of your boat and begin plucking fish after fish from beneath your craft. Sometimes, their success seems supernatural.

In this book you'll meet some of the biggest "sticks" in the country. These are the guys who dominate local angling scenes. Some are professional guides. A few fish tournaments regularly. The others are simply darn good fishermen.

Most of them you have not heard of. There's a good reason for that. We wanted to provide NAFC members with a book chock-full of fresh fishing tips, techniques and tactics that are unavailable to average anglers because they haven't been published in any of the national outdoor magazines. Editor Jay Strangis spent months locating the best anglers in the country and convinced them to share their secrets of success with you. Next, he commissioned the best outdoor writers in North America to present these valuable tips in a format that is easy to read and understand.

Strangis also has provided a closing section on catch and release written by fisheries aquaculture specialist John Daily. The future of North American fishing lies not only in the hands of fisheries managers like Daily, but with you, the angler. The catch-and-release ethic is taking hold across the land. Daily provides you with all the information you will need for handling our most prized resource: fish.

In closing, I can say with confidence this book will help you catch more and bigger fish. In fact, these pages contain the information you need to become a big stick yourself, no matter where you fish!

Within these pages you'll meet:
- Trophy bass expert Bob Stonewater (this Florida guide has more than 600 10-pound-plus bass to his credit!)
- Catfish pro Otis "Toad" Smith, long recognized as one of the best catmen in the country. His bobbering techniques will revolutionize catfishing.
- Wisconsin walleye guide Greg Bohn who has unraveled the secret for catching walleyes in weeds. He covers spring, summer and fall tactics!
- Emil Dean, an extremely successful Great Lakes area steelhead guide who does things a bit differently than other anglers.
- Legendary muskie hunter Len Hartman, whose deep-water techniques have led him to more 50-pound-plus muskies than any other man alive.
- South Carolina striper expert Dale Wilson. Dale has found the best bait for fooling massive rockfish. You'll be amazed how he does it.
- Montana trout guide Tim Tollett, who shares his deadly technique for drifting nymphs. Tim has been known to take fish from runs *after* other anglers have worked them thoroughly!
- Ron Kobes, a Minnesotan who baffles other fishermen by catching large northern pike from heavily fished waters.
And a whole lot more.

This book puts you on the water with these men. It gives you an opportunity to learn their secrets of success. One thing this book doesn't give you is a list of "magic" lures. They don't exist.

Will this book help you become a big stick? It sure is a step in the right direction!

Steve Pennaz
Executive Director
North American Fishing Club

Largemouth And
Smallmouth Bass

1

Shiner Magic

by Larry Larsen

ob Stonewater catches trophy largemouth bass. Lots of them. The "Shiner Man" from Florida has used large natural bait and his ability to "read" the water to account for more than 600 10-pound-plus bass. But more importantly, he is willing to share his deadly techniques so that you, too, can start catching bass most anglers only dream about.

"Fishing for big bass with shiners is just like pursuing them with artificials; you just learn to identify those areas with the highest potential for holding a trophy bass, and you fish them," said Stonewater, who guides on the famous St. Johns River. "If you're fishing a river, you have to realize what the current does, where it hits, where the drop-offs are formed and how the structure may be piled up on the bottom. In a lake, you need to be able to determine how the bottom slopes and whether any structure exists on the drop-offs."

Stonewater's clients are usually looking for trophy largemouths, so the guide is just not content with bass of lesser proportions. As a result, he uses the largest natural bait he can find: golden shiners. He has used shiners as large as 14 to 16 inches in length. Bigger baits catch bigger bass, he contends, and quickly offers proof. On one week's tally of 25 bass, only two weighed less than 6 pounds. Oversized shiners were responsible for such a catch.

"The giants usually want baitfish because they're a natural forage that they eat year-round," said Stonewater. "Of the more than

Florida largemouth expert Bob Stonewater drops lively golden shiners in the right places to catch trophy bass. He takes advantage of wind and current to move his bait to the bass.

200 10-pound-plus fish that I've taken personally (the rest were taken by his clients), fewer than two dozen were caught on artificial lures. Big shiners give off the slow vibrations that drive trophy bass wild."

The Proper Tackle Is Important

Stonewater has several suggestions for shiner-fishing equipment. Heavy, 7-foot rods with plenty of hooksetting backbone and conventional levelwind casting reels are normally chosen for this endeavor. Using lighter gear will handicap an angler seeking big bass. The giants have a knack for breaking the weakest link or not getting hooked in the first place.

Stonewater spools on 20- to 40-pound test premium monofilament line depending on the amount and type of cover he is fishing. Terminal tackle includes a strong 5/0 hook tied directly to the line. Variations include a weedless hook for dense cover and a pair of split shot or small rubber-core sinkers as an additive when weight is needed to work the shiner deeper. A cork, bobber or float is used when it is necessary to control or follow the path of

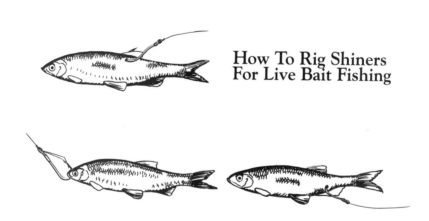

How To Rig Shiners For Live Bait Fishing

Hook a live golden shiner under the dorsal fin (top) with a 5/0 hook for still fishing. When drifting, or in current, hook the baitfish through the lips or tail. Use a hook with a weedguard to help ease the minnow through weeds or brush. Use of a float, or bobber, is optional.

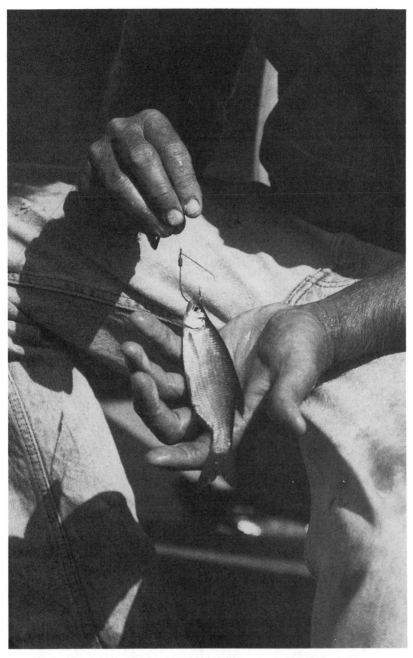

Golden shiners may reach more than 1 foot in length. They can be trapped with cast nets, caught angling or purchased from bait dealers. They remain very active when hooked and are a native forage in many waters that hold big largemouths.

the shiner. Otherwise the baitfish is allowed to swim on a free line.

Shiners can be hooked a variety of ways depending on the type of bait control needed. Hooking them under the dorsal fin allows the baitfish maximum freedom of movement but, correspondingly, may make it difficult for you to control it. Hooking a shiner through the lips is a practical way for trolled or drifted baits, or those placed in specific locations in current where the minnow might drown. Hooking the shiner just above the anal fin allows maximum directional control when "running" shiners under heavy floating cover, such as water hyacinths or water cabbage.

Where To Find Trophy Bass

Most flowages offer numerous "holes" carved out by the currents or created by small sinkholes. Bass fishing success in these depressions can be significant. An obvious surface key to locating structure in rivers is the bends. Contrary to some beliefs, creek and stream depths vary greatly, depending on where you are looking. Outer bends offer the most current and are generally the deepest part of a waterway.

On slow-moving tributaries, the outside bends are usually where big bass live. The successful shiner fisherman must pick those spots with the best big-bass potential. In stained waters, the areas should have at least four or five feet of water present with some form of cover, according to Stonewater. A deep creek flowing into or out of an even deeper channel is ideal. Even a four-foot-deep outlet with flowage only during high water periods can hold a big fish if the cover is sufficient.

"People won't go into places that are only 10 feet wide," Stonewater explained. "Lunker bass will, though, because it's the depth of water and amount of current that's most important, not the width of the creek. You'll catch them on natural bait, too.

"Big bass search for such spots to lay out of the current and feed," he continued. "Water no wider than 15 feet or so can be eight feet deep and offer a sharp, sloping shoreline that big bass like."

Stonewater guided me to one such place on a recent trip. The ditch was actually a main river fork that only flowed during relatively high waters. The small channel is actually dry in some places during normal water levels. The guide was right about there being big bass present that day. We caught four bass from 6 to 8$\frac{1}{2}$

Trophy largemouth bass prefer to ambush, rather than chase, their quarry. Placing live shiners within a bass' reach is Bob Stonewater's specialty.

pounds by drifting huge shiners along the bank.

Stonewater was familiar with that spot, but I've seen him ana-lyze other spots with which he had no previous experience and draw the correct conclusion regarding their harboring big bass. On another abbreviated fishing trip using shiners one year earlier, we had two largemouths of bragging size. Together, they weighed more than 17 pounds and came from similar locations, miles apart!

Patience comes into play when waiting on a giant bass to feed. It may eat a mouthful and not feed for another whole day. Large bass feed primarily on big items such as golden shiners when an opportunity presents itself. Since it is difficult to predict when the fish will feed, a successful angler may have to work a prime spot four or five times during the day. Sooner or later, the large predator will probably move to her feeding grounds.

Repeated casts with lively shiners are often necessary to entice a large bass to strike. If the depth, current and cover are right, there will be a big bass feeding there at some time.

"My dad fishes holes where he'll sometimes make 40 or 50 casts," says Stonewater. "Many times he'll catch an 8-, 9- or 10-pound bass on the last cast! Knowing what cover has the potential to hold the big feeding bass is the key."

Throughout the day, Stonewater will verify depths with his 7-foot rods by poking downward through stained water to reach the bottom. If the tip touches just before the reel is submerged, the affable 45-year-old will call that "reel deep." And that is potentially deep enough for the lunker bass he's after.

Along The Shoreline

In smaller or shallower waters, brush and fallen trees often provide the only shoreline cover available. The food base in the tiny waterways is primarily small forage fish and crustaceans. Big bass in these smaller waters are very aware of their environment and of their vulnerability to outside predation, so stealth is of paramount importance. Keeping noise to an absolute minimum, even when shiner fishing, is incredibly important.

Before casting that first shiner, determine the area from which you want to cast and identify the obstructions you will have to cast around or under to penetrate the big-bass hideout. A particularly good big-bass area is any point formed by the intersection of two tributaries. Currents create well-defined points where the greatest drops occur. Fish the shiner along the heaviest cover on the point before moving to shallower water. Stonewater suggests you fish such areas slowly and thoroughly for best results.

Aquatic plants are also prime cover for big bass. If the bank has a quick drop with overhanging weeds, a large fish can chase the forage fish up underneath the weed canopy and corner them. Fishing such areas effectively may require use of shiners "submarined" under the surface-bound vegetation.

Giant bass will normally wait in such areas for a forage fish to poke its nose under the darkened environment. Smaller bass actively feed several times a day, but as they grow older and bigger, they won't expend a lot of energy foraging.

Big bass, snug in their habitat, are lazy. Trophy largemouths in

The places Stonewater fishes don't have to be big waters. He likes to focus on small, deep pieces of river or canal and work them thoroughly.

rivers are no different. They realize that it's difficult to catch forage fish in open water.

Monster largemouths will move a little to feed on an enticing shiner, but not far. They prefer a feeding area with some current that will wash forage to them, according to Stonewater. Big bass want to be able to trap their food. An ideal feeding area would be a sand bank two feet deep that drops to 10 and then gets shallow again. Largemouths can lie in the deeper trough and move onto the feeding grounds to pin their prey against the bank.

When Stonewater has discovered such a productive big-bass spot, his experience shows that only three or four strikes are possible before the action slows. As a result, after the initial flurry, he quickly moves to a similar area that may offer the same size fish. While he may come back and fish the first area later, he believes his time will be spent more wisely by moving to a new flurry of activity. His strikes per hour increase that way and his clients have a better chance of catching fish.

To catch huge bass, Stonewater may rely on several shiner methods depending on the water conditions. In heavy currents, he'll drift shiners next to shore as his boat is swept downstream. In moderate currents, he'll anchor and allow the wind or current to drift the shiner into bass-laden pockets.

When he has a concentration of nice-sized largemouths located on waters with no current, Stonewater will anchor and work the school. Boat positioning and bait presentation are vital to getting continued action from a school of largemouths. Both ends of the boat are securely anchored, and he'll usually set out three or four baits if a second person is along to assist in monitoring the rigs.

This method is particularly useful over submerged hydrilla in open water or under floating vegetation such as hyacinths. The southern coastal states all have the latter, and hydrilla grows as far north as Illinois. Hydrilla, coontail moss and milfoil all may grow up from the bottom and not reach the surface. An ideal spot will have one of the weed clumps about six feet off the bottom in depths of 10 or 11 feet.

During the summer and fall, this anchor-and-cast method is one of Stonewater's favorites. Fish are quite active then, and live bait can attract and hold a concentration.

If wind and current conditions permit, Stonewater uses the drift method. The wind or current moves the boat along the shoreline, and the guide and his clients drift shiners through the deeper bends. Stonewater will usually set out three shiner rigs and drift through an area, pulling the bait into the prospective bass habitat.

This method is especially successful on days when fish are scattered on shoreline grass beds.

Where a good current exists, such as in a river, Stonewater will anchor his boat and let the shiner drift into bends. Springs, winds and tides can also generate water movement, and this method may be the most productive under these conditions. His boat is usually anchored up-current from the area to be fished. Anchors at each end will position the craft so that each angler can cast his bait upstream of the hotspot. The shiners are then positioned to drift into the productive area.

Seasonal Choices

To believe that large bass can only be caught during the spring is a mistake, according to this bass specialist. Using the giant baitfish fare has resulted in trophy catches year-round. Stonewater's

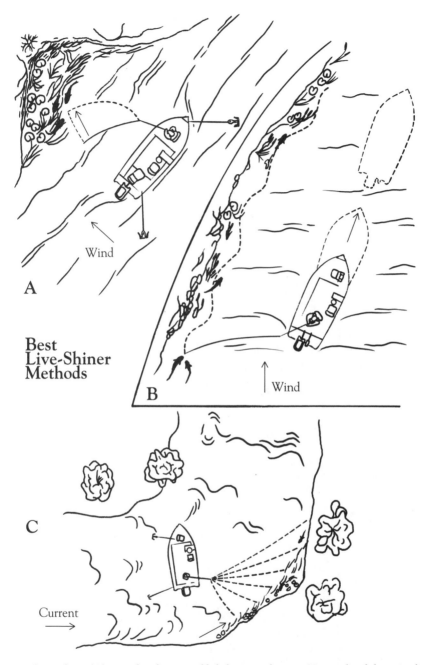

Best Live-Shiner Methods

A

B

C

Wind

Wind

Current

Anchor and cast (A) to work a shiner into likely largemouth cover. Use wind and the natural tendency of the shiner to seek cover to move the bait to the fish. Drift downwind (B), using a trolling motor to control speed, while working the shiner along likely largemouth hideaways, or anchor along riverbends (C) and work the shiner along deep outer banks, paying special attention to submerged cover.

Shiner Magic

"Bigger baits catch bigger bass," is the credo of Bob Stonewater, who, in one week, once caught 23 bass weighing more than 6 pounds each.

Complete Angler's Library

largemouth catches actually increase in the summer and fall, and the winter months also yield numerous trophy-class bass.

During the spring, he still catches plenty of big bass, but he is adamant about not fishing for bedding bass. Others at that time will be feeding, since not all large females spawn at the same time. In fact, big bass are often more concentrated in deeper water where they are unlikely to be harassed by the hoards of anglers who are out after a spawner in the spring. Such heavy angling activities and boat traffic can hamper productive trips.

Stonewater believes firmly in leaving spring's shallow spawners alone and practices catch and release on all others year-round. In fact, he allows his parties to keep only one trophy if they would like one for the wall. The majority of big bass caught and quickly released each month by his clientele are taken between 10 a.m. and 3 p.m., according to Stonewater's log. It reveals that fewer than one in 25 10-pound-plus bass is caught before 8 a.m.

So you see, shiners will take fish all year-round, not just during the spring when the majority of anglers are out. This year, avoid the crowds and enjoy trophy bass action every month of the year.

2

River Bass On Top

================== by Rich Zaleski ==================

"Topwaters aren't my specialty per se," said Terry Baksay, keeping an eye on his plug drifting along the shoreline. When it reached an eddy created by a partially submerged log protruding from the riverbank, he brought it to life with a gentle twitch of the rodtip. "But when you find aggressive, object-oriented largemouths in shallow water, surface fishing can produce more and bigger fish." The words had hardly left Baksay's lips when his lure suddenly disappeared into a frothy boil. "Aggressive, shallow-water bass," he grunted as he set the hook, "is what summertime river fishing is all about."

Baksay, a sporting goods store manager from Easton, Connecticut, is a member of bass fishing's equivalent of Hollywood's "Brat Pack", a group of young, talented and confident anglers reaching into the bass fishing limelight and staking their claims on fishing stardom in the '90s. He doesn't hesitate to cast into the face of conventional angling wisdom by relying on tactics like topwater fishing for river largemouths.

Conventional wisdom holds that the largemouth bass is a fish of still waters. But that belief has come up for review in recent years as anglers across the country have found exceptional largemouth fishing in flowing rivers from the St. Johns in Florida to New York's Hudson and the Sacramento River of California. They're finding that largemouth bass inhabit rivers and moving water of all descriptions, including the upper reaches of impound-

Terry Baksay drifts topwaters to favored largemouth haunts with tremendous success. The young tournament angler offers simple, but deadly, tips for catching largemouths in current.

River Bass On Top

ment tributaries. They're learning that largemouths in a riverine environment are rarely as severely turned off by unfavorable weather conditions as those in still water. And many are discovering an extraordinary connection between moving-water largemouths and topwater fishing.

"On big rivers," Baksay told me, "fishermen have always looked to the quiet backwaters for largemouth bass. That holds up in the spring and sometimes in the late fall. If there's real heavy weed growth in the back bays, some largemouths will use them all summer long. But in most river systems, plenty of largemouths will be out in the river during the summer and early fall."

Once you accept the idea that largemouths can and do thrive in current, tying on a surface lure is pretty much a common-sense strategy. Survival in the current requires more energy expenditure than life in still water. Since energy output requires fuel, it follows that river largemouths must feed more frequently than still water bass. To do so, they must feed more aggressively, a trait that should point the river bass angler toward shallow water, where most of the food is found.

Water Speed, Cover Are Keys To Finding Bass In Rivers

Consistent catches are a matter of concentrating your efforts on the right spots in the right areas. It's easy to read water on a small stream where differences in flow are visually evident among pools, riffles and runs. A big river has the same conditions, but on a bigger scale. The deeper and wider any particular stretch is, the slower the flow through that area, and the greater the chances of finding largemouths. Points or cuts in the bank, along with bars, wing dams and other sizable bank protrusions, alter the flow and further add to the attractiveness of an area. Within those areas, specific objects that break the current will determine the actual position of the bass.

Drift And Twitch Triggers Strikes

Baksay finds river largemouths easy to locate and easy to catch because they typically use areas of reduced flow and hold in eddies and slack water pockets created by objects or cover. They let the current bring their meals to them, rather than hunting for food. In moving water a fish only gets one look at a meal before it passes downstream, so it soon learns to strike quickly. It's a perfect appli-

Complete Angler's Library

Finding Largemouth In Rivers

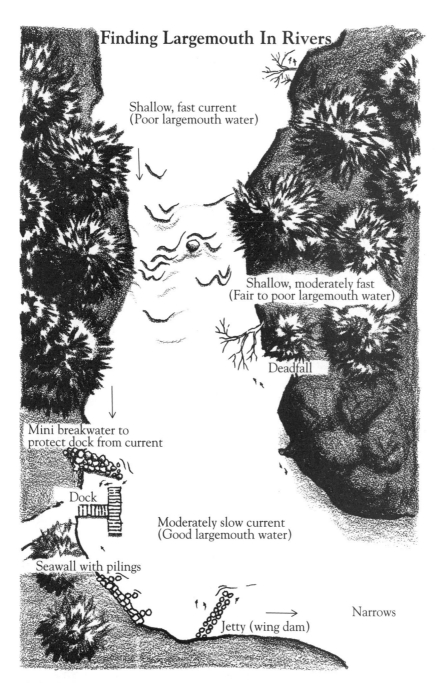

Shallow, fast current
(Poor largemouth water)

Shallow, moderately fast
(Fair to poor largemouth water)

Deadfall

Mini breakwater to
protect dock from current

Dock

Moderately slow current
(Good largemouth water)

Seawall with pilings

Jetty (wing dam)

Narrows

The best largemouth areas in rivers have moderate current and scattered cover. Any difference in the normal riverbank can attract bass, including docks, fallen trees, wing dams and small points.

cation for topwater tactics that will fool aggressive fish.

"The idea is to place your lure upstream of the object that's causing the current to shift directions," Baksay explained, "and let it wash the plug right to the fish's holding spot, just like natural food. I usually let it float free until just before it makes contact with the cover, then give it a twitch or a little movement of some kind. That's invariably when the fish will come out for it."

A surface plug drifting along aimlessly is easy for a bass to mistake for an injured or stunned baitfish caught up in the current and unable to flee. A rod twitch to create the appearance of panic as it's swept into an area where the flow changes enhances the "believability" of the presentation. A bass has little choice but to react to it as something with a high probability of being an easy meal.

Baksay takes this line of reasoning one step further. "When I'm fishing shoreline objects," he said, "I like the plug to bump right against the shoreline as it's being washed downstream toward the log, bush, piling or whatever I'm fishing. I think that the natural tendency is for creatures caught up in the current to struggle toward the shoreline in an attempt to get out of it. That's what I try to make my plug look like it's doing."

The object of the game is to let the natural flow of the current direct your lure to some type of object or cover. Once you fool that fish into grabbing your offering, you have to get it out of and away from the cover in a hurry, and the first few feet of the battle are critical. It follows that this is an application best filled by fairly heavy tackle. Because of the nature of the presentation, though, thick line can interfere with the lure's ability to look natural.

"In some ways," according to Baksay, "it's like fly fishing, because you have to be aware of the current drag on your line. Too much line lying out in the heavier current, away from the bank, will pull the lure away from shore and cause it to speed up. It'll blow by the object the fish is holding behind, instead of lingering there or bumping against it. The heavier the line, the more likely that is to happen.

"But you need fairly heavy line for the kinds of cover that largemouths use in heavy current—typically something along the lines of 14- or 17-pound test," said Baksay. "My solution is short casts and a long rod. Limiting my casts to 25 or 30 feet and holding a 7-foot rod pretty high keeps most of the line off the water as the

Drifting Topwaters For Largemouth Bass

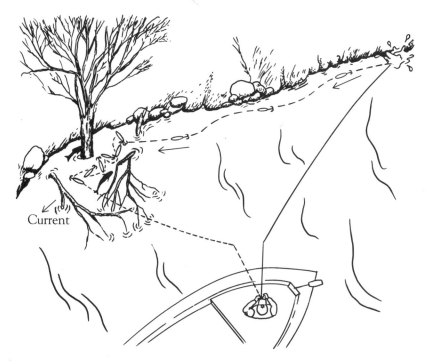

Cast a topwater plug upstream of likely largemouth cover. Keep the line out of the current as much as possible to avoid dragging the lure away from the bank. Twitch the lure slightly just before it bumps cover.

lure floats downstream at the speed of the current."

Lure placement and boat position are important aspects of Baksay's short-cast/high-rod technique. The nose of his boat is always pointed upstream, and he tries to get in ideal position before making a cast toward an object he suspects might hold a bass. "A lot of fishermen hurry too much, and as soon as they finish fishing one log they make a cast upstream past the next object. Nine times out of 10, the fish will hit on the first cast if the lure approaches it properly. But if it blows past a couple of times, or worse yet, if you get it hung on the cover and have to go in and unsnag it, the fish will be gone or totally spooked by the time you get in position to present the bait properly."

Instead of casting anxiously as soon as you spot a potential lie,

Baksay suggests investing the time to position yourself in the ideal spot and making the first cast count. You'll make fewer casts during the day, but more of them will properly expose your lure to bass that are ready to bite.

Baksay keeps his boat 15 to 20 feet off the cover or the bank and casts to the shoreline, 10 to 15 feet upstream of the target, from a position almost parallel with, but just slightly upstream of the eddy formed by the object. Keeping the rodtip high, he takes up excess line as the lure floats into position. When it reaches the high-percentage spot where he expects the strike to occur, the plug is slightly downstream of his rodtip. Any twitch of the rod now will cause the lure to hesitate in that spot and usually to turn. And it will usually draw a reaction from the bass. When he sets the hook, he's already pulling the fish away from the cover, not into it, through it or across it, as would be the case if his boat were downstream of the cover.

Unless he has some specific reason to suspect that a particular piece of cover is holding a fish, Baksay won't often make more than two or three casts before moving his boat into position to work the next object upstream. "Of course," he cautioned, "a lot of the objects you're fishing are pretty complex, like fallen trees, multiple pilings and so forth. You have to treat each limb, rock or whatever as a separate break, and you may only move the boat a few feet to get the right drift for the next target. But in a good bass river, there are plenty of targets, so don't waste too much time on one tree or rock pile if it doesn't produce something quickly.

"If you do catch a fish though," Baksay continued, "back off long enough to correct your position, and fish the break again. River bass are generally loners, but they often travel in small packs and larger schools."

Baksay points out that the rod you choose for this style of fishing is important, because it has several specific tasks to perform. You have to be able to make short, accurate casts; you'll need a stick with plenty of guts to pressure fish out of the tangles as soon as you set the hook; and it's imperative that the rod be long enough to keep most of the line off the water as the plug drifts.

Since the fishing is almost entirely visual, sensitivity isn't much of a consideration. Neither is the way the rod's action works your favorite surface lure. You're not so much retrieving the lure as picking up slack as it floats downstream; twitching it a few times

Casting to outside bends of the river works best for Baksay because the lure is carried close to the bank. He stations his boat about 20 feet from his casting target.

at most on each cast. Baksay chooses All Star's WR1, a graphite rod, not for its sensitivity, but for its ability to cast a wide variety of lure weights well.

"A long, fiberglass cranking stick would be just as good," Baksay explains, "except they don't handle as wide a range of lure weights." The importance of that factor can best be realized when we consider Baksay's standard arsenal of topwaters for river fishing. The Zara Spook he often chooses weighs almost $^3/_4$ ounce—the No. 11 Rapala he prefers in clear water, less than $^1/_4$ ounce.

Between those extremes are a non-traditional item called Slug-Go, a propeller bait similar to Heddon's Torpedo, and a larger minnow-type plug, a No. 11 Mag Rapala. The first is a soft plastic lure that's fished much like a stickbait. Baksay likes it for its erratic action, the way the soft body flows with the current, and especially for the fact that it's much more snag-resistant than treble-hooked hard baits.

The propeller bait comes into play in situations where the layout allows Baksay to let the plug drift behind pilings or tree limbs. "If I can get the plug into a tight spot like that and stop it with the line," says Baksay, "the current will work the propeller while the

River Bass On Top

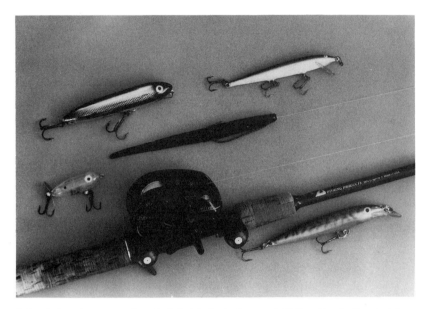

Baksay's favorite topwater lures include (clockwise from top left) Zara Spook, Rapala, Magnum Rapala, Heddon Torpedo and Slug-Go (center).

plug is just bobbing around, and that seems to really trigger bass. Getting them back out the opening the plug floated through can be a problem, but I'd rather deal with that than not get the fish on at all."

The slight diving action of the Rapala is often the most effective trigger. Let it float along lifelessly; then just as it reaches the eddy, it turns and dips beneath the surface a few inches and floats back up like a crippled baitfish struggling to escape the predator it has to know is lying in wait nearby. The small Rapala is superb in clear water, but it may not present a substantial enough target or create enough of a disturbance to be noticed in roiled water. That's where the heavier Magnum version comes into play.

While he utilizes variations in lure action to trigger fish, Baksay doesn't put too much stock in some other commonly held beliefs about what causes fish to strike a lure. He thinks, for instance, that at least in this application, lure color is only minimally important.

"The fish usually only gets a glimpse of the bait anyway, and the distortion caused by moving water helps camouflage it," Baksay said. "I experiment with a variety of colors, but mostly I like

Complete Angler's Library

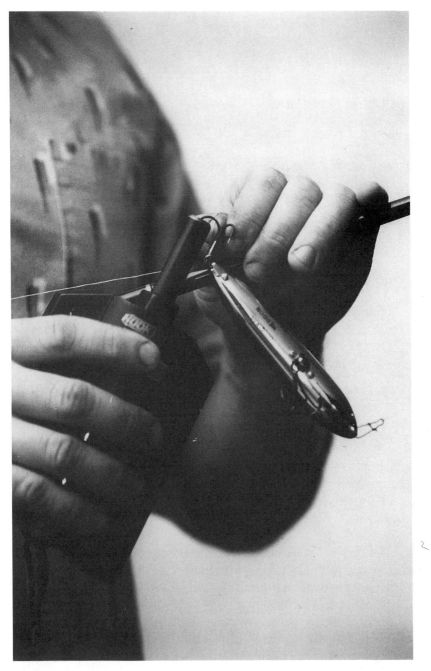

Sharp hooks catch more bass, especially in the case of topwaters, where fish may nip at the lure rather than inhale it. A portable, commercial hook sharpener keeps hooks in top shape.

Fishing with topwaters in current shares much in common with fly fishing. The line, the lure and the angler share a delicate balance. When they all come together—watch out, bass!

anything that looks like a minnow or shad, your basic white or chrome belly and a darker back. My next choices would be all black for very dark or very bright sky conditions, and something chartreuse for muddy water. You need that chartreuse in dingy water, and a lot of the best largemouth rivers are pretty muddy.

"Once you've learned to recognize the probable strike zone, let the current propel the plug and use the rod to guide it into position. Getting the fish to come up and take a shot at a lure isn't usually too much of a problem if you're anywhere near right with the color," according to Baksay. Getting a hook in them can be a problem though, at least until you have the moves down. Always let the fish take the plug underwater before you set the hook. With the lure that close to the tip of that long, stiff rod, missed hooksets can be dangerous. You won't miss many if you use super-sharp hooks and let the fish turn back toward its hideout with the plug in its mouth. There's a fine line, though, between setting too early and waiting so long that the fish drags your plug back into the cover."

To insure a hookup, Baksay replaces any plated hooks or beak-style trebles that come on the plugs from the factory, with short-shank, light-wire, "perfect-bend" bronze trebles. He attaches the new trebles with split rings, even if the factory hooks weren't so installed. And he sharpens each point of each treble before using the plug and touches them up with an electric hook honer at regular intervals during the day. They must be sharp enough to catch on contact, so that the plug "sticks" in the fish's mouth before you set.

Regardless of where you live, there's probably a sizable river not too far away. Odds are, it harbors largemouth bass. During the summer it's a good bet that those bass are ready and willing to take a surface bait. You may have to ignore conventional angling wisdom to get up the confidence to give it a try, but the fun and excitement are more than worth the time it takes to find out.

3

Mercurochrome And Sore-Mouthed Bass

by Chris Altman

P rofessional bass anglers are a creative bunch. All have worked long and hard to master the basics of the sport, and many of them have developed their own unique, often ingenious, techniques to catch a habitually elusive quarry under a variety of conditions.

Tom Mann, Jr., a full-time tournament angler from Buford, Georgia, is one such angler. A 15-year stint as a largemouth and spotted bass guide on the crystal clear waters of Georgia's Lake Lanier gave him ample time to perfect his craft and also led to the development of several innovative techniques. One of his best, a technique he calls "worm jerking," was born out of frustration.

"Each spring, I would see hundreds of giant bass cruising the shallows, but they would ignore every bait I tossed at them. It was enough to drive me nuts," the 36-year-old Georgian relates.

"Several years ago, I began swimming an unweighted plastic worm through the shallows. Even though the fish didn't jump all over the lure, my success with the worm was much better than with crankbaits, spinnerbaits or anything else I tried. The technique seemed promising, so I spent a lot of time perfecting it."

After the gaudy pink, bubble-gum-colored worms became the rage at Santee-Cooper and spread through the South like surface ripples from a cast plug, Mann began toying with offbeat colors. "I called Ed Chambers at Zoom Bait Company and asked him to put together some bright-colored worms for me. One of the colors that we eventually came up with was a bright, fluorescent orange,

Complete Angler's Library

Tom Mann, Jr. (no relation to the well-known baitmaker) finds unweighted, gaudy-colored plastic worms one of the best ways to catch bass in shallow water.

Mercurochrome And Sore-Mouthed Bass   35

which looks a lot like Mercurochrome. It's the brightest, oddest-looking worm you'll ever see, and the bass just cannot watch it pass them by!"

Mann has honed his "worm jerking" technique to an art, and it has played a vital role in his angling success ever since. He attributes several tournament victories on his home waters of Lake Lanier to the technique, as well as scores of in-the-money finishes. And in the 1989 B.A.S.S. Masters Classic held on the James River in Richmond, Virginia, Mann caught a limit of largemouths each day of the tournament by jerking worms for an 11th place finish in the most prestigious bass angling event in the world.

"Worm jerking is a shallow-water technique," Mann says, "so it's a natural for spring fishing. I start using it when the water reaches about 60 degrees and the bass start cruising the banks in search of spawning areas. I suppose every angler has encountered the situation in clear water: when you can see the fish, but you can't get them to hit. Worm jerking is the solution to that problem, and the bass will hit this worm when they ignore everything else. A fish in open water, whether it is cruising the shoreline or is actually suspended, is the hardest bass in the world to catch, but this technique will do that for you."

The worm Mann uses is a specialized version of Zoom Bait Company's Finesse Worm. This 7-inch, straight-tailed worm is manufactured with an extra amount of hardener, making the bait much stiffer and heavier than the typical plastic worm. "Zoom makes this worm especially for this technique," Mann says, "and really, it is good for nothing else. The worm is heavy enough to cast (unweighted) with baitcasting gear, and that is a big plus when you are dealing with big bass and heavier lines."

Zoom's 7-inch Finesse Worm is available in just three colors, Mercurochrome (bright, fluorescent orange), a bright white and a pink bubble gum. Most often, Mann tosses the Mercurochrome worm, noting that the worm's bright color makes it easy to see even when it is several feet under water. And since worm jerking is a visual technique, good visibility is a must whether you are fishing in clear or murky waters that may have a lot of vegetation or very little. Mann says that the orange color also tends to be the most productive, but there are times when the fish seem to have a definite preference for the others. He rigs different colors on different rods to determine what works best on a given day.

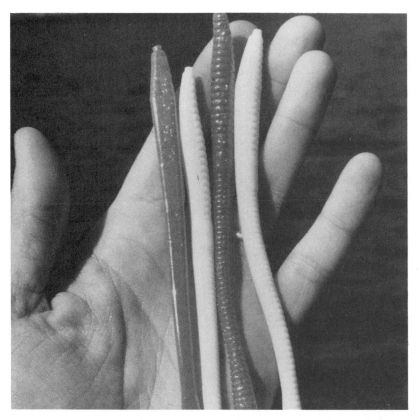

Mann uses the 7-inch Zoom Finesse worms in his worm-jerking techniques. Bright orange and white are his favorite colors.

What Gear Is Needed

Mann's worm jerking rig is the essence of simplicity. A barrel swivel is tied to the terminal end of the line, and a 4/0 Gamakatsu worm hook is tied to a 12- to 14-inch leader attached to the swivel. It is much like a miniature Carolina rig, except for the fact that no weight or sinker of any kind is used.

The worm is rigged in one of two ways depending on the retrieve and the abundance, or lack, of cover. When fishing relatively barren banks or areas with sparse cover, the worm is slipped onto the hook so that it is kinked and the hook is exposed. The worm spirals as it is retrieved, but the barrel swivel prevents a twisted line. When fishing around aquatic vegetation, brush piles, or other shallow water cover, Mann rigs the worm Texas-style to prevent hang-ups. Because the plastic composition of

Zoom's Finesse worm is a bit tougher than most, Mann recommends "skin-hooking" (burying the point just under the side of the worm) to increase your percentage of hooked fish.

Mann uses baitcasting gear exclusively to throw this little worm. "The best rod I've found for this technique is All Star's JR-1, a $6^1/2$-foot, heavy-action pitching rod. It has a relatively soft tip that facilitates casting, but still has plenty of backbone to haul a big bass out of the shallows. If I'm fishing the worm around really thick cover, I'll switch to All Star's SJ-1, a 7-foot, medium-heavy pitching rod." Most often, he uses 10-pound, clear Stren on a good baitcasting reel, but will upgrade to line as heavy as 17-pound test in thick cover and vegetation.

Mann's Three Methods For Presenting Worms

Through the years, Mann has developed three basic methods to fish this worm. The first, and the one he utilizes most often to catch bass cruising the shoreline during the pre-spawn period, involves an unusual jerking motion of the worm.

"I'll cast the worm, let it sink about two feet, and then start jerking the worm much like you would a Rapala or a Long-A Bomber (typical jerk baits). Ideally, the worm should stay a few feet under the surface all the way back to the boat. This worm, hook and swivel rig is heavy enough to hold the bait at the desired depth if you work it correctly. If the worm keeps popping to the surface you are working it too fast or jerking it too hard."

When retrieved in this fashion, the worm will dart and bob erratically under the surface, and you never know from one jerk to the next which way the worm will dart.

Another of Mann's worm techniques calls for retrieving the worm in a relatively straight line. He notes, however, that this retrieve is used only when the worm is rigged with an exposed hook. "The little bend in the worm makes it spiral as it comes through the water. Without that bend, it will come through the water like a stick." After the cast, the worm is allowed to sink to a depth of two to eight feet. Then a slow, methodical retrieve is initiated. The worm simply spirals in side arcs as it swims back toward the boat.

Mann utilizes these two techniques when the bass are cruising the shallows and not holding to any specific piece of cover. "In other words, I use these two retrieves when the fish are apt to be

Mann's Methods For Rigging Worms

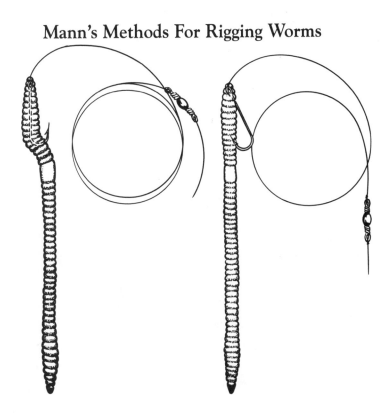

Mann hooks through the worm (left), giving it a slight bend which spins it through the water, or barely buries the tip, Texas style, for weedless rigging. A swivel keeps the line from twisting on the retrieve.

anywhere and I'm trying to cover a lot of water. The steady re-trieve version is the easiest to use when you keep your trolling mo-tor on and work your way down a long bank. When I'm fishing pockets or smaller areas, like you often do just before the spawn, I'll use the jerking technique."

Mann's third retrieve presents the worm rigged Texas-style (with swivel, no weight). "I use this rig when I'm fishing around heavy cover, any type of brush, rock or vegetation in shallow water. Around brush and rock, I'll simply cast the worm past the structure and retrieve it through the cover with short jerks of the rodtip. Sometimes I'll pause the worm and let the worm sink into the cover. The technique is great around vegetation because it allows you to pause the bait over the top of holes, or breaks in the

Mann recommends concentrating your efforts on small, sunny, sheltered coves and bays with sparse cover in spring. Later in the year, use the technique around shallow brush and weeds.

grass, where a bass may be lurking—something you can't do with most other lures."

When fishing the worm around vegetation, Mann says that most strikes do not come in the actual weedbed, but rather at a point somewhere between the deep edge of the vegetation and the boat. "I think the bass see the worm in the weeds and then follow it out. They don't like to stray far from their cover, so after following the worm, the fish will strike rather than letting an easy meal pass by." After pulling the worm over the top of the weedbed, pausing it over holes and breaks in the grass, Mann recommends halting the retrieve just over the deeper edge of the grass to allow the worm to sink a few feet before renewing the jerking retrieve.

Mann's worm jerking technique is not only extraordinarily productive and relatively easy, it is loads of fun. Fun, that is, if you

Jerking A Plastic Worm Around Weeds

Cast the worm past likely cover, letting it sink into open pockets during the retrieve. Bass often follow the lure out of the cover, so be sure to work it all the way back to the boat.

Mercurochrome And Sore-Mouthed Bass   41

Mann with a spotted bass that grabbed this white worm. The fisherman finds bright, un-weighted worms attract the fish when they seem to ignore everything else.

Complete Angler's Library

enjoy white-knuckled roller coaster rides, suspenseful movies and the butterflies that swarm in your stomach as your car begins to slide on an icy road.

"Ninety percent of the strikes that you will set on this worm will be visual, and most often you'll see the fish following the lure before he inhales it. It really is a lot of fun," Mann notes, "but it also tends to be stressful at times, especially in a tournament situation when you're already anxious.

"Knowing when to set the hook can be a problem because, quite often, the bass will dart up and grab the worm by the tail. Most of the time, the fish will inhale the worm after carrying it a few feet, so I find that it is best to wait four or five seconds after the fish first grabs the worm before you set the hook.

"If you keep missing the fish, let them run a little farther with the worm. I've seen instances where you have to actually strip line off the reel and let the bass run a long way with the worm before he actually takes it completely into his mouth, but that is the exception rather than the rule. You just have to experiment whenever you hit the water," Mann says.

Mann's worm jerking certainly ranks among the most productive of shallow-water techniques and is one of the secrets of bass fishing long kept from the general public. Now revealed, you can couple Mann's advice with a little Mercurochrome to give a bunch of bass sore mouths!

4

Jerking The Flats For Largemouth Bass

by Rick Taylor

His 10-year-old heart must have been beating like a trip-hammer. Everywhere he looked were bass, nice keeper bass, wallowing just a few feet under the surface of the shallow, clear-water cove. Yet every lure he launched from the borrowed rowboat swam back without the slightest hint of molestation.

Out of frustration, the die-hard adolescent tied on a Rapala sporting three treble hooks. If the bass weren't going to bite, maybe he could at least snag one. He fired the lure downwind as far as possible and began jerking it back with all his strength.

A sudden thud telegraphed up his line, and the water down yonder boiled. The excited youngster fought the largemouth's every run and ploy, then eventually lifted it over the gunwale.

To his amazement, the 2-pounder was not snagged. It was solidly hooked in the mouth. The bass had *hit* the lure!

For the next hour, the war-whooping boy from Ohio hauled in bass after bass on virtually every cast. But it had to be the Rapala and it had to be ripped through the water with monster jerks. Attempts with other lures and techniques produced zilch.

On that natural water of the Lake James Chain in Indiana 35 years ago, Larry Williams discovered a way to get inactive bass into the boat. Heretofore, that technique has proven to be a major factor in many of his fishing successes...which includes being a four-time qualifier for the B.A.S.S. "Classic" on waters across the United States.

Jerking minnow-imitating plugs over shallow flats triggers strike after strike for angler Larry Williams. See what this technique can do for your largemouth fishing.

Jerking The Flats For Largemouth Bass

When To Use The Jerking Technique

"It's kind of an ace-in-the-hole tactic that can help you out when nothing else is working," says Williams. "But it's most effective under a certain set of conditions.

"First, there needs to be a bright sun to warm the shallow water and bring up the bass. Next, you need some wind, because if the water is like glass, the bass will spook before you can get near them. Then all you need is a good, shallow flat and you're in business!"

Perhaps the real beauty of this technique is that it's well suited for that particular weather phenomenon notorious for sending anglers home with nothing more than a good excuse: the cold front. Warm air turns cold, water temperatures drop, the wind switches around to the north-northwest, and cloudy or hazy skies become bright blue.

"Many people think this drives the bass deep and turns them off," says this part-time pro angler from Lakeview, Ohio. "While that may be the case for some fish, others will be looking for relatively warm water. And they'll find it in certain areas of the lake where the shallows are sun-baked and maybe sheltered a little from the wind!"

Cashing In On Seasonal Patterns

Water clarity can also be a factor. In clear lakes, like the one he learned the technique on years ago, Williams has found that the best time for jerking minnow-imitating plugs is in the early spring...in fact, as early as just after ice-out. Apparently, the sun's warmth better penetrates the water and thus better soaks into the lake's bottom. In murky waters, it gets absorbed in the first few feet, or even inches.

In summer, however, clear-water bass are usually looking for cooler regions, not warmer, so they'll avoid the sunny flats. Interestingly enough, this is the time that jerking the flats works for Williams in those muddier waters, such as the Ohio River, where he was the 1989 Ohio points champion on the Redman tournament circuit. Flats are a major structure here this time of year, and Williams says the baitfish will come right up on them and get quite active, even in high water temperatures and under a hot sun. The baitfish bring in the bass, and the bass bring Williams.

"Jerking the flats doesn't seem to work all that well in the fall,"

Williams' technique requires a lot of work, but it makes disinterested bass suddenly smack at a lure in an instinctive reaction.

warns the 45-year-old family man. "It might be that other tactics, like topwater, work so well that there's no sense wearing yourself out by jerking."

That's a good point to reemphasize: This tactic is designed to make otherwise disinterested bass suddenly smack at a lure in an instinctive reaction. If they are in a feeding mood, there may be a number of ways to catch them that require less strain on your part.

Perhaps another reason jerkin' minnow imitators doesn't work as well in the fall is because the weather, the water temperature, the bass' desire to be in shallow water and their need to feed are all on a natural, downhill trend. So, those sun-baked shallow flats, which are not warming all that much anyway, have lost some of their appeal.

Conversely, in spring, the bass, the water temperature and

everything else are on their way up, ready to start a new year. Even if the main lake is only 40 degrees, a good, shallow flat inside a cove can be as much as five degrees warmer. The best places to look for such coves are on the northern side of the lake; since spring winds are predominantly from the south, they blow the sun-warmed, upper layer of the lake to northern areas; and by facing south, these shorelines are also more open to direct warming from the sun.

Finding The Right Flats

"If you aren't familiar with the water," says Williams, "look at a good map and circle those areas where the contour lines are far apart. Ideally, the flat will be about five feet deep, but it can be as much as 15 feet, depending on water clarity. It will be on or near a north shore and have deep water nearby. In a man-made impoundment, that deep water is usually a submerged creek or river channel."

Williams explains that it's a bonus to have some kind of cover on the flat, even if it's only scattered. Weeds or brush piles will better attract and hold both prey and predator. Still, cover is more relative than mandatory. If a lake has little or none, a bare flat may do just fine.

The slope of the flat is also relative. Williams prefers one that doesn't drop more than a few feet in a hundred yards. But again, it all depends on what the rest of the lake has to offer. As for size, he says a 30- to 40-acre flat is ideal, five acres is too small, and no flat can be too large.

Working The Flats To Catch Largemouth

"I usually start out near the shoreline," reports Williams, who has been fishing professional tournaments since 1978. "I'll keep making passes and work my way out until I locate the main bass concentrations. It's hard to use a depthfinder in shallow water, but if the bass are on a deeper flat, I may scout it electronically first."

A major key to this jerking tactic is to drift with the wind. If you're trying to follow a specific contour, use your trolling motor to stay on line. When a pass is completed, fire up the outboard, run back upwind and start over...perhaps 50 feet farther out this time. Unless the wind switches on you, it shouldn't be too difficult to keep each pass parallel to the others and thus thoroughly cover

Jerking Minnow Imitations On Flats

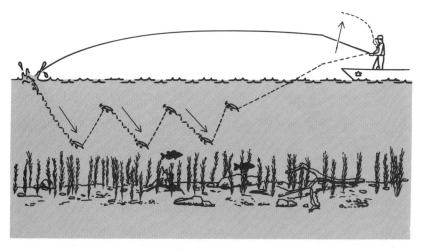

Cast a floating, minnow-imitating plug as far downwind as possible while drifting. Jerk the lure with a sweep of the rod to make it dive, then twitch it slightly as it rises, and repeat.

the flat. Be sure not to motor across the flat between drifts.

You should also cast with the wind and make them as long as possible. Since the wind will be blowing you toward your target, the true length of retrieve will end up being much shorter than the cast. Occasional angle casts are also recommended, wind permitting.

As soon as the lure splashes down, Williams says to start reeling as fast as you can while jerking hard with four or five sweeps of the rod. The purpose here is to get the shallow-running lure down to its programmed depth immediately. Then, just stop for about one second, and give five or six little twitches of the rodtip. This makes the lure quiver and, according to Williams, is when most strikes will come.

If nothing hits, resume fast-cranking once again. Jerk hard a few times, then pause before applying the quiver. Keep this up all the way back to the boat.

"Basically, this is a numbers pattern, not a big-bass pattern," Williams says. "You'll take a lot of bass in the 1- to 3-pound range. My biggest has been 4 pounds. Big bass are lazy; they don't want to chase something that's shooting through the water, acting like a

Spinning reels with large spools cast farther and have a high retrieve ratio. Williams prefers them for his bait-jerking technique.

Complete Angler's Library

How To Drift A Flat

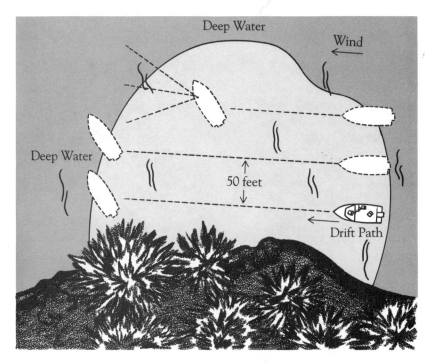

Work a large flat by starting on the shoreline side, upwind of the flat. Drift and cast the length of the flat, then motor back over deep water to avoid spooking fish. Set a course for each drift about 50 feet farther out than the previous drift course.

baitfish that will be very hard for them to catch."

When conditions are right, Williams jerks the flats to fill his limit, then goes after larger bass with other tactics. This has won him many club tournaments and placed him high in a number of national pro events. Last year at the B.A.S.S. Invitational on Lake Guntersville, Alabama, the first day he brought in a limit (five) of "jerked" bass, weighing more than 17 pounds—an average of more than 3 pounds each. Unfortunately, on the final two days of competition the wind went dead, and so did the flat Williams had found the largemouths on.

"The only time a wind can get too strong," says Williams, "is if it's riling up the water. Otherwise, if you can cast and keep the boat drifting in the right direction, you can effectively jerk a flat.

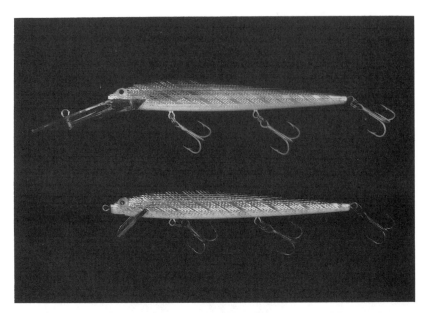

Williams' favorite minnow-imitating lures include models like these Rebel floating minnows: (top) deep-diver; (bottom) shallow-runner.

Your enemy is no wind; you need at least a good chop on the surface to keep the fish active in the shallow water.

Lures And Equipment For "Jerking"

When selecting a lure for jerking, Williams goes first to the No. 13 floating Rapala. His favorite color is black and silver, followed by black and gold, then blue and silver.

His second choice in lures is Bomber's Long-A, which has a gold or silver insert, causing a lot of flash and looking quite natural in the water. Being a little heavier, and with slightly more lip, the Bomber casts farther and runs a little deeper.

If even more distance, or depth, is required, Williams opts for the Bang-O-Lure in the same lengths and colors. And for those very deep flats, he's lately found success with the Rebel Spoonbill, which gets down to 10 feet or more.

"Any number of rods and reels will work with this tactic," notes Williams, but he prefers spinning outfits. "I've always been partial to spinning outfits, so that's what I use. I like a $6^1/_2$-footer with a fairly soft tip, because it helps cast those lightweight lures a long ways. If I'm working deeper flats, I'll go to a stiffer action rod

When drifting flats, Williams keeps a number of rods rigged with lures of different colors and sizes, switching from rod to rod until he finds what produces best.

to help me get a quicker, harder hookset."

He uses the Mitchell 300 spinning reel because it takes a broader, shallower spool, which allows longer casts. He fills it with 10-pound test monofilament. At the end of the line Williams uses Berkley's Cross-Lok snap, contending that a snap, as opposed to tying directly to the lure, gives the crankbait more wiggle. A snap also allows for much faster lure changes.

Williams recommends one more thing for jerking the flats: conditioning. If you're not in fairly good shape, both mentally and physically, it may not be for you.

"It's a hard-work tactic that really tires you out," he laments. But judging Williams' success with this tactic, it is one any fisherman who likes to catch largemouth would do well to adopt.

5

The Meanest Worm In The West

by Ronnie Kovach

Anglers in the far western United States have found that soft plastic baits account for more bass than any other offering. It's no accident. Since anglers like Southern Californian Mike Folkestad have applied themselves to Western largemouth fishing, worms, grubs and feather-like reapers have found a new home, and new uses, in the desert Southwest.

A veteran touring pro, Folkestad has pioneered and refined many of the so-called "finesse" strategies now associated with Western-style tournament fishing. Besides being a proficient competitor in high-stakes competitions, he is also a renowned big-fish expert. Working the small, heavily pressured reservoirs of Southern California, he has tallied more than 50 largemouth bass topping the 8-pound mark.

Although Folkestad's finesse methods were pioneered in the West, they will work for you on practically any lake where largemouth are found. And they will help you to not only catch more, but also larger, bass.

Stitchin' With Baitcasting Gear

Many of the impoundments Folkestad plies in Southern California are small, 1,000-acre lakes. They are inhabited, however, by mammoth Florida-strain largemouths. It is not unusual, for example, for a reservoir like Lake Hodges near San Diego to yield more than 300 nine-pound-plus bass annually. Specimens weigh-

Bob Folkestad uses soft plastic baits to catch monster Florida-strain largemouth bass in Western reservoirs, including this pair, a 12-pounder and 8-pounder.

The Meanest Worm In The West

ing in the double digits are common in this area.

That's the good news. The bad news is that these lakes see heavy use by all kinds of boat traffic, including fishermen. Plus, the Florida bass are by nature highly selective and temperamental feeders. To catch them, a slow, methodical approach is critical.

"Big Floridas won't move too far or too fast to attack a bait," Folkestad said. "This is why I've done so well with a slow-crawled worm using the stitchin' method!"

A line-retrieving technique similar to that used by expert fly fishermen, stitchin'-a-worm is usually practiced with a medium- to heavy-action baitcasting outfit. The reel is spooled with light 8- to 10-pound monofilament. Folkestad prefers to use large 6- to 10-inch plastic worms. These baits are literally handmade by small, local manufacturers. The texture of the worm is extremely soft compared with commercially produced, injection-molded baits. Many Western pros firmly believe big Florida bass will hold onto the soft worms longer. Preferred colors are earth tones such as tan, cinnamon, crayfish, mottled green, purple or black.

Standard Texas-rigging is used with the stitchin' strategy. A $3/16$-ounce bullet weight slides above the worm, allowing for

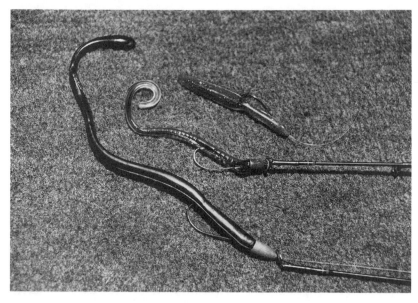

Some of Folkestad's favorite lures include (from top) a reaper, 4-inch plastic worm and the longer, 10-inch snake. He applies scent to plastic baits to encourage bass to hold them longer.

Complete Angler's Library

Folkestad retrieves line with a "stitching" method, much like a fly fisherman, giving him added feel for the tap on the line that signals a largemouth has inhaled the lure.

greater line sensitivity. After the bait hits bottom, Folkestad begins the retrieve by slowly pulling the line in with his left hand.

"I actually pull in about 12 to 14 inches of line every few seconds," he said. "Then I pick up the slack in my hand by winding it up with the reel handle. I continue to use the reel to move the worm along until it bumps into the next piece of structure. Then I start to slowly stitch it through the cover once again."

This process is repeated until the worm is "stitched" back to the boat. Frequently, the bass will gently tap the worm as the angler is pulling in the line by hand. When this happens, simply release the monofilament and quickly pick up the slack using the reel handle. When you feel the pressure of the fish, swing and set.

Folkestad carefully coats his baits with liquid fish attractant to insure bass will hold onto the worm while he winds in slack.

"Chirp" To Trigger Strikes

Instead of pulling the worm by hand, Folkestad often uses a simple cast-and-wind retrieve. But again, this is done slowly. "I'll barely inch the worm through every piece of rock, brush or rubble it comes into contact with," he noted.

The Meanest Worm In The West   57

Here's the secret to this slow-crawl presentation. Once he feels contact with some sort of prominent obstruction, Folkestad lets the bait rest motionless for a few seconds. Then he gives the reel handle a quick $^1/_4$- to $^1/_2$-turn twist. This makes the worm jump from the submerged cover as if it is panicked and under attack. The subtle ploy of using the reel handle to give the bait the erratic jumping motion is termed "chirping." Sometimes this additional motion is what it takes to trigger a strike from unusually lethargic Floridas.

Split Shottin' Your Way To More Fish

A variation of the Carolina rig, the split-shot rig has often been heralded as the best set-up to consistently catch bass in the West. The basic split-shot rig is typically fished on light- to medium-action spinning or baitcasting outfits using 6- to 8-pound test monofilament.

A smaller 4-inch worm, curlytail grub or 2-inch long reaper or leech are favored split-shot baits. Folkestad rigs each of these soft plastic lures Texas-style, embedding the points of smaller worm hooks into the baits to make them weedless.

Next, a medium-size lead shot is crimped 12 to 18 inches above the lure. As the worm, grub or reaper is retrieved, the lure will seductively rise and fall off the bottom, trailing the lead shot. This mimics the movements of small crayfish or threadfin shad, which are indigenous to these Western reservoirs.

This basic rigging works fine at depths down to 30 feet. But when probing the extremely deep terrain of many Western lakes, Folkestad modifies the rig to maintain bottom contact all the way down to 60 feet.

"I begin by rigging my worm, grub or reaper Texas-style with a $^3/_{16}$- to $^1/_4$-ounce bullet weight," noted Folkestad. "But then I slide the bullet sinker up 18 to 24 inches above the bait and crimp the nose portion of the sinker tight to the line. This gives me a very snag-free bait capable of maintaining excellent bottom contact at great depths."

Some anglers may be hesitant to crimp the bullet weight to the fine diameter monofilament, fearing it may nick the line. But in reality this rarely occurs if the crimping is done smoothly.

If the bass are not aggressively grabbing the bait, or if the bottom is particularly smooth, Folkestad will fish his modified split-

Deep-Water Jigging Rigs

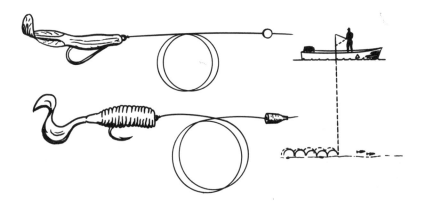

For deep-water jigging, Folkestad rigs a reaper Texas-style (top), or a twister tail on a plain hook. He crimps split shot, or a bullet sinker (in deeper water) 18 to 24 inches above the hook to make the lure trail naturally along the path of the bouncing sinker.

shot rig with an open hook. Instead of using the traditional plastic worm hook, he switches to an Eagle Claw No. 181 long-shank baitholder. The hook is threaded into the worm, grub or reaper, leaving the point totally exposed. Two miniature barbs along the shank of the baitholder keep the soft plastic lure from sliding down the hook.

On hard or muddy bottoms with few obstructions the bass practically hook themselves on the open-hook rigging.

Jigging With Darters And P-Heads

There are times when the bass on these man-made Western reservoirs suspend off the bottom in a non-feeding mood and must be coaxed with small baits and erratic movement to get them to bite. Under these conditions, Folkestad prefers to use minuscule $\frac{1}{8}$-ounce jig heads, compact 4-inch worms, 6-pound monofilament and light-action spinning outfits.

The leadheads are available in either an arrowhead-shaped "darter" or a round "p-head." The small worms are threaded onto the darter or p-head jigs leaving the hooks exposed. The darters actually "dart" from side to side as they sink, while the p-heads fall

Folkestad shows a high level of patience and concentration when he is perched over good large-mouth habitat. One of the keys to his success is a light touch.

Complete Angler's Library

Jigs For "Shaking" In Cover

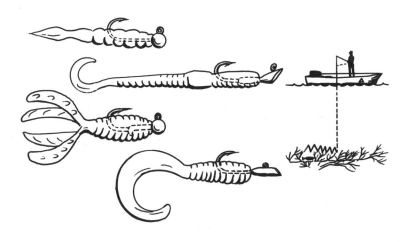

Lures Folkestad uses for shaking in cover include soft, plastic bodies on p-heads (left) or on darter heads (right). He uses line no heavier than 6-pound test and jig heads $^1/_8$ ounce or less.

in a straight line. The worms also add action to the bait.

"The object," said Folkestad, "is to rhythmically shake these little baits as you swim them through the strike zones. Always be prepared for pressure bites as the bass gently mouth the darters or p-heads on the fall. If in doubt, swing and set."

When tight-mouthed bass are stationed near bottom rather than suspended, the tiny leadhead combos can produce terrific results. Try to position your boat vertically above the zone your graph or flasher shows the fish are holding. Lower the darter or p-head to the bottom, and use your rodtip and wrist to vigorously shake the little bait around the structure.

Folkestad utilizes this ploy frequently in the dead of winter when he wants to "shake" the bass out of their doldrums. "By really shakin' the little darters or p-heads I can sometimes irritate wintertime bass into attacking the worm. This is a prime strategy in my deep-water tactics using soft plastic baits," he said.

The Other Ingredients

Mike Folkestad may share his expertise for fooling Western bass using an array of soft plastic worms, grubs or reapers. But it is

An expert on big largemouths, Folkestad has developed his techniques based on their temperamental habits.

the many little things Folkestad does, perhaps unconsciously, that make his presentations so potent. Some of his specialized approach is mechanical; the rest requires the right frame of mind as much as anything else.

First, Folkestad is particularly precise in matching his tackle to their methodology. Specialized techniques like stitchin', chirpin', split-shottin' and tiny darters and p-heads dictate perfectly matched rods, reels, monofilament, sinkers and hooks, as well as the lures themselves.

Secondly, his finesse methods require maximum concentration and perseverance, because bass fishing out West is tough, with limits few and far between. You cannot expect many strikes during the day and each must be made to count. In observing Folkestad fishing with his finesse presentations, I have found his attention level extremely high from dawn to dusk. He misses few strikes and his confidence level remains high despite what other anglers might consider tough conditions.

If Mike Folkestad's four basic strategies for using soft plastic lures can produce on busy, Western impoundments, imagine what you can do on your own more quiet waters! Fish these techniques with patience, confidence and perseverance and watch your largemouth bass tally climb!

6

Night Fishing For Smallmouth Bass

by Don Wirth

I n some parts of the country, particularly in the Southeastern states, night fishing for smallmouth bass has assumed a
cult status. Local anglers often fish from sundown to sunup,
show up for work, then repeat the process the following
evening. Surprisingly, in other parts of the U.S. and Canada,
night fishing is practiced only rarely. It's hard to imagine this dis-
parity across the land when it comes to such an enjoyable and effective fishing technique.

After dark—oh, after dark! Something wild and wonderful
takes place. The big smallmouths creep from their deep-water
haunts and move onto shallow, fishable structure such as ledges,
weedbeds, points and humps. Some experts say these big smallies
take advantage of two feeding patterns daily during the summer
months. By day, they feed on schooling forage fish that suspend
near the thermocline, often 40 feet deep. By night, they move
onto rocky banks and weedy areas that harbor nocturnal crayfish.
As the crayfish get active, so do the smallmouths.

On the Tennessee/Kentucky border sits scenic Dale Hollow
Reservoir, a sprawling turquoise-colored impoundment noted for
big smallmouth bass. Make that *giant* smallmouth bass: Dale Hollow gave up the world record smallie in 1955, an 11-pound,
15-ounce behemoth that some feel will never be equalled. Dale
Hollow guide Fred McClintock, however, isn't a member of that
group. He's convinced even bigger smallmouths are swimming in
Dale Hollow right now, and he believes fishing at night may be

Complete Angler's Library

Fred McClintock feels the world record smallmouth bass mark can be broken, and night fishing may be the way to do it. The smallmouth expert has developed strategies for catching smallmouths after dark.

Night Fishing For Smallmouth Bass

one of the best ways to catch such a fish.

McClintock has been a guide at Dale Hollow since 1985. A Pennsylvania native, he was originally attracted to the deep lake because of its legendary muskie fishing. As a foreman at Bethlehem Steel, McClintock often fished for muskies in Pennsylvania and New York on his days off. But once he began fishing Dale Hollow for a living, he found that the lure of catching a giant smallmouth bass was highly addictive.

Since then, he's become the most sought-after guide on the reservoir. He's landed smallmouths approaching 8 pounds, as well as muskies more than 35 pounds and walleyes more than 15 pounds, from the lake.

McClintock's fishing expertise has been featured frequently in such publications as *North American Fisherman*, and other major national fishing publications. Put simply, few anglers possess the natural abilities for catching big smallmouth bass that Fred McClintock has.

Basic Approach

"Night fishing for smallies is a whole different ballgame from fishing in the daytime," McClintock said. "I've seen many expert smallmouth fishermen who just couldn't catch quality fish after dark. Likewise, I've fished with some terrific night fishermen who simply didn't care for daytime fishing. Night fishing is an acquired taste. You either love it or you hate it."

One way to learn to love it is to pre-plan your night fishing trip so that you're not groping blindly for the right approach. "The two most common failures of anglers who try night fishing are not knowing what they're doing, and not knowing what to look for," McClintock said. "Obviously, you can't concentrate on catching fish if you're lost. And getting lost is a very easy thing to do when you're night fishing if you don't know the water."

McClintock always recommends arriving at a new lake early in the afternoon and cruising potential fishing areas while you can still see where you are going. "Don't try to fish an entire lake or reservoir after dark, especially when you first get started night fishing," he said. "Know the water you wish to cover, and cover a confined area." He suggests using a topo map to find a smaller area that has everything a fish needs for survival: a deep-water sanctuary, a good food supply and a place to spawn.

Locations For Smallmouth Fishing At Night

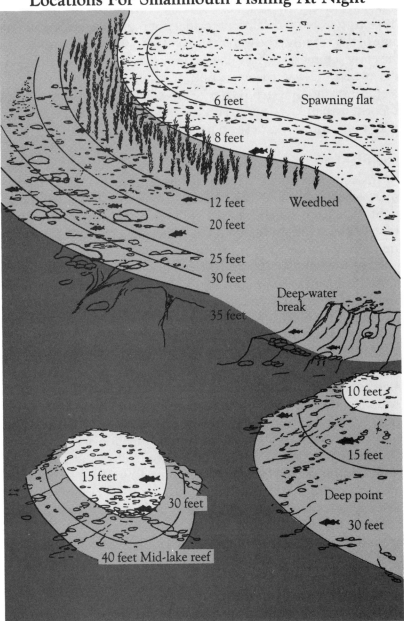

6 feet — Spawning flat

8 feet

12 feet — Weedbed

20 feet

25 feet

30 feet

35 feet

Deep-water break

10 feet

15 feet

15 feet

Deep point

30 feet

30 feet

40 feet Mid-lake reef

McClintock's preferred night fishing locations take advantage of the smallmouth's tendency to move up from deep-water sanctuaries when the sun goes down. Edges of flats, tops of isolated reefs, points and breaks all have potential for harboring fish.

Not knowing the right kind of places big smallmouths use after dark can also tip the scales in the favor of the fish, not the angler. "It's easy to fish too shallow or too deep at night, depending on the time of the year and the water temperature," said McClintock. "In the early summer, the fish may be very shallow. Late in the summer, when the water is at its hottest, the fish may be extremely deep. Knowing that depth they're most likely to be using is more important than knowing what kind of jig they're hitting or what color pork rind works best, in my opinion."

The Right Stuff

In deep, clear waters daytime fishing is done mostly with spinning gear and light line. But this tackle may only lead to trouble at night, McClintock believes. "There's really no good reason to use light tackle and wispy lines after dark, because, to me, the name of the game is boating fish, not just getting strikes," he said. "You must use the light stuff during the day because on clear lakes even 10- to 12-pound test may look like well rope. Six-pound line is the gold standard for daytime fishing when using the most popular daytime lures (grubs and small hair jigs), but at night you'll boat more big fish with heavier gear."

McClintock favors baitcasting tackle and 14-pound line for night fishing with spinnerbaits and heavy jigs, his two favorite nocturnal lures. Most of his rods are 6 feet in length, and none "wimpier" than medium-heavy action. He uses heavy-action rods when fishing the heaviest (up to 1 ounce) spinnerbaits and jigs.

McClintock uses Stren fluorescent fishing line, which he couples with black lights. "Black lights have made night fishing far easier for the average angler, since they illuminate fluorescent lines and make them glow like neon tubing," McClintock said. "They're especially critical when fishing drop baits such as jigs."

When fishing late in the summer, McClintock might choose a longer rod, up to 7 feet. He says that the longer sticks let you move more line when you sweep back to set the hook, thereby increasing your odds of burying the hook point in the leathery jaw of a big smallmouth that may be down 35 feet or more.

Compared with daytime fishing, you need less tackle to fish after dark. "In fact, having too many rods and reels only creates tangles and confusion," McClintock said. When fishing from his Stratos 201-PRO bass boat, McClintock seldom keeps more than

Getting to know the water in daylight and picking a specific area to fish are important ingredients to successful night fishing.

three rods ready. "I like to keep rods pre-rigged with the lures I'm going to use when night fishing, because changing lures is more trouble after dark," he said. "Snaps would make lure changing easier, but they're a no-no when fishing single-hooked lures like jigs and spinnerbaits."

McClintock insists that all his tackle be in perfect working order before hitting the lake at night. "Because we're after big smallmouths at night, I don't want to take any chances with a malfunctioning drag or clashing gears," he said. "It's well known among night fishermen that if anything can go wrong with your tackle, it will at night. Ever try to tear down a baitcasting reel in the dark? It's no fun at all!"

McClintock's Lure Choices

McClintock uses only a few lures after dark. All of them have single hooks. "Stay away from treble-hooked lures at night, unless you want to try a topwater bait like a black Jitterbug," he said. "First, a big smallmouth can more easily throw a treble-hooked lure. They seem to get a lot more leverage against the hook. Use spinnerbaits, jigs and similar lead-bodied baits at night."

Night Fishing For Smallmouth Bass

McClintock likes spinnerbaits for several reasons. "They vibrate when you retrieve them slowly, which may be more important to the fisherman than to the fish," he said. "I like to be able to feel my lure when I'm casting it into total darkness, and at night a spinnerbait feels like something's thumping on the end of my line. As the blades turn, they flash, reflecting any ambient light—from the moon, stars or surrounding man-made sources. That may not seem like much light when compared to what the sun produces during the day, but remember the best night fishing for smallies is in extremely clear water. On a moonlit night, I believe these fish can see even a minute light reflection quite well."

Spinnerbaits, at least the ones McClintock uses for night fishing, are heavy lures. "I often fish a 1-ounce spinnerbait in late summer, when smallies are deep," said McClintock. "The heavier your lure, the better you'll be able to feel it and keep track of it when night fishing. Plus, a heavier lure is easier to cast on a stout baitcasting rod. You'll backlash less with a heavy spinnerbait than when trying to cast a lighter lure, such as a $1/4$-ounce jig. That's important when you're out there in the dark."

On moonlit nights, McClintock likes a light-colored spinnerbait, such as white or chartreuse. If he's fishing during the dark moon, he'll switch to a darker lure, such as black or purple. Early in the season, he will use a lighter lure ($3/8$-ounce) with small blades, always in a short-arm version. He has good luck with the long, thin willow-leaf spinnerbait blades as well as the more common Colorado or Indiana styles.

As the water warms and the fish go deeper, McClintock will stay with them by gradually increasing the weight of his spinnerbaits. He has caught big smallmouths at depths exceeding 35 feet on 1-ounce spinnerbaits. If the fish are striking short, he will add a pork trailer, always a No. 11 Uncle Josh frog, staying with the general shade of the spinnerbait he's using, but varying the color a bit. For example, if he's using a black spinnerbait, he may use a brown or purple pork frog; if the spinnerbait is white, he may add a chartreuse frog. McClintock believes this slight color contrast helps make the lures more visible in the dark.

The manner in which McClintock retrieves the spinnerbait varies with the season and depth. "The short-arm spinnerbait is especially effective at night because it can be dropped or helicoptered down ledges and drop-offs," he said. He casts the lure toward

You don't need many lures to catch big smallmouth bass at night. Lures you do need include hair jigs, spider jigs and spinnerbaits.

shallow water, and with the rod at a 45-degree angle, allows the spinnerbait to sink on a tight line. When it reaches the bottom, he lowers the rodtip, takes up slack with the reel and sweeps the rod back to 45 degrees. This retrieve is repeated back to the boat.

When smallies are using shallower cover, such as weedbeds at the end of a spawning flat, McClintock often swims or "slow-trolls" the spinnerbait. The lure is simply retrieved at a slow to moderate speed and kept just off the bottom or right over the top of the cover. The speed of retrieve will increase or decrease as the depth contour rises or falls.

In shallow water, McClintock allows the lure to settle to the bottom on a tight line. Then the rodtip is pulled back with a short stroke, no more than a foot, and the lure is allowed to sink again. McClintock said this retrieve is dynamite when big smallies are up shallow and feeding.

Leadhead jigs are also included in this angler's night fishing repertoire, but McClintock steers clear of the lighter leadheads used so extensively in daytime fishing for smallmouths. "Many of these have thin, wire hooks that can be easily straightened by a big smallmouth," he said. He relies on heavier jigs, often up to $^1/_2$

ounce, and always dresses them with some sort of trailer.

"Here in Tennessee, we fish a lure known as a fly 'n rind," he said. "It's basically just a hair jig with a pork rind trailer." Early in the season, McClintock will stick to lighter jigs, usually $1/4$-ounce, with a U-2 or 101 pork trailer. He will often "swim" these lures at the edges of flats in shallow water at the beginning of the night fishing season. The swimming retrieve requires as long a cast as possible, and the lure is reeled back to the boat with the rod at a constant 45-degree angle. This is a painstakingly slow, but extremely fluid and natural way to fish a jig, a retrieve that is often interrupted by a trophy bass.

As the water heats up and the bass move deeper, McClintock will go to heavier jigs. He'll fish a $3/8$-ounce jig when the smallies move between 20 and 30 feet on deeper structure, then a $1/2$-ounce jig when they're deeper than 30 feet. If the bass are on vertical structure, such as deep ledges, he'll use a "drop" retrieve, letting the jig fall slowly on a tight line.

Hair jigs are universally preferred by smallmouth night fishing addicts, but lately McClintock has had good success experimenting with a rubber-legged jig dressed with a soft plastic trailer, such as Hale's Craw Worm. This lure can be retrieved in short, erratic movements right across the bottom to simulate a live crayfish.

Another lure McClintock employs after dark is the so-called spider jig. "These lures are known locally as 'creepy crawlies,' and they are deadly on lunker smallmouths at night," he said. McClintock's favorite spider jig is the Hoot-N-Ninny, manufactured by Zorro Baits. "This lure combines a leadhead jig with a strong, sharp hook and a soft plastic trailer with twin twist tails," he said. "There's a round, tentacled collar that fits behind the leadhead. This is perhaps the most critical design feature of this type of lure. When a smallmouth mouths the bait, it closes its jaws around that spongy collar and will very seldom blow out the lure, as often happens with a regular leadhead jig." Because the bass tend to hang onto a spider jig longer than a standard jig, you miss fewer fish, McClintock has found.

McClintock likes to fish spider jigs by dragging them right across the bottom. The erratic, darting action mimics the movements of a crayfish perfectly. On moonlit nights, McClintock prefers sand, smoke, light green, red or chartreuse spider jigs. During a dark moon phase, he'll switch to black, purple, dark green or

On moonlit nights, McClintock chooses a light-colored spinnerbait.

pumpkin, but he tries to keep his choices simple.

"It doesn't take a big tacklebox to be an effective night fisher-man," McClintock believes. "A paper sack full of jigs and spinner-baits and a couple of bottles of pork rinds are all you'll need."

Seasonal Patterns That Work

McClintock has found that certain patterns pay off time and again when he's night fishing, and he's agreed to share them with smallmouth anglers who are dedicated to catching bigger fish.

"Early in the season, when the surface temperature is barely bumping 80 degrees at Dale Hollow, I'll look for big, submerged weedbeds," he said. "Weeds are usually overlooked by smallmouth fishermen who think all these fish hang around is rock. You won't find weeds in many Southeastern highland reservoirs, but when they're present, they will absolutely outdraw every other type of structure in the beginning of the night fishing season."

Big weedbeds adjacent to smallmouth spawning flats can be found in midwestern mesotrophic lakes and Canadian shield lakes as well as southern reservoirs. "Often when the spawn is complete, these fish will hang around the flats for a few days, then move out to the edges of the flats and look for a place to hold," McClintock said. "A big weedbed provides perfect sanctuary for

Night Fishing For Smallmouth Bass

these post-spawners." He has caught some of his biggest smallmouths at night in shallow weedbeds, often by running a big spinnerbait right over the tops of the weeds. "Just let the blades barely tick the tops of the weeds and hang on, 'cause when that big girl comes blowing out of the grass, she's liable to jerk the rod clean out of your hands!" McClintock promised.

Let's say you succeed in locating a good weedbed close to a spawning flat, but can't connect with fish. "Two things are happening: you're either fishing too deep, or you're not fishing a weedbed that's close to deep water," McClintock said. These two statements may sound contradictory at first, but the guide explained: "The best weedbeds are close—a cast or two away—from deep water. But even though they may be close to deep water, this doesn't mean that the bass will be holding in the deeper portion of the weeds. On the contrary, they're actually in the shallower areas at the beginning of the season. The bass like to have that sense of security that comes from having deep water close by, but they won't necessarily use deep water all of the time."

Once the water warms and this weedy pattern fails to produce, McClintock shifts gears and begins seeking out deeper structure. He'll look for ledges and drop-offs, areas that fall off into deep water. "After the weeds no longer produce, I'll resign myself to the fact that I'll have to slow down and fish down to 20 feet or so," McClintock said. Leadhead lures like the fly 'n rind or spider rig are the first choice now, although the spinnerbait will also be used. "If there's a ledge or drop fairly close to a big spawning flat, particularly a big flat with weeds in it, that's the first place I'll look," he said. "Big smallmouths don't roam all over the lake—they're homebodies. I like to fish areas with a lot of good habitat close together for the best fish."

Black lights make this deeper fishing easy and fun, according to McClintock. "Often a big smallmouth will inhale a falling jig and you'll never feel it. The black light makes even the slightest line movements show up so you can pop the hook into 'em quick."

Besides drops and ledges, McClintock likes to fish deep points. "A point is always a good bet in a deep body of water and especially so at night," he said. "I like the points that drop off at a sharp angle into deep water. Don't just fish the tapering end, but cast to the deeper sides as well." McClintock fishes points down to 35 feet or so in hot weather.

McClintock might use light spinning tackle when fishing in daylight, but after dark he relies on stout baitcasting gear. He feels the heavier tackle is more forgiving.

Perhaps McClintock's favorite midsummer smallmouth structure is a deep hump. "Most fishermen pound the banks, so offshore humps stay unfished much of the time," he says. "If you can locate them, you're likely to have a great smallmouth spot that will last you all season, maybe several seasons, if you don't take too many fish off it."

McClintock uses all the lures previously mentioned when fishing a hump, but especially likes a heavy spinnerbait. "Maybe it's because I'll gear up with heavy line and a very stout rod when fishing a heavy spinnerbait. You get a feeling of confidence, a feeling you can handle even a giant smallmouth with this kind of tackle," he said. "Of course, the fact is, you can still get your line broken by a good smallmouth, even when it's 17-pound test." McClintock likes humps with a few stumps peppered along their expanse for his biggest smallmouths and has found humps to produce when fish are holding below 30 feet or as shallow as 10 feet. "Humps are probably the best structure I can think of for a truly giant smallmouth simply because there's so much deep water surrounding them, and giant smallmouths really hang in deep water," he said.

Night Fishing For Smallmouth Bass

Beautiful smallmouths, like this 6-pound fish, are what keep guide McClintock fishing until the crack of dawn.

Complete Angler's Library

McClintock believes that smallmouths may go below 35 feet in extremely hot weather at night, but he does not like to fish for them when they're that deep because "it's too hard to stick 'em."

Conservation Measures

Night fishing in hot summer weather has its positive side, but there are negatives as well. Foremost among these is the toll it takes on the fish. "When the water surface temperature is in the 80- to 90-degree range, as is very common in my area in the summertime, it's very hard on smallmouths you may be carrying in your livewell," McClintock said. "I never carry any fish around in my livewell except for a single trophy a client wishes to mount."

Local club tournaments held at night are especially deadly on the smallmouth population, he believes. "On the morning after a typical summer night tournament, you might spot 20 or 30 dead smallies floating around the dock where the fish were weighed in," he said. "This happened because the water was just too hot and the fish went into shock. I think it's a real waste of our precious smallmouth bass resource. If you must fish night tournaments or hold smallies in your livewell in hot weather, take the necessary precautions to keep them cool, and treat the livewell water with catch-and-release compound, which calms the fish and slows down their metabolisms to help prevent shock."

The Right Time For Smallmouths

If you're after a trophy smallmouth bass McClintock believes nighttime is the right time! But follow his advice: Do your homework. Learn the lake; find the areas with the most potential for big smallmouths. Use a few good lures. Fish slow. Fish smart. And above all, be kind to the fish. "Take only what you need, and handle the rest with tender, loving care," McClintock advised.

Panfish

7

Crappies: The Rest Of The Year

by Rich Zaleski

Each spring, the world overflows with crappie fishing experts. Your Uncle Joe, the "dock bum" at the marina, even the little kid down the block—the one with the $4.98 fishing outfit. Everybody catches their share of these panfish in April and May.

Crappie fishing experts are a lot harder to find in late June, and by August they are few and far between. They will be plentiful again by next May, but to whom do you go for crappie fishing advice in the meantime?

Meet Doug Eriquez. The only time of the year he does not do much crappie fishing is when the fish are thick in the shallows during the spring.

"May and June are so busy with bass tournaments and good fishing for other species," he explained, "and there are so many fishermen pounding on the crappies, that I'd rather wait until summer and fall to catch mine. It's nothing like spring fishing, but it can be very good."

According to Eriquez, the penchant spring crappies show for shallow water and cover keeps too many crappie fishermen in the shallows all year long. "Summer crappies," he explained, "use cover, but only to rest in. When they're feeding, they're on the move in open water.

"And even when they do use cover," he added, "it's not the shallow bushes and weeds they're around in May. Summer crappies use deep weed edges and fallen trees that reach into deep

Except during the spring, schools of crappies like to roam a body of water. Knowing their boundaries and how to search for them will help you catch more.

Crappies: The Rest Of The Year   81

water. Standing timber can also be good, but it's not too common around here."

"Around here" for Eriquez is the northeastern part of the country. He lives in New Milford, Connecticut, between Candlewood Lake and Lake Lillinonah, a pair of impoundments that offer impressive crappie fishing. But he especially enjoys fishing for crappies in natural lakes.

Deep cover is hard to find in these glacially formed bodies of water, making it difficult to locate fish. So I asked Eriquez to describe how he goes about finding open-water, natural-lake crappies in the summertime.

Summer Surveillance

"Even when in open water," he told me, "crappies relate to something. When I can, I like to figure out what they're relating to, but sometimes you just can't."

Eriquez believes that crappies relate to the edge of the hard-bottomed shoreline shelf, the edge of the weeds or a water-color break, and often a nearby school of baitfish. The baitfish relate to plankton, which is moved by current and wind and changes depth according to how much sunlight there is. Therefore it can look like crappies are wandering aimlessly, but they're really just following their food. Since plankton—the first link in the chain—is the thickest on the downwind side of a lake, Eriquez starts his search for crappies there. He relies heavily on his depthfinder to pinpoint where crappies are holding.

"I just kind of wander back and forth from the deep basin to the shallows, with the gain on my flasher cranked way up so I have a second echo," said Eriquez. "The location where the bottom signal weakens and the second echo disappears is the edge of the basin, or silt line, where the bottom composition changes from hard to soft. From that edge, to the edge of shallow-water weeds that reach the surface, is the crappie zone. If the weeds end in a wall right at the drop-off, I look for someplace where there's an extension of the flat beyond the weeds, like a point or bar.

"I look for one edge where the weeds stop reaching the surface," continued Eriquez, "and then another edge where the lower, deep-growing grass ends. There may even be a third edge where the sand and gravel of the shoreline shelf meet the silt of the basin. I just make note of the depths, and about how far they

Locating Crappies In Summer

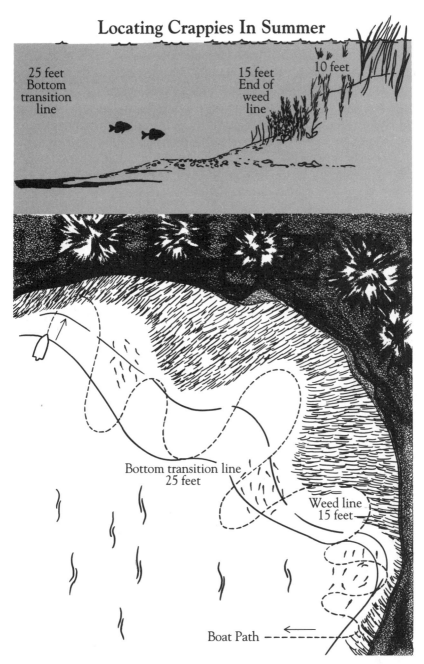

25 feet
Bottom
transition
line

15 feet
End of
weed
line

10 feet

Bottom transition line
25 feet

Weed line
15 feet

Boat Path

Eriquez searches for schools of crappies using the weedline and the deeper, bottom transition zone as parameters. Using a zigzag course, he throws markers as he moves over fish and returns to the largest school after exploring a complete section of water.

Crappies: The Rest Of The Year

average from the shoreline and from each other.

"You might not want to waste time like this, especially if you fish the same lake a lot," Eriquez conceded. "But summer weedbeds aren't the same after a cold, wet spring as they are after an early, warm spring, and the crappie movements will be different too. Also, late in the summer, different species of weeds are blossoming at different times, and things are changing again, so it's something you should try to keep track of."

On a good crappie lake, you'll see fish blips on the screen while you're doing this reconnaissance work. Eriquez believes it's a mistake to stop and fish every time you see a suspended fish or two. He likens it to spending a nickel as soon as you get it. You're not going to get much for your money. You might catch a few crappies that way, but they're going to move, and you'll have no idea where. "I like to get the lay of the land first," he said, "to find out what they're relating to. It's like investing those nickels until you get enough to buy something a lot better.

"If I see a really big bunch of fish, I might stop and fish," Eriquez continued, "but usually, I just toss a marker buoy near them. Sometimes, you'll see two or three big groups of fish while you're zigzagging back and forth along a quarter mile of drop-off, and drop a marker on each one. When that happens, take a look at the pattern of the marker buoys, because most of the time it was the same school, and the markers can tell you how they're moving and help you figure out what they're relating to.

If Eriquez doesn't see any schools of fish worth marking, he concentrates on developing an idea of what breaklines there are, and how they relate to each other, as he makes a mental note of the seemingly scattered, individual fish blips. Later, he tries to view the blips as a whole, to get an idea of the right depth range and the distance from breaklines most of the fish seem to be.

"Ignore any fish that appear real shallow or real close to bottom, and the ones that are within a few feet of the weed edge," he suggested. "Most of the rest will fall into a pretty narrow depth band... say, from 12 to 17 feet, or from 15 to 18 feet. That's the depth you want to fish, because that's where most of the fish are.

"Develop a mental image of how the bulk of the blips within that depth range were positioned," said Eriquez. "Over the drop-off? Along the edge of the basin? Fifty feet or so from the weedline? Look for a common pattern, and don't worry about a few excep-

A flasher-type depthfinder works fine for locating schools of crappies. Graphs do a better job of indicating numbers of fish in a school.

tions. You're concerned with what the biggest bunches of fish are doing, not a few stragglers."

On the bigger bodies of water, Eriquez uses a bass boat to fish for crappies. But on the smaller, natural lakes where he does much of his fishing, he finds a cartopper with an electric motor more than sufficient. The paper graph recorder in his big boat is great, but he does just fine with the flasher in his pond boat. "The only thing I can't get used to is a liquid crystal unit," he said. "You have to be able to read the signal strength to recognize fish and to find the edge of the basin. Flashers and graphs show signal intensity, but with the LC jobs, a pixel is a pixel. It's either on or off."

Since he's convinced that crappies are mobile, Eriquez only anchors on exceptionally windy days. More often, he uses the electric motor to hold himself in the area of a school. By backing the boat into the breeze, with the stern-mounted electric motor on a low speed setting, he hovers in place over or next to the school.

Since you're dealing with crappies that are on the move, contact with the school may be interrupted. The quicker you can figure out which direction they are moving, the faster you can regain contact each time they move out of range. The first time Eriquez loses contact with them, evidenced by four or five casts without a hit, he'll spin the motor around and proceed in a forward direction, making a loose, ever-expanding oval pass around the spot he last "saw" them, with the "stretched" side of the oval running parallel to the breakline.

It may take a few minutes to regain contact with the school, but once this is accomplished, he has a good idea which direction the fish are moving. From then on, he tries to slide the boat along the breakline with the fish, while keeping the stern pointed roughly into the wind.

Keeping your lure at the right depth is critical with this technique. If you are not getting bites you need to know if the school has vacated the area, and not just whether you're working too far above or beneath the fish. Generally speaking, you should always work the upper half of the depth range that you believe the crappies are using. "They'll come up for a bait," Eriquez said, "but they won't go down. A foot under the fish, and you've missed them. But you can be three feet over them and still get bit."

"Ninety percent of the time, I use an $^1/_8$ ounce jig. I know that it sinks a little less than a foot per count, and I know how fast to work it to keep it moving more or less horizontally," said Eriquez. "Sometimes, they won't hit something moving that fast, though, and you'll have to go to a $^1/_{16}$. I find it tougher to gauge the depth of a lighter jig, and the wind can affect it too much, so if I can possibly catch 'em on an $^1/_8$, I feel a lot more confident."

Crappie Lures—A Simple Selection

In this age of myriad color combinations, metal flakes and what-not, this crappie expert's lure selection might seem a little sparse. "I use plain, old-fashioned, chenille and marabou-tailed crappie jigs almost exclusively, and if I have yellow, white and black, I'm all set," Eriquez said.

Actually, he uses yellow jigs almost all the time and only tries black or white if the fish aren't responding. Plastic curlytails, tube style jigs, and plastic-bodied, marabou-tailed jigs all catch crappies. But Eriquez believes the marabou/chenille jig works as well, so why confuse the issue with additional choices?

"The more different jig styles and colors you have," he suggested, "the more time you spend second-guessing yourself and tying on new lures. The answer to catching them is locating them, not trying to turn them on with a fancy color."

Complete Angler's Library

Eriquez likes the control he gets from a ¹/₈-ounce jig, including the fact that he can count it down and move it horizontally without being overly bothered by wind.

There is one additional style of lure that Doug Eriquez uses to catch crappies, but he uses it more during the fall than the summer. "They move so steadily in the summer that it's tough to get right on top of them long enough to fish vertically," he explained, "but if I can, I'll drop a No. 5, jigging model Rapala — the one that's designed for ice fishing — right down to them. You get to use it a lot more in the fall, though, when they settle down more."

As the water cools in the fall, crappies do not move shallower right away. The first change in their behavior is to spend more time each day resting at breaks than moving. The movement patterns are similar, but they will usually be closer to the breakline, and when they encounter a fairly sharp turn in the weed edge, or a rock pile, a patch of deep vegetation or another such condition, they are likely to hang around it for a while.

They will still hit the jig, but if you can get right on top of them, you can clean house by fishing vertically with the jigging Rapala. Eriquez has found that crappies most often hit the Rapala while he tries to hold it motionless in the water. "I've had them nail it while the rod was resting on the gunwale," he told me, "but usually, I'll lift it a foot or so, hold it there for a few seconds, and

Eriquez took this big crappie in the fall from a small lake. He will use a cartop boat to get into lakes that have no public ramp if the water shows signs of holding large crappies.

Complete Angler's Library

then drop it back very slowly. Then I'll let it sit for a minute before repeating the action. If you jig it steadily the way you do for trout or perch through the ice, you won't get many crappies."

In some lakes, there is a period in the fall when crappies move back into shallow cover...usually just after the surface matted vegetation starts to fall back from summer levels. "I guess that when the weeds start to die off it exposes a lot of prey," Eriquez theorized. "When the water temperature drops down to about 55 or so, the crappies will be right back where they were during the spawn, except maybe not as deep. But it's a lot like spring fishing, because you're casting jigs at shallow cover."

That shallow movement only lasts a few weeks and in some lakes might not even happen at all. Once it's passed, the fish move back out to the open water, often settling in areas much deeper than they used in the summer. "In later fall, the crappies don't move as much and tend to hold around deeper cover—sometimes, as deep as 40 feet. That's when the jigging Rapala really gets a workout. They'll change depth, moving almost straight up over the cover they're holding on, and they could be 15 feet down over 50 feet of water. The next day, they could be 35 feet down, but they're still in the same spots, at least until the ice starts to form."

Catching crappies all season long is possible. Adopt Doug Eriquez's theories and methods, and you'll catch crappies in summer and fall. Combine it with what you already know about springtime crappie fishing, and you're home free for the entire open-water season. If you need help with springtime crappie patterns, ask your Uncle Joe or the kid down the block. Crappie experts are easy to find in the springtime.

8

Spider Rigging For Crappies

by Steve McCadams

Where spider rigging was first conceived, no one really knows. It is now being utilized all over the country though known under a number of different names such as seining or trolling.

The label is easily understood once the technique is observed in action. Multiple poles of various lengths extend from the boat, mimicking the appearance of a spider's legs; hence the name spider rigging.

"With my style of spider poles I can offer crappies several different baits at the same time and at different depths," said veteran crappie angler Morris Blackburn of Springville, Tennessee. Blackburn applies his tried-and-true method on his home waters of Tennessee's Kentucky Lake, branded through the years as the "Crappie Capital" of America.

Long known for their selective and curious nature, crappies often require a bait presented to them on their terms; namely the right lure and lure color, presented at the proper speed and depth.

"A double-hook rig, consisting of either minnows or artificial jigs, is my favorite bait presentation," said Blackburn, who fishes frequently from a 28-foot pontoon where several poles are rigged and lures are trolled slowly. "It's really surprising how one color or type of jig will produce better than another on a given day. With the multiple pole approach, I can offer the fish a wide variety, letting them choose which is best."

With the use of an outboard motor or an electric trolling mo-

Consistent catches of open-water crappies fall to the "seining" method of Morris Blackburn, and the technique has caught on among many anglers.

Spider Rigging For Crappies

Blackburn prefers the comfort of a pontoon when he fishes his spider rig method. The boat moves forward, and on calm days, can easily be controlled with an electric trolling motor.

tor, the boat is moved at almost idle speed. The rigs are designed to be fished at the depth of choice, which in most cases means the angler will stagger them from close to the bottom to just under the surface. With the use of sonar equipment the angler can monitor what's below in the zone he is fishing.

Stagger Tackle To Find Scattered Fish

The double-hooked crappie rigs are usually tied some 12 to 18 inches apart, with the same distance allowed to a bell sinker tied at the terminal end of the rig. When fished vertically, the rig effectively reaches the fish holding deep near cover or the suspended crappie schools meandering about in search of forage.

Another advantage of spider rigging is that it allows even the novice angler to effectively cover large segments of a lake or reservoir. Big waters often intimidate anglers, and they're lost before they start. With spider rigging, anglers can slowly troll areas and find fish while monitoring depthfinders or graph recorders and reading topographical maps.

Spider-style fishermen use marker buoys as reference points in open water when they locate a school of active fish. Going back

Complete Angler's Library

over the area and making a sweep with the buffet-line of baits will likely yield success time and again. By using the process of elimination, anglers can formulate a pattern of depth and bait selections based on what the fish have chosen and not chosen. Simple changes can increase productivity instantly.

The so called post-spawn period of crappie fishing often gives even veteran anglers gray hair, but spider rigging again comes to the rescue when fish suspend and choose not to relate to structure. It is well known that crappies are structure-oriented fish, given half a chance. They prefer to seek refuge in stumps, brush piles and other natural cover most of the time, but some phases of the year see them change habits temporarily.

When crappies are scattered, anglers have to cover lots of water before they can hide the ice in the cooler with a layer of fish. Even depths of 10 to 20 feet can be fished with spider rigs, because the sinker on the terminal end holds the rig down no matter what depth is desired. An angler simply has to adjust the size of the sinker to reach the desired depth while maintaining a relatively constant trolling speed. Even the lightest head jigs or minnow-baited hooks can be effectively held at the proper depth using this

Crappies have a universal appeal to both young and old anglers alike, and beauties like these are what crappie fishing is all about.

Setting Up For Spider Rigging

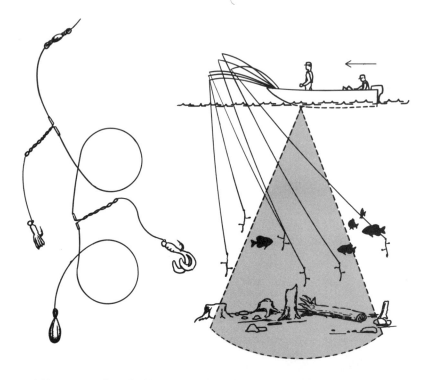

Available commercially as double-wire panfish rigs (left), these can be rigged with plain hook and minnow, plain jig or minnow-tipped jig. A bow-mounted, or through-the-hull transducer, offers a view of the bottom, and in some cases, the depths of the baits themselves, for better lure control.

method. Experiment and see what works for you.

Blackburn uses rods ranging from 10 to 14 feet in length held by permanent rod holders. The rigs are widely spread to avoid tangles. He prefers monofilament line in 10- to 12-pound test, but recommends lighter sizes in clear waters. He attaches baits to the line with drop loops that allow the baits to trail away, resulting in a higher hooking percentage. Commercial panfish rigs, on which small wire is tied and offset so snell or drop loops can be tied, also work well for holding both minnow-baited hooks and jigs.

Long Rods Aid Hookset

The hook almost always sets automatically as a crappie takes

Blackburn offers crappies a buffet of baits and colors at different depths with his spider rigging method.

Spider Rigging For Crappies

Spider rigging is catching on because the method covers a lot of water in a very manageable way. Once the lines are set, an angler simply has to sit back and control the course of the boat while occasionally making depth adjustments.

the bait and turns against the resistance of the weighted line. The slight bends in the rods and their springy length help cushion the hookset and prevent the hook from ripping out of the fish's mouth. "Watching the rod's tip is the best indicator of even the lightest strike," Blackburn said, "but usually an instant bend of the pole will indicate when the fish is on.

"Getting more than one on at a time really gets you busy and sometimes you'll have three or four hit at once," he said. Blackburn spends many of his retirement days watching the end of his telescopic poles for a bend of a rod's tip. "I use a Micronar color video unit and you can see the schools of fish as you're going over them and pretty much know which pole is going to produce. At least by watching the screen you know how deep to set the rigs, and you know whether or not there are stumps or other structure in the area you're fishing."

Mobility, Added Lines Improve Catches

Spider rigging has been used in crappie tournaments across the country as well as by anglers probing new waters. Some states limit

Complete Angler's Library

the number of poles allowed by the individual, but most are liberal enough to allow two anglers to fish four to six poles from an individual boat. However, anglers should consult their state's fishing regulations on the number permitted.

For filling the cooler with the tastiest of all panfish, spider rigging is a hard method to beat. It's a multi-purpose technique allowing the angler to offer suspended crappies a selection of bait type and color. Maneuvering over open-water areas with this many choices seldom fails to produce something. And the technique offers anglers the mobility to explore submerged creek channels, rock piles, weedbeds and a host of other fish-holding terrain.

The open-water crappie fisherman no longer has to make the choice of live minnow versus artificial jig. He no longer has to wonder which color in his box is better than the one he has in the water. Spider methods allow presentation of a veritable smorgasbord to the crappie. Once a certain color or pattern begins to produce fish consistently, similar tackle can be added to the spider rig. Try this method and see if it doesn't improve your crappie-catching success many times over.

9

Sunfish Continental

by Homer Circle

U ltra-light tackle? I thought I had been using it for
years. You know, 2-pound mono and itty-bitty
$^1/_{64}$-ounce jigs...then I met Mick Thill with his super-
ultra-light methodology, and it blew my cool!
Our meeting took place at the annual show of the American
Fishing Tackle Manufacturers Association. Thill was there to
promote European match fishing techniques and, over coffee, he
described how lethal they were for small European species such as
roach, tench and perch. He told how thousands of spectators
would line stream banks to cheer on their favorite anglers, many
of whom would catch more than 100 fish a day. "Those species
must be very easy to catch," I said.

Thill responded: "On the contrary, they can be very difficult.
It's the method that induces them to feed even when they're lethargic and hugging the bottom. And it will work the same on
American species such as bluegills, trout, perch, catfish, grayling,
crappies...in fact, all of your panfish. I'd like to show you just how
deadly it is sometime."

While I was listening, my mind was on an old phosphate pit
near my home in Florida. During the rainy season the water turns
slightly murky, making it easy to catch all the bluegills we need for
a meal. But when the dry season sets in, the water is gin clear and
the bigger bluegills are easily spooked and hard to catch. A lively
cricket fished deep is a sometime producer.

I knew this would be the acid test for Thill's match fishing art,

Complete Angler's Library

Mick Thill's super-ultra-light techniques produced these lunker bluegills when usual methods fell flat.

Sunfish Continental

so we made a date. I told him I would call when things were tough-est, and he smilingly replied, "That's the kind of challenge I like."

The day before Thill was to arrive, I checked with the pit ex-pert. He answered: "They've got clear-water lockjaw. So bad they won't even take worms, crickets, mini-jigs or flies. You'll be wast-ing your time!"

European Methods Call For Super-Ultra-Light

When we arrived at the pit the water was flat calm and we could see bottom 20 feet down. While Thill was unpacking his match-fishing gear, I quickly rigged my ultra-light outfit. To a 10-foot, sensitive graphite pole was attached an equal length of 2-pound monofilament. A small bobber suspended a No. 10 Aber-deen hook on which was impaled a lively cricket. One BB-size split shot was attached a foot above the bait to hold the bobber upright. I felt confident I could equal Thill's match-fishing catch.

He paid no attention whatsoever to my preparations, totally absorbed in rigging his 16-foot graphite rod with $1/2$-pound monofilament line. I could hardly see it and marveled at his per-ception as he tied it to a No. 16 Model Perfect hook. Most fisher-men have never seen a size 16 hook, let alone fished one.

Then to further boggle my mind, about a foot above the min-uscule hook he added two of the tiniest shot I had ever seen, about the size of this "o"! When I commented on the itty-bitty hook, Thill said, "Oh, when fish are really being difficult, we drop down to a size 36 hook. They are approximately half the size of this 16!"

He reached into a Styrofoam chest where he kept the bait cool. As he popped the lid off a ventilated container he said: "These are Eurolarvae. See the two tiny black eyes? That's the head end where you insert the hook...right between the eyes. They live surprisingly long."

Instead of Eurolarvae, American anglers would call them mag-gots, spikes or grubs. Ours are slightly smaller and have been used for years by ice fishermen. An unusual feature of his larvae was the red, yellow and blue colors they had been dyed. It did not affect their liveliness.

He surprised me by rigging three on one tiny hook, one natural white, a yellow and a red. He explained that it is necessary to care-fully insert the hook only into the outer skin. Go too deeply and you have a blob of larvae innards on your fingers.

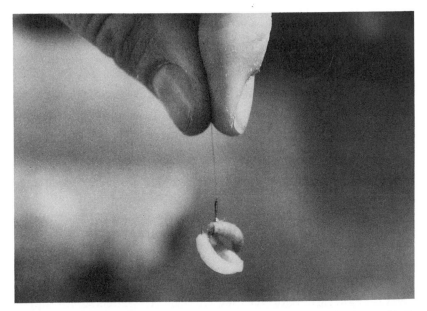

Eurolarvae to Thill, but maggots to many American anglers, are the potent bait he uses for all panfish. Dyes are used to tint some of the larvae red, yellow or green, and help attract bluegills.

Sensitive Floats And A Keen Eye Needed

Now, let's examine the most important item in Thill's super-ultra-light angling system, the bobber, or float, as he called it. The slim body is about two inches long, made of epoxied balsa, and has a stainless wire protruding about two inches from either end. The top end is covered with a red fluorescent sleeve about the thickness of a pencil lead.

It is attached to the wispish line by threading it down through a minute eye in the bobber's side, then affixed to the bottom wire stem with a tiny plastic sleeve.

Now, while all of this was going on I was observing, but at the same time dunking a cricket around nearby cover. I had one offer when my bobber nodded meekly, nothing more.

Then Thill gently dipped his triple-grubbed hook into the clear water and let it settle until the weight of the mini-sinkers pulled the bobber upright. Thill stooped to peer closely. He grunted, "Uh-huh!" Then he raised his pole to give line tension and let the bluegill do the hook setting. Soon the scrappy sunfish was circling on its way to the surface, and I was wondering about all the things I had yet to learn about sunfish.

Bobber's "Attitude" Important

As he played the fish, I asked: "Mick, I was eyeballing that bobber very closely and it never nodded its head at all. How did you know a bluegill was on?"

He replied, "In match fishing, we call this the science of float reading. Until you become keen at interpreting the nuances of movements, you won't even place in the money. You were watching the bobber, while I was watching the attitude of the center wire."

He hoisted a 9-inch bluegill to his waiting hand and, as he removed the barb from its lips, continued, "This fish sucked in the grubs from above, which nullified the downward pull of the lead shot. This caused the bobber to rise only minutely, but enough for a professional eye to detect. Setting the hook a second later could mean a missed bite."

I was impressed, and my respect for his system grew with each hefty bluegill he caught. He asked how many we needed for supper and I suggested about a dozen. He quit at 13, and they averaged from 8 to 12 inches, one pulling the scale down to the 2-pound mark.

He showed me his bobber kit and it contained varied shapes from long and slim to short and squatty. Some were designed for

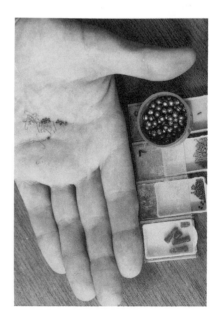

A normal hand indicates how tiny the No. 16 hooks and miniature lead sinkers are. The assorted plastic sleeves are used to affix wispy line to the bobber.

Super-Ultra-Light Rigging For Sunfish

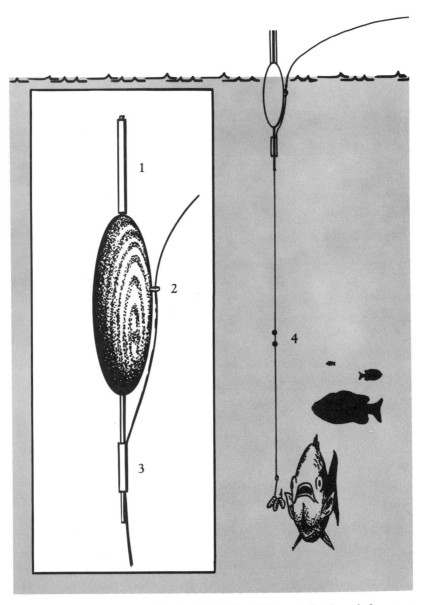

The stainless-steel, upper wire of the ultra-light bobber (1) is covered with a red, fluorescent sleeve for high visibility. One-half pound line is threaded through a minute eye on the side of the bobber body (2). A plastic sleeve (3) affixes the line to the bottom wire, permitting adjustment of the bait depth. Mini-lead-shot sinkers are added to the line (4) until only the tip of the bobber body appears above the water surface.

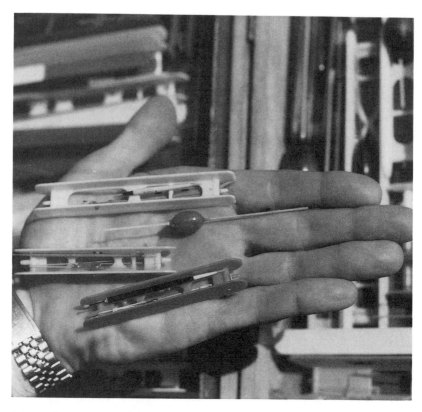

Bobber selection ranges from mini to mid-sized to meet different conditions including flat water, moving water and wind chop.

use in moving current, windy days or even night fishing. All had highly visible center posts for detecting vertical or lateral shift-ings.

Like the capable tutor that he is, Thill showed me what he meant by the "nuances of movements" and if you aren't aware of them lost fish will result—fish you don't realize are lost because you never know they are inhaling the grubs.

And inhale is the correct term. For instance, with the bobber resting vertically, should a bluegill be above the bait and gently open its mouth as it flares its gills, the bait rises barely enough to negate the weight of the lead shot that hold it upright. So, think of the rising effect on the bobber being as little as a few millimeters. It demands keen sight and constant concentration.

It's so subtle at times that Thill will keep adding shot until the top of the bobber is actually below the water's surface. Then the slightest change in the bait's attitude will cause a surface dimpling by the rising or shifting of the bobber body.

If the top end of the stainless wire stem should tilt to the left, it signals a take from the right down below. Vice versa on a tilt to the right. And when the stem dips out of sight, a bluegill took the bait from below.

Getting Bluegills In A Feeding Mood

As an old saying goes, bluegills are where you find them. But, there are times when you've found them that they stop feeding after a couple are caught, as if the head bluegill says: "Okay, guys and gals, at ease!" Thill has a clever tactic for such times.

He carries a magnum slingshot with rubber bands to propel a pouchful of grubs up to about 50 feet. He fires a volley, then waits to see if feeding action results. If not, he lays a pouchful in another direction. Once he triggers even one bluegill to begin eating these decoy maggots, others are sure to follow.

Although he prefers to fish from shore where most match fishing is done, he is just as adept moving about in a boat, seeking bluegill hangouts wherever they might be. He showed me a clipping in his scrapbook, written by Bob Bledsoe, outdoor editor of the *Tulsa Tribune*.

They set out on a frigid November day on the Illinois River when even the veterans were getting zilched. Thill uncorked his super-ultra-light bag of grub tricks to come through with nine species of fish! Bledsoe's column gave a glowing appraisal of Thill's skills.

Design An Ultra-Light System To Suit Your Needs

After that afternoon with Thill, I find that certain variations better fit my mobile fishing needs. For instance, the long pole is okay for bluegill fishing around our home base because it telescopes for handiness. But since it would be too long for air transportation, I use another super-ultra-light rigging in my travels.

Available are ultra-light spinning and spincasting reels that will handle the threadlike line, and 5-foot graphite rods that telescope to about a 14-inch length. These are packed between layers of clothing for protection and I've never had a breakage problem.

As to the durability of the grubs, I have kept them in the refrig-

Thill's 16-foot graphite rod brings a wide arc of water coverage within reach. This is an important advantage when clear water makes fish skittish.

Complete Angler's Library

erator for six weeks without a noticeable decrease in vitality. When transporting them over a period of hours, a small foam chest with plastic ice packs will keep them in a dormant state. When exposed to outside air they revive surprisingly fast.

With this ultra-light outfit I am prepared to panfish for meals when bigger gamefish are hard to find. It has come through on so many occasions that I never travel without it. The tougher the fishing, the more sense fine lines and small lures make.

Super-ultra-light fishing is not for every bluegill fisherman because it is a demanding technique. It is not the kind of pursuit two "good ol' boys" engage in because the intensity of concentration allows little time for bantering or story telling.

It is for the angler who enjoys the challenge of mastering a new tactic when bluegills just are not taking old, time-tested, traditional baits. And once you acquire the skill you will know the feeling of excelling in an age-old sport that has challenged mankind since primordial days.

If your local tackle stores do not stock the grubs, bobbers, line and hooks mentioned, and you would like to know more about the finer points of match-fishing presentations, contact the American Fishing Tackle Manufacturers Association, Barrington, Illinois.

One thing I can tell you from personal experience: When this technique doesn't catch bluegills, it's high time to stay home and "catch up on your behinds," because nothing is likely to produce fish when super-ultra-light offerings fail!

10

On The Trail Of Trophy Bluegills

by Jack Gulnetti

The sport of fishing has grown by quantum leaps in recent years. Technological advancements—sonar, graphite rods, spider-thin fishing line—have surely helped, but so have fishing tournaments. They spawn specialized experts who, in turn, teach the rest of us more than we ever thought possible about bass or walleyes or salmon.

But what about panfish? Where can we find expert advice on what could well be the nation's favorite fish, the bluegill? Good question. Although more angling hours are devoted to this species than any other, there is a definite shortage of reliable, scientific information, particularly on the specifics of finding and catching large 'gills.

This conclusion is precisely what led Jeff Murray, an outdoor writer from northern Minnesota, on a relentless pursuit of solid information about trophy bluegills. What Murray has learned might surprise you. It may also help you locate and catch the finest bluegills your area has to offer.

"What started it all," Murray recalled, "was the day I latched onto my first 1^1/$_2$-pound 'gill. It happened while I was backtrolling for walleyes. I mean, the fish looked like some sort of mutant, but in a striking sort of way. It had that same menacing glint to its eye that all true predators have. From that moment I was hooked!"

But Murray soon found out that the trail to bluegill nirvana was littered with obstacles. The biggest was the deficiency of information in fishing literature on the habits of pound-plus 'gills.

Jeff Murray spent years learning the kinds of conditions that create big bluegills. He's come up with a set of conditions you will want to look for where you live.

On The Trail Of Trophy Bluegills

"I quickly realized that very few anglers—and biologists—knew much about large bluegills," Murray said. "They were like me—the ones they caught were accidents, and the others taken on purpose were, well, embellished somewhat. Everybody, it seems, thinks $1/2$-pounders are 1-pound fish. Few have come face to face with a true trophy 'gill!"

Bluegill Factories Share Common Traits

This left Murray with only one option: Search scientific records—journals, doctorate theses, test-net surveys, fisheries reports—in hopes of finding a formula that would lead him to trophy bluegills. After a two-year investigation, he found a formula.

For example, according to one study, the growth rate of bluegills along the Minnesota/Wisconsin stretch of the Mississippi River was significantly faster than on the Iowa/Illinois portion to the south. One would expect the opposite, with warmer waters and a longer growing season farther south.

Said Murray, "You don't need to be a biologist to tell if a water body is fertile. Start with the drainage system of the general area. Lush croplands and healthy forest lands are one tip-off.

"Next, wetlands within the immediate drainage pattern of the water body should be relatively undisturbed. This provides a stable water source, acting as a sponge-like reservoir in times of drought and times of flooding. More important, swamplands are food factories, providing microscopic organisms that panfish need!"

So, the less development surrounding a lake or river backwater, the better. But nutrition alone won't lead to overstuffed bluegills. The predator/prey relationship of a water body has an even greater impact on the size distribution of panfish.

"Because bluegills are such prolific spawners, something has to offset their ability to overrun the food chain," Murray said. "As a rule, I avoid lakes with a lot of runts. They're a red flag that stunting has occurred. You're just wasting your time!"

One factor limiting bluegill numbers is a stunted bass population. According to the 56-page pamphlet, *Producing Fish And Wildlife From Kansas Ponds*, farm pond fishermen who wish to grow huge bluegills, can. It's easy and fun. Simply stock bass with the 'gills and release every bass you catch under 15 inches.

In many northern lakes, Murray believes perch help keep

Complete Angler's Library

Use a slingshot to attract bluegills and get them into a feeding mood. By tossing larvae into the water in a 10- to 15-foot circle, you can create a feeding frenzy.

bluegill numbers in check. Research into the relationship, conducted by Dennis Anderson, a fisheries biologist from Brainerd, Minnesota, suggests lakes of more than 300 acres with sparse vegetation favor this relationship.

"I never appreciated the role perch play until I caught a handful last winter on a favorite bluegill lake," Murray said. "Each one was coughing up $^1/_2$-inch 'gills on the way up the ice hole. Perch are more predacious than I'd given them credit for!"

Besides the predators themselves, an environment favorable to efficient predation of bluegill fry and fingerlings is important. Murray recommends medium water clarity that is favorable for myopic bluegills to feed on tiny crustaceans as well as for predators—bass, perch, northern pike—to prey on overabundant 'gills.

Spawning habitat should also be restricted, since bluegills patrol their beds and don't need a lot of space to repopulate their underwater world. Sand (or gravel) shorelines are ideal. Lakes with a lot of muck and rock to balance things out help restrict panfish propagation.

Still, quite a few sand/gravel lakes support saucer-sized bluegills. But they must experience a periodic drawdown. Flowage lakes are excellent examples, where utility companies control riparian rights, and water levels fluctuate on a seasonal basis. The result is just what trophy bluegill seekers dream of, said Murray.

"During low-water conditions, young bluegills are forced out of shoreline vegetative cover and into open water, where predators can feed efficiently and keep the population in check," Murray explained. "But the drawdown is typically short-lived so that there are enough survivors. If you've got a flowage lake within driving distance, check it out as soon as possible."

Add it all up—good nutrition, adequate predation, medium water clarity, limited spawning habitat, periodic drawdown—and you should have big panfish. But you still have to find them, which, Murray said, is even easier than picking a good lake. A study he learned of on Michigan's Third Sister Lake yields some clues.

Here, 18 of 27 tagged bluegills hadn't moved more than 65 yards from the point of original capture. The reason is a bluegill's sedentary nature; if its surroundings meet its basic needs, it will stick around.

Here is Murray's five-point description of bluegill "heaven:" (1) A small bay (with enough weeds to grow plenty of freshwater shrimp); (2) Within a larger bay (hopefully with a southern exposure and a few offshore humps); (3) Plenty of overhead cover at the shoreline (particularly wood); (4) A sandy bottom; (5) Access to nearby deep water.

"I recently built a house on a flowage lake that has two areas meeting these criteria," Murray said. "Throughout the year I can usually find bluegills pushing a pound, and it'll be within a half-mile radius. February is the toughest month. May and June are the easiest."

Getting Big Bluegills To Bite

"Spawning 'gills are no match for a neutrally buoyant presentation," Murray continued. "I like shoreline blowdowns in calm back bays. But you can't pull it off with standard spinning gear. Start with a featherweight rod—a fly rod blank about 8 feet long, tied with single-foot spinning guides. It shouldn't weigh much more than two ounces. Add 2-pound mono and a small but smooth-casting reel, such as Daiwa's SS 700. With this outfit, a variety of baits can be flung without having to add extra weight.

Habitat For Trophy Bluegills

Bluegill heaven: A small bay with weeds, within a larger bay with southern exposure and access to nearby deep water. Overhead cover along the shoreline provides additional security.

"Bluegills of all sizes attempt to spawn, but the biggest fish intuitively select superior spawning sites. Invariably, they'll be just deep enough so you won't see them, and logs, fallen trees and brush will be chosen over barren stretches.

"Simply keep a low profile, turn off the motor well before you reach your intended target, make long casts and avoid spooking the fish as you play them away from their beds," advised Murray.

Post-spawn 'gills, and those in deep-summer holding patterns, are fish of a different scale. At one time, Murray used to rely mainly on drifting tiny leeches below slip bobbers, but lately he's found other ways to tempt finicky bluegills.

"The problem with summer fish," he said, "is their on-again, off-again moods. One moment they'll hit a radish peeling, the next ignore the most tantalizing offering. This is especially true

The best trophy bluegill lakes have sufficient numbers of predators and periodic drawdowns to restrict access to cover, keeping the population thinned and reducing competition for food.

for fish more than a pound. If you're lucky enough to find the fish in a cooperative mood and ready to hit any morsel that crosses their path, use whatever you want. The leech is a great bait because it does all the work for you. But shrimp imitations are often more effective, although you'll have to sort through more smaller fish."

Shrimp imitations?

"You know, freshwater shrimp. Most big bluegill waters are full of them. They're ¹/₄ to ¹/₂ inch long. I hear all this talk about minnows or Daphnia, but shrimp are the ticket!" said Murray.

Not only are shrimp a preferred 'gill target but, according to Murray, shrimp are easy to mimic.

"Just use a ¹/₆₄-ounce jig with a fake grub body. No bait needed. Cast it out—again with light line and a long rod—and let it settle

Complete Angler's Library

into the strike zone. Use sonar if possible. Then, jerk the jig back in short, quick two-inch strokes.

"This presentation accomplishes two things. First, it mimics the way shrimp propel themselves through the water. And second, it helps register a bite before the fish has a chance to exhale your jig. You can use an electric trolling motor and vertically jig a weedy hump, but I prefer long casts worked back to the boat!"

The recent surge in European tactics involving maggots, specialized balsa floats, telescoping poles (or 10-foot-plus rods) and light line, is deadly on big bluegills, too. But Jeff Murray feels that few anglers are using the system to full advantage.

"Maggots are a great bait," he said. "They're tough, lively and, best of all, a natural offering; panfish of all sizes never tire of larvae. However, maggots can be incorporated into a triggering presentation that causes a literal feeding frenzy.

"If you've got the fish cornered, toss out a couple dozen maggots in a 10- to 15-foot circle," said Murray. "A small slingshot might be necessary. Let them settle and toss out your bait below a properly balanced float; in calm water the tip should barely be visible. Repeat until you get some action.

"Before long, the fish will find the smorgasbord," Murray continued. "Once that first one commits, the rest will turn on. The only drawback is competition from smaller fish higher in the water column. When they bug you, try a ledgering system or let the maggots crawl into small slices of bread before throwing them overboard. By the time they wriggle out on the way down, they'll be below smaller fish and visible to the larger ones!"

Evidently, there's a lot more to bluegill fishing than soaking a worm below a bobber. Now that you know how to find big-bluegill waters close to home, you can use these tactics to catch panfish too big for an ordinary frying pan.

11

Finding Great Lakes Perch

by David Richey

G reg Wilkins is a Lake Michigan enigma. While others head out on the big lake to catch brown trout, steelhead, coho and chinook salmon, Wilkins putt-putts a half-mile offshore to catch his limit.

Wilkins, of Honor, Michigan, cares little for the pot-bellied gamefish that prowl Lake Michigan. His species of choice is the yellow perch, and when it comes to catching these tasty gamefish, no one is better than this angler.

Yellow perch are one of modern day fishing's miracle stories. Once extensively netted by commercial fishermen on the Great Lakes, Lake Michigan's perch numbers dropped dramatically. Even the burgeoning fishery off breakwalls and piers along the big lake's shoreline soon went down the tube.

The commercial fishermen took some of the blame, and rightfully so. But they weren't the only culprit in the demise of the Great Lake's yellow perch.

The early 1960s were witness to an alewife invasion. Millions of these forage fish swam into Lake Michigan, found it to their liking and prospered. Young alewives feed on plankton, and as they grow older they feed on tiny perch fry and perch eggs. Alewives killed millions of perch before they had a chance to grow.

"The stage was set for destruction of our perch population," Wilkins said as he shoved his boat into the water at the Platte River mouth near Honor before moving offshore to his favorite reefs and rock piles. "Perch numbers plummeted in the 1960s, and

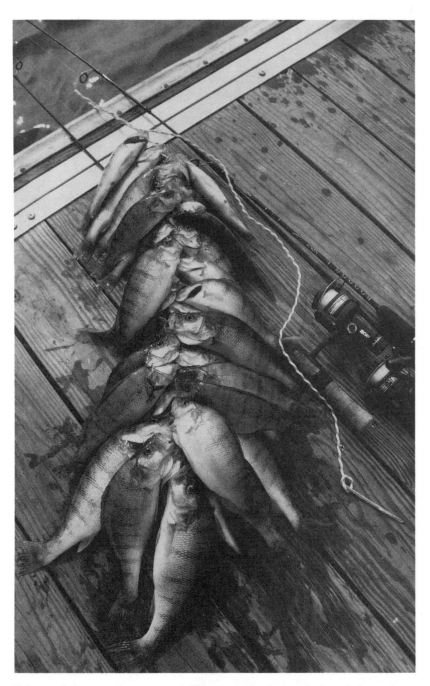

Yellow perch this size make a great meal. There are perch aplenty in the Great Lakes, and once you find them you can catch them by the stringer-full.

Finding Great Lakes Perch   117

to catch even one perch was enough to rate local headlines."

Then, Wilkins said, chinook and coho salmon began consuming alewives in astronomical numbers. Lake trout, brown trout, steelhead and even yellow perch started making inroads on the small alewife fry, and soon alewife numbers began to dwindle as predator gamefish populations grew.

"A partial alewife die-off occurred in the early 1980s and perch began recovering," said Wilkins. "Where we once were content with catching tiny perch and felt bad about keeping any, we now catch numbers of yellow perch, some that measure up to 17 inches. In fact, some of these yellow bellies are so fat and so long, inexperienced anglers think they are catching walleyes. Two-pound perch are not uncommon."

Keys To Finding Great Lakes Perch

Wilkins maintains that even though northern Lake Michigan now holds a bountiful supply of jumbo yellow perch, it isn't always easy to catch them. The way to a cooler full of perch is to first find them.

"If you can find 'em, you can catch 'em," Wilkins said. "Perch are nomadic gamefish to a certain extent. Granted, they don't wander all over the lake like a school of coho salmon, but perch do move around as they search for food."

The eastern shoreline of Lake Michigan, and particularly the 120 miles of shoreline from Ludington north to Leland (which includes Platte Bay where Wilkins often fishes), is now home to some of North America's finest yellow perch fishing. The perch are present, but the day-to-day problem is locating the schools of fish, and it can be difficult.

"A small Loran-C is used to facilitate finding my favorite rock piles," Wilkins said. "I've committed most of the submerged rock piles to memory by triangulating their location with objects on shore, but by punching in the coordinates on my Loran-C, it's a simple matter to leave the rivermouth and be anchored over the rocks in a matter of two or three minutes."

He believes the one big secret to consistent jumbo yellow perch catches is learning the exact location of these major fish factories. Perch frequent the reefs and rock piles for just one reason—to feed on the abundant forage base.

Rocks and submerged reefs are usually situated along major

Al Holmes of South Haven, Michigan, admires a jumbo yellow perch caught while fishing rock piles on Lake Michigan.

drop-offs near deep water, and the water depth over this underwater structure will range from 12 to 22 feet in most areas. The rocks—usually large boulders—occurred either naturally or were placed in these locations during dredge-and-fill operations off large rivermouth areas when the U.S. Army Corps of Engineers constructed breakwalls, piers or harbors of refuge many years ago.

"The placement of these rocks on the lake bottom has been a real lifesaver for perch fishermen," Wilkins noted. "The submerged rocks and reefs attract emerald shiners, alewife fry and crayfish, and this forage base attracts and holds yellow perch."

Wilkins noted that although the locations of these forage-producing rocks may be well-known to local anglers, they can be difficult to find for fishermen new to the area. But, he said, perch fishermen are gregarious, and usually are willing to let newcomers anchor nearby once they locate a school of active fish.

Finding the fish means more than just knowing where the rock piles are located, Wilkins said. A fisherman must know how large the underwater rock formations are. They must also know where nearby muck beds are found because the perch will feed on the larval insects emerging from the mud. Anglers need to be able to experimentally fish several areas over the rocks or near the muck beds until they find schools of fish.

Finding Great Lakes Perch   119

"Perch may frequent a specific rock pile for days on end," Wilkins said. "Then, for no apparent reason, the fish may move 20 yards, or as much as two miles, to feed over another similar underwater structure. Consistently catching these fish means knowing where two or three reefs or rock piles are located, and then fishing near bottom in several locations over each one until the fish are found."

Wilkins relies both on his Loran-C and an electronic flasher to pinpoint schools of fish under the boat. The Loran-C gets him to the underwater structure and the flasher allows him to detect the presence or absence of fish.

Rigs And Baits For Jumbo Perch

Three types of bait—emerald shiners, softshell crayfish and wigglers—are used on one of two basic rigs to take perch. A two-hook perch spreader enables the angler to catch fish two at a time. A single hook rig can also be used.

"Perch spreaders are used to separate two hooks," Wilkins said. "A wire framework with two arms is attached to a $^1/_4$-ounce bell sinker to hold the rig on bottom while the angler maintains a tight line. Leaders with a No. 8 or No. 10 gold long-shank hook are attached to each arm of the spreader to fish bait at two different depths near the rocks. A tight line from rod to bait enables anglers to feel the dainty bite of the perch."

He said the single-hook rig features a bell sinker on the bottom with a dropper line about 12 inches above the weight. A gold long-shank hook is used to hook the bait and the dropper line should be about six inches long.

Wilkins said the well-equipped perch fisherman will be prepared for any eventuality when it comes to having the proper bait. He usually carries three or four dozen 2-inch emerald shiners in an aerated bait well.

"Minnows are steady producers at times but it's wise to be prepared," he said. "I usually purchase 100 wigglers (larvae of the *Hexagenia limbata* mayfly) before each trip, and if soft-shell crayfish are available, a trip isn't complete unless at least three dozen are aboard. There are times when crabs are the desired bait."

Crayfish are hooked lightly under the tail while shiners are hooked once in the tail or lightly under the dorsal fin. When Wilkins uses wigglers he puts two or three on each hook.

Perch Rigs

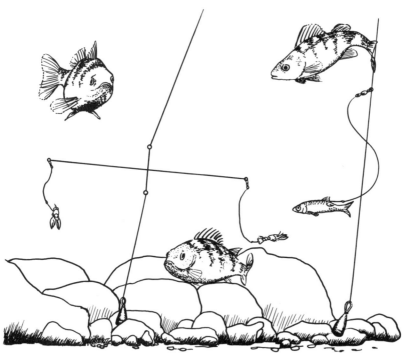

The perch spreader rig allows more than one fish to be landed at a time. Commercial spreaders are available, or some anglers like to rig their own with wire, swivels and monofilament line.

Electronics And Boat Position Target Perch

Wilkins uses two anchors on his boat. One is used to tether the bow of the boat in the proper location while another is used on the stern to prevent the craft from swaying in the breeze.

"My normal procedure is to motor offshore while watching my Loran-C," he said. "When the unit tells me we're over a rock pile and that I suspect holds perch, I switch on my flasher unit.

"I study the flasher for tiny blips that appear and disappear, an indication of perch swimming below the boat," continued Wilkins. "Once we've determined that perch are present I nose the boat into the breeze and have my fishing buddy lower the bow anchor."

Wilkins then uses the motor to cautiously nudge the stern around until the boat parallels the wind direction. He lowers the stern anchor, double checks to make sure it is securely anchored to the bottom and shuts off the engine. Anchoring in this manner prevents yawing or drifting, and perfectly positions the boat directly over the school of perch with the bow into any breeze.

Perch Fishing Is A Numbers Game

Wilkins uses 7- to 8-foot, light-action spinning rods to catch perch. Open-faced spinning reels filled with 6-pound monofilament are ideal. A handful of $^1/_4$- to $^1/_2$-ounce bell-sinkers are needed because the sinkers often wedge in the rocks and cannot be freed. A box of No. 8 or 10 gold long-shank hooks are needed because perch often swallow the bait, and when fish are biting it's easier and faster to tie on a new hook than to free one that has been swallowed.

"The name of the game once we find perch is to catch as many fish as fast as possible," Wilkins said. "Perch hit well for 15 or 20 minutes and then swim off."

The day I fished with him we watched his flasher unit as blips appeared and disappeared off the screen. Perch fed hungrily below us. Wilkins used a perch spreader, baited up each hook with three wigglers and lowered the bait to bottom. I followed suit but chose to try emerald shiners as bait.

The sinker took his bait to bottom, and once slack formed in the line, Wilkins reeled up excess line and kept the sinker just touching bottom. He stared intently at his rodtip, and within seconds it dipped an inch. He set the hook and kept the fish coming to the surface.

"Open the cooler," he hollered. "I want these fish kept on ice."

The cooler lid came up, the fish was taken off the hook and dumped in the box. The rig again sank quickly to bottom. Seconds later two 13-inch yellow perch came flashing out of the water and into the cooler. There are no wasted movements when Wilkins boats fish. They're in the boat, unhooked and into the cooler without a moment's delay.

The fish then began feeding on my minnows. I felt a faint tug, lifted the rodtip an inch or two, and felt another nudge on my line. The hook was set, and the rodtip sagged as twin 12-inch perch broke the surface and were lifted over the gunwale to be unhooked.

Catching jumbo perch is always a thrill, and these gamefish

Locating rock piles on the Great Lakes means using locational equipment like Loran-C or following good triangulation from shore and lake markers.

are a big enough drawing card that I wanted to study them briefly before catching more. The perch from Lake Michigan are often paler than those from other waters.

Most perch from inland lakes are a golden bronze color with vivid black bars extending down their sides. Many of the perch we caught that day were a light gray color with black bars, and the colors are not as pronounced as on other yellow perch although we did catch some fish with the normal coloration.

Many anglers seem to think the paler coloration is in keeping with other Lake Michigan gamefish like steelhead, northern pike and walleyes, which lack the deep and vibrant coloration of fish caught in shallower inland waters.

Be Willing To Move To Sustain Action

The action continued to produce good sport for 20 minutes before someone threw a switch on the fishery. One moment we were bringing in one after another and then the perch disappeared without warning.

"Let's go to another rock pile," Wilkins said as he lifted the stern anchor. "These fish have moved on and you might like to see

Perch this size make good sport and food. Small crayfish, minnows or jigs tipped with grubs can all be used to bring perch to the boat.

how we prospect for fish." He was right. I did.

My anchor was raised, and we peeled away from other boats that had gathered and began checking nearby reefs. The wind had died, so we didn't anchor but merely bobbed on the surface over two rock piles before we found more action.

The next productive rock pile we found was on the edge of a sloping drop-off. The bottom plunged down another 10 feet from the bottom of the pile and we had to anchor on the rocks to keep from drifting out of the area. Wilkins' flasher unit showed rapidly appearing and disappearing blips on the screen and he was sure they were yellow perch.

We anchored, baited up and again sent our bait spiraling toward bottom. I tightened my line, jigged the bell sinker up and down twice on the bottom to make sure the bait was in the proper place, and a hard tug had me setting the hook. A dandy 14-inch perch came to the surface, and we again started icing perch.

The action continued until a stiff breeze came up, blowing down from the Manitou Islands, and Wilkins said we should call it a day. We motored back to the rivermouth. Minutes later we were loading the boat on the trailer and heading for the nearest coffee shop with a great catch of yellow perch.

Perch fishing is nothing new to the Great Lakes. What is new is Wilkins' approach to finding Lake Michigan's yellow perch and staying on top of them long enough to catch a good mess for dinner.

"Don't get me wrong," Wilkins said. "I enjoy a big king salmon ripping out 50 yards of line, and I enjoy the aerial acrobatics of catching a Skamania steelhead.

"But for sheer fun and delightful eating, there is nothing finer than locating a big school of hungry yellow perch, catching them and cooking up a huge batch for an evening meal. The meat is sweet, tender and flaky, and a fisherman is hard put to find any better eating."

That, folks, is what keeps avid perch anglers like Wilkins coming back for more.

12

Winter Perch Tricks

by Craig Bihrle

"There's one," Dave Jensen grunted as he snapped his right wrist upward, his 2-foot ice fishing rod bent like an upside-down U. Seconds later a fat Devils Lake perch splashed up through the eight-inch hole and flopped about on the ice.

As Jensen unhooked the small, $^1/_{32}$-ounce jig we estimated the weight of the fish at about 1 pound. I stood up so Jensen could toss the fish in the bucket I was using for a chair. Five similar-sized perch were already in the bucket.

None, however, were mine.

Frustration began to set in. I fully expected Jensen would out-fish me, but six to zero to start the day, and our holes were only six feet apart?

When Jensen explained what he was doing, I listened. He has been successful at catching winter perch for more than 30 years. Much of his early experience came on North Dakota's Lake Ashtabula, which from the late 1950s through the mid-'60s was one of the better Midwestern perch lakes. In the late 1970s and early '80s, when Devils Lake turned into a winter perch fishing mecca, Jensen was on top of the action, and he authored an article in a prominent outdoor magazine that turned this northeastern North Dakota lake from a local secret into a regional hotspot. If anyone could show me a good day of Devils Lake perch fishing, I figured Jensen could. I was right.

"Drop your lure all the way to the bottom," he directed after I

When the ice comes on the lake it is jumbo perch time. Dave Jensen catches these overstuffed panfish with persistent searching and adaptable presentations.

Winter Perch Tricks

prodded him for his secret. "Raise it up a foot or so, then let it sink to within four to six inches of the bottom. Then start jigging constantly. Every once in awhile, lift your jig up a foot or so and let it settle back."

After following Jensen's advice for about five minutes, I saw the spring bobber attached to the end of my rod twitch, then bend. I set the hook and pulled my first perch of the day through the ice.

My problem was that I hadn't been giving the lure enough action, and my jig was probably too far off the bottom. Jensen suggested that I pull my spring bobber all the way out to the end of my jigging rod, which increased my ability to detect light-biting fish.

For the rest of the day, the action was steady. Not fast and furious like Devils Lake can be, but not bad either, considering the inactivity of the anglers around us. We quit about 2 p.m., after four hours of fishing, with a bucket full of fat perch. A few pushed $1^{1}/_{4}$ pounds. My luck changed for the better, too. I had nearly equalled Jensen's total by the end of the day.

Finding Perch When Others Fail

On our three-hour drive back to Bismarck, I asked Jensen about our success.

One key, Jensen said, was that we had moved around until we found fish. The other was that we were using spring bobbers on our jigging rods, which allowed us to pick up light-biting fish that other anglers using conventional bobbers and "stick-on-a-spike" rigs were not getting.

He sure was right about the moving around part. We had started near the Towers, an area of the 50,000-acre lake crossed by a power line. Then we headed to East Bay, where we had been told perch were hitting the day before. Each of the four spots we tried produced the same results: no fish—and cold feet.

A cold front, which included 40-degree-below windchill, was buffeting Devils Lake and nobody, apparently, was catching fish. We had Jensen's Eagle X7200 LCD in the back of the truck, but even that didn't seem to help. So we used a different fish-finding machine: the telephone. Jensen called one of his most reliable local contacts. "Ziebach Pass," came the answer. "Try 12 feet of water in the old channel."

I had hoped we'd find a school of fish in classic fashion on the LCD. Jensen had done it many times before, but when it doesn't

Jensen checks the depth and looks for marks indicating perch from a portable, liquid crystal graph unit mounted in the back of his vehicle.

work, you have to be willing to try something else.

On Devils Lake, or any other lake for that matter, Jensen said the first step to finding perch is to stop at a bait shop and find out where the fish have been biting. If, for instance, perch were being caught at a certain spot the afternoon before, that might be a good spot to head for in the afternoon. You don't want to head for the nearest cluster of permanent houses and start drilling holes. Most people with permanent houses don't move a lot, Jensen said, and a gathering of permanent houses doesn't mean fish are biting there.

The theory is, Jensen said, that perch in a lake move in large schools. If anglers are fishing the school, they'll move too.

"If you watch the fishermen, they're just like a herd of cattle," Jensen noted. "They'll keep drilling holes and moving with the school of perch."

The herd approach to catching perch can be productive, but it also creates a lot of commotion and activity above the ice. That tends to keep the fish moving, especially if they're in shallower water. "That's not the fun way to catch perch," Jensen said.

Getting Away From The Crowds

When first hitting the ice, Jensen may head for the nearest group of anglers he sees fishing outside or in portable houses. He'll

Winter Perch Tricks   129

take a depth reading, and maybe fish for a few minutes, but he'd rather fish away from the crowds. The depth reading lets him know how deep the fish are, and when he starts looking for a new spot, he'll work similar depths first.

A depthfinder is not a necessity when ice fishing, but a portable unit powered by a 12-volt motorcycle battery, or the battery in your vehicle, can save a lot of work. You can drill a hole and let down a weighted line to find out how deep the water is, but it is a lot quicker to place a transducer in the hole or just stick your transducer in a pail of water (Jensen often uses the minnow bucket), set the pail on the ice, and take a reading. (This method works well only if the ice is less than two feet thick and has a smooth surface.)

Jensen almost always has his depthfinder along when he's after perch. If the ice is not safe to drive on, sometimes he'll set the unit on a wagon and tow it around. If deep snow restricts vehicle access to certain areas, he'll put it on a toboggan. Whichever method is used, the primary purpose is much the same as in the summer: to locate the right depths to fish and also to locate schools of fish. Finding schools, though, is not as easy as finding depth.

"If you use a locator and spend a lot of time at it, you can be successful at finding schools of fish," Jensen said. "You move around a lot, and you drill a lot of holes."

Early in the season and again later in March, especially early or late in the day, shallower water in the 10-15 foot range is a good place to start looking for perch, Jensen said. At those times of year, you're more apt to find active perch. In mid to late winter, you are more likely in deeper water (20 to 30 feet in Devils Lake).

In deep-water situations at midday, where you are over a school of fish and suddenly the fish are gone, Jensen said you should move around and use a locator to try to find the school again. "Drill some more holes and stay with them," he suggested.

How long do you stay in one spot? Jensen said 15 to 20 minutes is long enough. If you haven't had any bites by then, it's time to think about moving. "There are a bunch of fish someplace," Jensen noted. "It's just a matter of finding that school."

Using Spring Bobbers To Detect Bites

It is obvious that you cannot catch fish unless you find them, but there are also times when you find fish on your locator but you cannot catch them. Perhaps a cold front has just gone through, or for some other reason the perch are not real active. At these times a spring bobber puts perch on the ice when nothing else seems to produce—even a jigging rod fished with no bobber at all.

A spring bobber is simply a thick wire or thin metal bar that acts as a super-sensitive extension to your rod. Some ice fishing rods come with the spring bobber attached. All you do is thread the line through it and extend it out as far as it will go. You can also buy similar devices which clip to the rod.

There are two other types of spring bobbers you can purchase commercially. One is a four-inch wire with a colored bead attached to one end. To attach this bobber you slide the wire through the last line guide and clip the plain end of the wire to the rod. The fishing line threads through a guide under the ball.

Another spring bobber looks like a spring from a ball-point pen. The spring is attached to the end of the rod, and the line is threaded through it. It is from this device that the spring bobber gets its name.

Most spring bobbers are relatively inexpensive. For between $1 and $2 you can get a single or double pack, which should last a

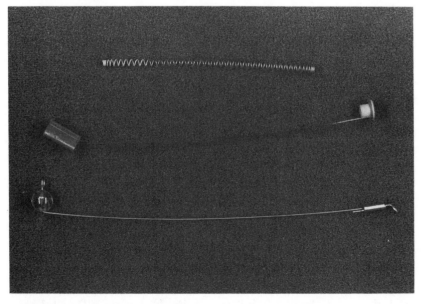

Three types of spring bobbers available commercially include (top to bottom) spring, flat wire and light wire with bead.

Winter Perch:

Fishing With A Spring Bobber

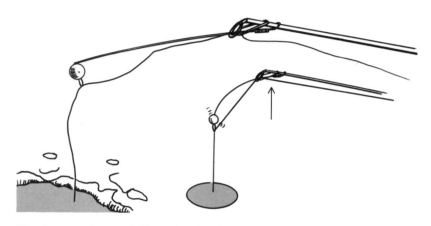

The advantage of a spring bobber: When the fish is holding the bait, but not moving it, raising the rod slightly will reveal the bite, allowing the angler to set the hook on many fish that would otherwise be missed when using a conventional floating bobber.

lot longer than your average ice fishing jig.

All types of spring bobbers give you greater ability to detect a strike than with a plain jigging rod. The springs are so flexible that even the slightest line movement will jar them. A hit that won't even jiggle most conventional floating bobbers will move a spring bobber.

The advantage of a spring bobber can be obvious even when no movement of the spring is detected. By slowly lifting the rod-tip, the bobber will drop if a perch is holding onto the bait. This type of bite detection cannot be achieved with even the lightest floating bobber.

Jensen has been using spring bobbers to catch perch for some 15 years now. "The reason I started," he remembered, "was that after observing both trout and perch under the ice—watching their movements and how they bit—we realized quickly that (floating) bobbers weren't going to cut it."

When fish are active and the weather is stable, Jensen said, small floating bobbers work fine. It is likely that most Devils Lake perch are caught by anglers using bobbers.

But, Jensen said, "when you have a cold front, and the fish aren't real active, they will inhale the bait and then quickly spit it out. We saw this demonstrated a number of times while watching perch at the bottom of a lake. Fish can take these lures in and spit them out and not even move the bobber.

"By using the spring bobber, you're able to detect the slightest indication that a fish is holding the bait. You want to set the hook as soon as the bait is inhaled."

Jensen likes to set the hook with a short, stern flick of the wrist, rather than a big sweeping arm movement. That way, he said, if you miss the perch you can drop the lure back down quickly and go after the fish again. "It doesn't take a six-foot arc to find out if you've hooked a fish," Jensen said. "And if you keep your hooks sharp it doesn't take a hard set to get the point embedded in the perch's mouth."

A spring bobber alone will not guarantee that you will catch fish. If you are not jigging the lure properly, or if you don't have the lure at the proper depth, you will not catch as many fish. My initial experience fishing with Jensen was evidence of that, and I wasted some valuable fishing time figuring this out.

Some of Jensen's favorite winter perch tackle include (l to r) a small Russian spoon, a variety of small ice jigs and a small Swedish pimple with single hook. He keeps a hook sharpener (background) within reach.

This jumbo yellow perch fell to a light-colored ice jig with a black dot. When active, perch will hit big baits, but during periods of inactivity, the smallest baits must be used.

Getting The Bait Right

Jensen will usually use two jigging rods. Sometimes he will jig both; other times he will jig one and use a minnow and bobber on the other. The secret, Jensen said, is that a moving bait attracts fish. By jigging, you are actually trying to attract fish from a distance.

Using an ice jig with some flash to it helps to attract fish. Jensen likes small teardrop jigs or ice flies, in either $^{1}/_{32}$- or $^{1}/_{16}$-ounce, and a No. 8 or 10 hook. Jensen likes light colors in shallower water, and dark colors in deeper water. "But," he said, "movement, to me, has always been more important than color."

To dress up a jig, Jensen will always use a wax worm or perch eye when using the spring bobber and occasionally will use this combination under a floating bobber. Wax worms under a bobber will generate bites, Jensen noted. "But the bites are not as numerous. When there's a lure moving, you're attracting those fish in from a distance. If it's just sitting there still, you've got to rely on their eyesight, and they almost always have to pass within a foot or so of the stationary lure to notice it."

Minnows, 1 to 1¹/₂ inches long, are the best choice under a floating bobber, but Jensen thinks it takes too long for the average perch to get a minnow in its mouth. "When they do take it," he said, "many times their mouth is too small and they've only got the minnow by the head."

When he uses minnows, Jensen likes to fish them below small Swedish Pimples or Russian spoons. "Something that has a little flash to it," he explained. "They'll be working all the time for you, as opposed to a plain hook."

Much of what Jensen told me held true on our fishing trip. Both of us caught fish using ice jigging rods with spring bobbers, fishing small white ice jigs and wax worms. In holes within reach we set up our second rods with small minnows suspended under bobbers. Jensen caught two perch on minnows and missed a couple of others. I noticed only one quick bite on my minnow all day.

Perch fishing isn't always so tough. Some days you can fish anywhere and catch fish on just about anything you drop down the hole, with a big bobber on top besides. But when the perch are finicky and hard to find, your odds will improve if you drill a few more holes, move a little more and slip on a spring bobber.

Better yet, leave the spring bobber on all the time. It works great when the fish are active, too.

Catfish

13

Fresh Bait
For Giant Cats

by Gerald Almy

blood-red sun nudges its way above the cypress-rimmed horizon in the east as Bob George steers the 20-foot fishing boat in tight circles, studying his depthfinder intently. Suddenly the flasher lights up red for 15 feet. George jerks the big outboard into neutral, cuts the motor, and with one deft movement eases a huge sea anchor overboard.

We are seemingly in the middle of nowhere—miles from shore—on sprawling Santee-Cooper Lake in the lowlands of central South Carolina. But to the seasoned guide, we are on the perfect spot to catch a giant blue catfish or perhaps even a channel or flathead.

And if anyone should know where and how to catch giant open-water cats, it's George. Each year his clients pull dozens of fish in the 30- to 60-pound range, plus hundreds of slightly smaller ones in the 10- to 25-pound class from these fertile lake waters—fish that George puts them onto with his keen knowledge of catfish habits. The techniques this catfish master uses can be productive on large open waters wherever these bewhiskered fish are found.

"This is part of an old canal wall that the slaves built," said the laconic guide. "It's 40 feet down but comes up about 15 feet off the bottom. Big cats love vertical structure like that."

Steaking a fresh herring he caught the day before in the locks at the nearby dam into five chunks of fresh bait, the guide deftly

Each year guide Bob George leads clients to scores of giant catfish like the one the author caught (above). He uses fresh bait and knowledge of underwater structure to do it.

Fresh Bait For Giant Cats

slips each one onto a 6/0 Eagle Claw Series 42 RP hook. Eighteen inches above the hook is a stout swivel, above that a 1-ounce egg sinker.

Lowering the bait to the bottom with the long baitcasting outfit, George feels the weight touch the lake floor, reels up a foot and places the rod in a holder. Five times the ritual is repeated, and before guide and angler have even had a chance to pour a cup of coffee from the green, metal thermos, one of the rods bounces sharply in its holder and bends into a deep, throbbing arch.

Jumping from my seat, I grab the outfit from its holder, set the hook and feel the incredible weight and power of a huge cat bulling toward cover. There is nothing to do but hold on and hope for the best during the first few minutes as the wild cat rampages deep. But finally I gain a bit of line and work the cat near the surface. Seeing the boat, the big catfish surges back deep, stripping 30-pound line from the reel like sewing thread.

I bring the fish back to the surface again. This time George swiftly engulfs it with the mesh of the landing net. Struggling, we hoist aboard 47 pounds of sleek blue catfish.

It is a massive fish but for George, one of the premier catfish guides on South Carolina's 170,000-acre Santee-Cooper Lake, it's just another good cat, one of countless huge fish his customers take every season. And there are others—even larger fish—that never are subdued.

"I was out with a party striper fishing, but the rockfish (stripers) weren't doing anything," said George. "I said to those boys, 'Let's get over on some real action!' We went to one of my favorite catfish spots and I set out five lines. Before I could put out the sixth outfit, all five of those rods bent double. We never did get any of those fish. Every cat that bit broke 30-pound line."

Fortunately, not all cats tear up his tackle quite so badly. With fish capable of doing what those five cats did, however, George insists on stout gear for challenging big blues, channels and flatheads.

Gearing Up For Giant Cats

George recommends using an 8- to 9-foot medium- or heavyweight graphite casting rod. "The long rod is helpful for keeping baits separated and is also effective for pulling fish out from beneath the boat during a fight or keeping them away from the pro-

Fresh Bait Rig

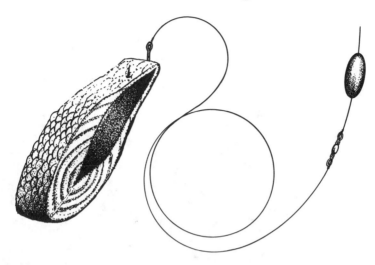

A simple herring steak on a 6/0 hook is George's favorite catfish bait. He rigs the hook 2 to 3 feet below a sliding egg sinker and swivel.

peller blades," said George. "A long handle is best so the rod can fit easily in a holder and be wedged under your arm when fighting a huge cat. This latter point is particularly important, since battles with lunker catfish might last 20 minutes or more when a particularly big fish is hooked."

A levelwind reel with smooth drag is George's choice, spooled with 25- or 30-pound monofilament. To this the guide attaches a 2- to 3-foot, 30- to 50-pound test leader connected to the main line with a stout No. 3 swivel. Above the swivel on the main line he threads a $1/2$- to 2-ounce egg sinker. For hooks, George uses Eagle Claw Series 42 RP, though he says any good strong bait hook will work. Sizes 4/0 to 7/0 are useful, depending on the size bait you're using and the size fish present.

Besides quality rods, reels, swivels, hooks, weights and fresh line, you'll need a good boat for open-water catfishing. A seaworthy craft of 17 feet or longer is preferable, though in smaller waters a 15- or 16-footer might do. The boat should be deep-sided, since rough weather may develop in the open-water haunts you'll be fishing for big cats. Many of the boats designed for striper fishing and inshore saltwater fishing are perfect for catfishing on large

Guide George studies his depthfinder as he circles over potential catfish-holding locations. He prefers rough, vertical structure.

lakes. The bigger the boat, the more you can spread your rods out and cover a wide area with the baits.

Any boat you have should be rigged with a compass, depthfinder, anchor, cooler, fillet knife, cutting board, topographic maps, spare tools and terminal gear. A large fish box or heavy-duty stringer will be required to handle catfish that might weigh 50 pounds or more. Besides these items, a good catfishing boat needs quality rod holders.

Nothing Tops Fresh Bait

With the proper boat and correct tackle, the only item needed to begin searching for big cats is bait. Countless brands of commercial and homemade catfish baits are used to take old whiskerface, but George says there is nothing that can top fresh, natural baits. He recommends choosing offerings that are native to the waters you fish and obtaining the freshest bait possible.

Starting in mid-February, locks on the Santee-Cooper dam near Pinopolis are opened, letting anadromous herring into the lake. These thin, silver fish from the Atlantic Ocean can be dipped or caught with cast nets near the dam. This is the Santee-

Cooper guide's favorite offering from midwinter through spring. Cats will hit whole live herring, and flatheads especially like these large baits. However, for blues and channels, chunking the herring into four or five steaks about three-quarters of an inch thick is best. The head also makes a good bait.

If you don't have herring in the waters you fish, shad is an excellent alternative. Either whole or cut shad, depending on the size, can be used. Catch them with throw nets, dip them or snag them and always use the freshest bait you can obtain. Either keep the bait alive or place it on ice immediately after obtaining it.

In summer months, catalpa worms start appearing on shoreline trees and cats feed heavily on them. Amazingly, fish up to 45 pounds will take these small offerings fished on the bottom. Freshwater mussels are another good catfish bait. But nothing, in George's opinion, tops fresh cut bait, particularly an oily variety such as herring or shad.

Finding Giant Cats Through The Seasons

When searching for big catfish, George stresses the importance of finding a lake that has a history of producing exceptional

George cuts fresh herring into 1-inch-thick steaks. Head and tail sections also work, and on occasion, he may use an entire fish.

George hoists a smaller cat, about 15 pounds, on Santee-Cooper Lake in South Carolina.

sized fish. NAFC members should consult their state fishery department, local F.I.N affiliates, wardens and biologists to ferret out these top spots for lunker cats.

Once you have selected a body of water, purchase a topographic map of the lake and study it to find possible catfish hangouts. Then go out in your boat and locate those spots with the depthfinder. Search for actual fish, too, which will appear as large inverted U's or V's on a graph or thick bands on a flasher, on or near the bottom.

In spring large catfish often move into surprisingly shallow water, according to George. "I've caught huge ones in as little as three feet of water in March and April," he said. "Other times they might be as deep as 12 feet." Long, sloping points, flats, bars, old roadbeds and shallow, flooded timber all are worth prospecting for spring catfish. Anchor and cast to the area where you expect fish to be, put the rods in their holders and wait. When a fish takes the bait, give him a few seconds, then set the hooks with a hard sweep of the rod.

As the water warms up in summer, look for big cats in deeper water where the fish seek out their preferred temperature range and better oxygen supplies. Shallows still can produce a flurry of

Complete Angler's Library

George's Hotspots For Giant Cats

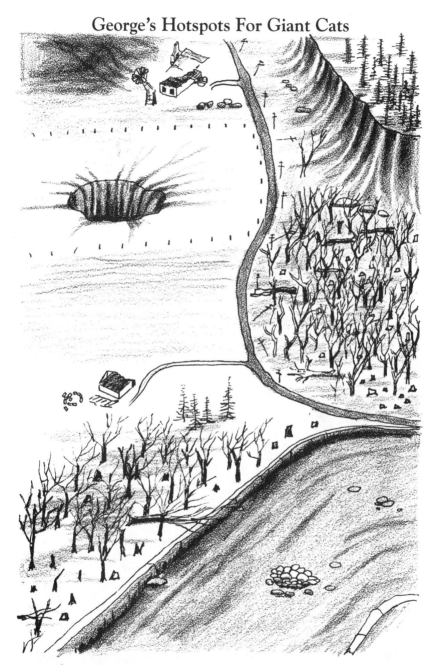

George uses a topographic map dated before the flooding of the reservoir to locate favored underwater structure, including old buildings, canal walls, cliffs and roadways. During summer, fall and winter he searches sharp breaks for signs of cats.

It takes two deckhands to get a catfish of nearly 50 pounds into the boat, but George (right) and his clients have managed the feat many times.

action early and late in the day, but for the most part, deep water is the payoff zone for the largest summer catfish. Depths of 20 to 60 feet are optimum, according to Bob.

But depth is only part of the formula. "Old flooded bridges, canals, roadbeds, buildings, cemeteries, sharp drop-offs, holes, timbered bars, anything rough—that's what a big cat will hold around," George said. "They seem to like tall structure, like a wall on a flooded building or canal. When the depthfinder lights up red for a 10- to 15-foot span, you're on top-notch cat cover!" A uniformly flat bottom that suddenly drops off five or ten feet into a hole is another choice spot for finding jumbo summer catfish.

Anchoring, Drifting Techniques Both Catch Cats

Once you have located prime, deep-water catfish structure using your topo map and depthfinder, two fishing methods can pay off, according to George—anchoring or drift fishing. Anchoring works particularly well when you have a small, specific piece of structure you believe fish are holding on such as a flooded building or sharp drop-off. This is the best way to stay exactly on top of that bottom cover. If it's a particularly windy day, anchoring works best.

At other times, George may drift fish. This is particularly true if he's covering a broad area where cats could be more scattered. Drift fishing allows you to cover lots of water and puts the offering in front of many fish.

If you thought cats were too lethargic to chase and catch a moving bait, think again. Some of the biggest cats fall for this technique. They aren't a bit timid or lazy about chasing a bait pulled in front of them. Just wait until you hook into a 40-pounder using Bob George's fresh-bait techniques. You'll see for yourself. Big cats are anything but lazy.

14

Cats On The Rocks

by John Phillips

The drag complained once more, and my rod pretzeled as it had all morning long. However, this time there was no stopping the charge of the catfish. The fish was too big and powerful, and the drag was set too tight for a fish that surely weighed more than 20 pounds.

When the line fell back limp, Bob Holmes of Trenton, Tennessee, chuckled and said, "I told you you'd get hold of a good one before the day was over."

Holmes, a local catfish expert, and I were fishing the rocks on the Tennessee River during the spring spawn. Catfish, just like all other species of fish, have seasonal migration patterns, Holmes told me. During the spring, blue cats and channel cats move into rocky shorelines to look for holes in which to lay their eggs.

"Cats on the Tennessee River usually spawn in late April, the entire month of May and early June," Holmes reported. "The cats prefer water temperatures in the low- to mid-60s when they spawn, and fisheries biologists in most any area can tell you when that normally occurs."

Besides providing nest sites for the cats, the rocky structures usually warm up first because of the ability of the rocks to hold heat and warm up the water around them. One of the best man-made areas to find catfish is along riprap, which generally is composed of large limestone rocks used to hold the shoreline around bridge approaches, dam faces, causeways, breakwaters and marinas. Other places where cats will spawn in the spring include

By knowing when catfish spawn and where to look for them, Bob Holmes catches plenty of "no-scales" during the spring season.

Cats On The Rocks

Rigging A Slip Bobber For Catfish

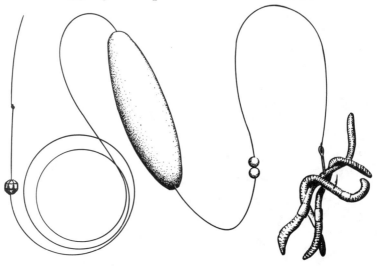

A slip bobber with small stop knot allows Holmes to cast freely and fight catfish all the way to the boat, no matter what depth he is fishing.

natural rock bluffs, rock slides, rocky points or exposed layers of underwater shale. The most productive sites include rocky spawning regions close to deep water like river channels, creek channels or dredged channels. Although monster-sized catfish may be taken along the rocks during the spawn, the average fish will weigh from 1 to 5 pounds.

"Even though cats will hold in one to 30 feet of water during the spawn, depending on weather and water conditions, I usually take most of my fish in five to 10 feet of water," Holmes explained.

Most of the time, Holmes suspends his bait off bottom with a slip bobber and fishes along the edge of a break where shallow rocks drop off into deeper water. He likes to work the bank by moving his bait parallel to the shoreline, following the same depth contour.

"Cats will show up on rocky banks that face south or southwest first, because these banks are the quickest to warm up," Holmes said. "Spots where you catch the most catfish will have a moderate to light current. A current circulates the water through a bedding region better, and the baitfish seem to hold tighter to the rocks when the water is moving."

Rigging For Cats On The Rocks

"Although I have caught cats on 5-, 6- and 7-foot rods, recently I have refined my techniques and have started using a 10-foot, medium- to heavy-action pole," Holmes said. "I prefer the longer pole as well as a medium-size spinning reel like the Mitchell 300 or a Lew's Speed Spin Three. I fish with 10- to 20-pound test Berkley XT line because I need a line that has enough abrasion resistance to keep the sandpaper-like teeth of the catfish from damaging the line and breaking off. This line will also hold up better around sharp rocks. With a 10-foot pole, I can use my slip cork and fish all the depths from 0 to 20 feet."

Holmes likes to fish with either a styrofoam or balsa slip bobber that's 3 to 4 inches long and $1^{1}/_{2}$ to $1^{3}/_{4}$ inches in diameter. He

Finding Catfish On Rocks

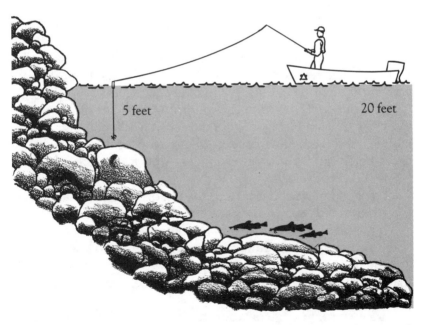

5 feet

20 feet

Holmes fishes rocky shorelines with a slip bobber rigged to a shallow depth. He probes a piece of shoreline at that depth, then sets the bobber deeper and repeats until he locates catfish, usually somewhere between 5 and 15 feet in springtime.

particularly likes the corks made by Float High in Alexander, Kentucky, which he considers some of the best. Holmes also utilizes a Knot-Tight bobber stopper to position the cork at the depth he wants to fish. He prefers this type of bobber stop because its small size allows it to travel easily through the guides of his poles.

Either No. 1 or No. 3 split shot are the sinkers Holmes uses to carry his bait to the bottom, depending on the weight needed to balance the cork. On the end of the line, he ties either a No. 4 or No. 6 treble hook, which he has found holds the bait tighter and improves hooking ability.

Check Local Catfish "Menu" Before Hitting The Water

Holmes' menu of favorite baits includes night crawlers, frozen catalpa worms, bait shrimp, strips of river herring or the gut of cut gizzard shad, depending upon availability and the mood of the fish. Across the country, anglers successfully fish for catfish with a wide variety of baits, including chicken livers, live minnows, hellgrammites, hot dogs and cheese that has been saturated in some type of catfish attractant. He says marina operators and bait shop owners in the areas he has fished usually know the most productive catfish baits at any particular time. Holmes always adds a commercial fish scent such as Fish Formula Catfish Scent or Fish Formula Shad to his baits. Although he normally only fishes for a half-day when he goes after cats, Holmes will catch from 10 to 30 cats in that half-day's outing. He rarely gets skunked.

"If an angler fishes from early morning until late afternoon on a day the cats are biting, he will often catch 100 pounds of cats," Holmes observed. "I've caught 15- to 20-pound catfish on the rocks before and know other anglers who have taken 50- and 60-pound cats there."

The good news about fishing the rocks is that once an angler locates a catfish spawning site in rocky structure he can often catch catfish in that same region for four to six weeks, because different catfish spawn at different times. Anglers who know how to fish the rocks and have learned the rocky shoreline where catfish spawn every year can fish the same rocky sites year after year and fill their coolers with catfish.

"I know some anglers who only fish for cats during the six weeks of the spawn," Holmes said. "During that time, they catch all the cats they want for the year."

Holmes impales his gob of worms, a favorite bait, on a treble hook. He advises fishermen to check with local bait shops to learn the best bait in their area.

Pinpointing the correct depth is the key to taking cats on the rocks. During the spring, the fish tend to hold at the same depth. Floating your bait in a depth zone where cats are feeding can make the difference between catching fish and not catching them.

"I usually begin by controlling the boat with my trolling motor as I cast to the bank," Holmes explained. "I'll set my cork at five feet to begin and fish 100 to 200 yards of the bank at that depth. If I don't take a catfish, I'll turn my boat around and return down the same bank with the cork set at eight feet. I'll continue this process until I've fished all the water from five to 20 feet deep. When I catch a couple of cats at a certain depth, that's where I'll fish."

The conditions that cause cats to feed shallow or deep are the same that make bass move up or down. Holmes has found that the warmer the water, the shallower the catfish will be. In clear water, look deeper to locate the cats.

Catfish can be caught in shallow water when the water is rising, but will be taken in deeper water when the water level is falling. Finally, he notes, more catfish will be caught on points than along the banks when the water level is falling.

In areas where both channel catfish and blue catfish are in a river or a lake, channel catfish will show up on the rocks first—often as much as a week or more before the blues. Because channel catfish will leave a spawning area first, anglers are more likely to catch blue catfish later in the season.

"An angler who wants to have great sport can use 6- to 8-pound test line and an ultra-light rod," said Holmes. "The only problem with light-line tactics is that the fish will wear the line much quicker, and an angler must retie after every cat. Also, you'll generally hook at least one fish a day that will take all the line off your spool without ever stopping!"

More Than One Way To Skin A Cat

John Hill of Fisherman's Resort in Town Creek, Alabama, below Wheeler Dam on the Tennessee River, fishes for catfish in the rocks using a different technique.

"In early spring, if our area has had flooding conditions, the big blue cats will move up to the base of the dam and begin to spawn in the rocks below the dam where lots of riprap and large boulders are located," Hill said. "If spring rains bring the water up early, big blues will show up as early as March."

Hill has learned the biggest catfish of the year in his region often are the first spawners. Although anglers do catch these trophy-sized catfish using rods and reels, Hill prefers to fish jugs.

"Most of the water below the dam is between 8 and 10 feet deep," Hill commented. "By setting out eight or 10 jugs with lines at different depths, I usually can determine the depth the cats are feeding by which jugs are producing fish. When I pinpoint the depth the cats prefer, I either shorten or lengthen my lines so my baits will hold in that depth of water."

With 50 jugs out, Hill is busy chasing jugs and catching catfish all day long. The key to landing a big catfish on a jug is not to try to overpower the fish.

"I approach a jug as quietly as possible when I think I have a big cat on," Hill explained. "Then very gently I lift the string to lead the cat to the surface. If the cat gets excited and starts to fight, I release the jug to avoid tearing the hook out of the fish's mouth or breaking the line. If the cat's calm, I slip a net under it and bring it to the boat.

"One of the main reasons people lose big catfish is they try to fight the fish into the boat. If you're holding a jug with a straight line to a cat, and the fish weighs 50 pounds or more, 99 times out of 100, that fish either will break the line or straighten the hook.

Rocky, riprap points or banks draw Holmes, as well as spawning catfish. He also finds riprap along bridge pilings to be productive locations in the spring.

Therefore I let the jug play the cat and attempt to be as quiet and gentle as I can with a big fish until I have the net under it."

Hill, like Holmes, believes the best cat-catching occurs when the cats are actually spawning. Tailrace fishing for catfish in most parts of the country seems to be highly popular throughout much of the spring and summer. But successful cat anglers know how, where and when catfish go to the rocks along the points, rocky banks and riprap to spawn. If they use Holmes' or Hill's techniques for catching cats, they're likely to catch the most and the biggest catfish of the season.

15

Floatin' On For Cats

by Rick Taylor

What could be finer than lying back in the plush greenery of a riverbank...watching your line twitter against the gently flowing current...dreaming of some barbel-faced behemoth sliding away with your bait? To many of us, fishing doesn't get any better.

It's relaxing. It's Americana at its best. And according to one of this country's top catfishing experts, it's relatively unproductive.

"The best way to catch a lot of big cats," points out Otis "Toad" Smith, the subject of numerous articles and the co-author of *Channel Catfish Fever*, "is to get to areas that most other fishermen don't or can't. And that usually calls for a boat."

It doesn't have to be anything big or fancy, contends this captain of a modest, 14-foot aluminum vee-hull with a 15-horsepower outboard. In fact, the smaller and simpler, the better.

"The other thing you need is a river that's just large enough to navigate," continued Toad. "If the river's too large, there may be a lot of boat traffic. If it's too small, anglers can get to any part of it on foot."

A boat also gives the catfisherman the ability to quickly establish his quarry's daily pattern(s). These fish can be in brush piles, cutbanks, holes, ripples, slow current or fast current. It may depend mostly on the time of year, but their location can change from day to day. So mobility is a must.

"With a boat you can cover the entire river," said Toad. "The

Toad Smith with a string of average-run river cats. Smith takes the bait to the catfish, rather than wait for the cat to come to him.

Floatin' On For Cats

same is true for any brush pile, hole or similar fish-holding structure. If I were walking a river, in a day I could work maybe one mile of one side. With a boat I could cover eight to 10 miles and both sides. And I wouldn't have to put up with all the mud and bugs shore-walkers do."

Toad has fished dozens of rivers across America, including a few outside our borders. His main stomping grounds, however, are the small-to-medium flowages of northwestern Iowa and southern Minnesota. From places like the Big Sioux River in Iowa and the Minnesota River, he consistently takes cats in the 4- to 12-pound range.

Seasonal Patterns Of River Cats

This 40-year veteran of the sport has found that early spring is the time both flathead and channel cats migrate upstream to fast-water areas. They hold in places just out of the current, like the first deep water below a dam, and move up in schools to feed around that structure periodically throughout the day. NAFC members can also find them on the top (up-current end) of holes and working into ripples.

By summer, most rivers have dropped and stabilized, and the cats will generally move to brush piles, bank cuts, the bottom of ripples or the down-current side of holes. Toad feels the pre-spawn period of June and early July is the best time for catfish, because the larger fish are more aggressive. They become less active during the spawning period of mid-July and return to their active ways in August.

By September the river is usually at its lowest and the water temperature is cooling. This tends to push baitfish toward the deepest holes, so naturally catfish will follow. This is when Toad relies almost exclusively on freshly cut or live bait, placing the offering right in the heart of the hole. The fish are still quite active until the water temperature drops to about the 55-degree mark.

"In the course of a year, the key to finding active catfish," said this 48-year-old family man from Sibley, Iowa, "is to go when the river is rising, which is usually the case in spring. Fresh food is being washed in from the surrounding countryside and this really turns cats on. The fishing can be pretty good during periods of stabilized water, too. But when the river is falling, they are tough to catch."

Seasonal Catfish Locations In Small Rivers

During active periods, such as spring, catfish may move into the current at the head of a ripple (A). More often they will settle behind a large rock out of the current (B). As river water rises and warms in the spring, cats move upstream in search of food (C). An anxious cat may be found at the head of a deep hole (D), while a few may roam the hole (E). The front side of snags is a preferred location (F). Inactive cats hold in the deeper part of the hole (G), or within the snag. Occasionally they will hold behind a snag, or at the rear of the hole (H). After early fall, most cats feed and rest in the deeper part of the hole (I).

Selecting The Best Baits

Cats rely far more on their sense of smell than sight to locate food, so water clarity means little to these fish. As Toad Smith quips, the catfish is like "one giant taste bud:" it can pick up even the slightest scent through both its barbels and skin. The fish is probably more aware of a piece of food upstream than is any other fish in the water.

Consequently, Toad, whose credits include channel cats more than 30 pounds and flatheads nudging the 50-pound mark, is particular about his baits.

"Stink baits are okay," he said, "but they generally catch smaller fish. I'll take more and larger cats on freshly cut chubs, suckers or whatever the primary forage is in that particular river. And there are times during the hot months of July and August when a blood bait works quite well, too, especially at night."

Toad, who once caught a 6-pound channel cat on a piece of his own heart (following open-heart surgery), keeps his live bait in the boat's aerated livewell. Any that die are put on ice. Freshness is the operative word.

Once his boat is in position and holding—via one of his two 20-pound anchors—he cuts a 3- to 4-inch-long chub in two at an angle. Making this wedge shape, and hooking into the corner of the wider end, keeps the bait from spinning and twisting the line. With larger baits, such as a 10-inch sucker, Toad fillets one side and cuts this slab into two or three pieces, again at an angle.

Some Of The Best Bait Is Homemade

Toad's other favorite catfish attractor is blood bait, which he makes himself. He brings home buckets of congealed blood from a nearby chicken plant and pours it on a screen for drying. The substance is then cut into $10x1x^1/_4$-inch strips and frozen until required for fishing.

Using a No. 6 Eagle Claw 374 treble hook, he ties a 10-inch tag line onto the eye, then wraps the blood bait around the shaft in a crisscross fashion. After securing the bait on one of the hooks, he wraps the tag line around it and finishes by tucking the line under one of the hook's barbs. This holds his blood bait in place for casting and working in currents.

"The nice thing about chicken blood," says Toad, "is that during summer when the cats are holed up behind brush piles, it

Fillet a baitfish, removing the meat on each side, and use each strip to bait a hook. The exposed fillet releases scent more quickly than a whole baitfish.

works like a triggering device to fire them up and coax them out from the tangles. As soon as it hits the water, the blood trails down current. If nothing happens, I may even take a handful of blood and throw it out in front of that brush pile I am fishing."

If you have been working a school of catfish regularly and the action is declining, your quarry may be getting used to your standard offerings. This is one time when Toad may try live bait. Yet rather than just toss in the chub or sucker, he often makes a number of tiny cuts on its body with a razor blade. This increases the prey's scent and has proven an excellent nighttime tactic as well.

"Keep the hook exposed," warned Toad. "Catfish don't have the faintest idea what a hook is and don't seem to mind its feel. And since you hold the bait a few feet away from any brush pile or snag anyway, the hook doesn't need to be weedless."

Tackle For River Cats

Toad prefers the Eagle Claw 84 Hook in the 3/0 size for channel cats and 5/0 for flatheads. He's pretty adamant about using Trilene's new Solar XT high-visibility green line, because it helps him see strikes before he feels them. His choices are 20-pound test

Blood strips are formed by laying coagulated chicken blood on a screen and cutting into strips. Finished strips should be about 1 inch wide, ¹/₄ inch thick and 8 inches long. Freeze them in containers for later use.

for channels and 30-pound test for flatheads.

"The rod is very important," said Toad. "I like a two-piece European rod because it's light enough to cast a long way, yet it has enough backbone for a good hookset, even during those times I've drifted my bait 100 yards downstream. I use a Garcia 6500 reel because it has a star drag and a free spool with a clicker, which comes in handy at night when you can't always see your line." It may also seem odd, but Toad often uses floats when fishing.

Catfishing and bobbers may not seem synonymous. But when used correctly, slip floats can be very effective. One of those times is when the cats are active, say in the spring, and feeding off the bottom. Another is when you are trying to work the bait into a tight spot. And do not overlook using them when you are having trouble seeing or feeling a strike.

But best of all, floats allow you to drift the bait steadily, accurately and relatively snag-free along the bottom as you search for active fish. Need to change depth quickly? Just reel in, slide the floatstop up or down your line, and cast back out.

Slip floats come in a number of shapes and sizes. For heavy

baits and/or heavy currents, Toad likes a rounder, pear-shaped style, such as the Wazp Gazzet. The one he uses most often, however, is called the cigar. Shaped as the name implies, its more streamlined form handles a medium to light current quite well.

Toad prefers the bell sinker, because it holds better on the bottom in current than an egg sinker. If you can't find this style, a walking sinker is a fair substitute. For split shot, Toad says buy the round, soft ones. If they have "ears," they move erratically in the water and tend to snag more. If the shot is soft enough, you'll have no trouble pinching it on or taking it off your line.

The Art Of Scouting For River Cats

Since your boat frees you from the land, there is little point in scouting areas that have been fished readily by shorewalkers. Ignore the obvious. Go past that bridge or that snag-infested bank with a beaten path and scattered soft drink cans.

After Toad has eliminated these, he looks for meandering stretches of the river, as opposed to straight ones. Holes are the foundation of cat hangouts and you'll find most of them cut by the curving current.

By moving, observing, fishing, Toad tries to find that one- or two-mile section of river with all the best ingredients, namely large, deep holes relatively close together and quality structure and cover, such as brush piles, cutbanks and ripples. He also looks for a tributary or two to help keep the catfish populous re-stocked during changing water conditions. The best time to scout is when the river is low; you often find good spots that are hidden by high water. Yet the search doesn't end there.

"After doing your research, there's only one true way to locate cats," Toad said. "And that's by fishing. Don't spend too much time in any one place. Move quickly at first, looking for the active cats. You'll be surprised how many fish this can put on your stringer.

"Then, after you've learned that stretch and feel pretty sure where the best holes are," he advised, "you can set up and fish them for longer periods."

Working A Likely Spot

The time-honored way to run a river is upstream. By going to your farthermost spot first, you can idle or drift quietly down to the next with little disruption. And in the unfortunate case of motor trouble, it's always nice to know the current is in your favor.

When his eye is on, say, a fallen tree at the top end of a hole, Toad usually anchors his boat 20 to 40 yards directly upstream of the area. The exact distance hinges on a number of factors, such as speed of current, layout of the snag and depth of water.

From the rear of the boat he casts straight back, then feeds out the appropriate amount of line to set the bait five to 10 yards upstream of the cover. The idea at first is to see if any cats will swim upstream to take the bait, well clear of the obstacles.

If nothing hits in a few minutes, Toad will let the bait drift back a few more feet. This continues until he is as close to the snag as he dares. If there is still not a taker—and the spot looks good—he pulls up the anchor and repositions his boat to the side of the tree or hole. From this vantage point, he can either cast upstream at an angle and bring the bait back through the target area, or he can flip forward into other places where fish have not yet seen or smelled the bait. Except when water temperatures are below 55 degrees, Toad rarely fishes the center or deep part of a hole, since this is mostly the cat's resting area.

Toad's final attempt here is aimed at the back end of the hole, casting upstream. Eddies often form here, so his bait may actually drift up into the hole. Normally, this is the least likely place for an active catfish, but Toad has seen times when they all seem to be here.

"Like I said, if you're just scouting, don't work this hole more than a few minutes," said Toad. "But if you've already established that this is a good spot, give it 20 or 30 minutes before moving on. Don't write it off. An hour from now you may have all the action you can handle."

Best Times Of Day For River Cats

Being less dependent on sight (and therefore, light) for feeding, cats can go on the feed just about any time of the day or night. As a rule during the main fishing months, you may see a slow, steady increase in the action from noon to dusk. From then on, a sharper rise can be expected throughout the night, peaking at dawn and tapering off for the rest of the morning. As Toad advises, do not get too comfortable around the campfire, but move frequently, fishing proven spots longest.

Smith pulls a cat from below a brush pile. He places his bait at the leading edge of the cover to lure cats out.

Putting The Final Touches On Your Catch

Toad's final advice concerns the final stage of your outing: cooking your catch. Fillet the catfish and—if it is a large one—cut the slabs into frying-pan size. Then, before breading or cooking, boil those pieces for two minutes. This isn't necessary with flatheads, but a channel cat's meat tends to be a little oily. Boiling it will enhance its flavor.

Toad's catfishing techniques require a bit more work than most fishermen are willing to put in. That is precisely why they work so well. Try them yourself and see.

Walleye And Sauger

16

Walleyes On Wire

by Darl Black

"C"an't say I've ever felt anything like this before," I told
my instructor as I brought a nice walleye to the boat. "I
can feel every twist and turn the fish is making. The
sensitivity is incredible!" Even more incredible was
the fact it was a fiberglass rod, not a state-of-the-art graphite.

Every movement of the fish could be detected because of the
special line. It wasn't monofilament or Dacron—but wire.

I would never have believed it if I hadn't experienced it myself. Wire! Not the thick Monel or braided wire that had been
used years ago for lake trout fishing. I had tried that stuff before in
Canada and swore I would never do it again. No, this was fine diameter, stainless steel wire wound on a conventional baitcasting
reel.

My instructor for this wire line session on Lake Erie was Art
Lyon of Conneaut, Ohio. I met Lyon at a sport show where he was
doing a seminar on wire-line fishing. Somewhat skeptical, I asked
him dozens of questions. He suggested most would be answered if
we went fishing.

That was in 1984. Lyon has continued to refine his technique
and to promote wire-line fishing. It is now in widespread use
across the central and eastern basins of Lake Erie. It also has application for inland waters, although acceptance there has been
slow.

Art Lyon took this walleye on wire line. The light wire takes plugs deep without the use of downriggers.

Walleyes On Wire   169

Getting To The Bottom Fast

"The first time I became interested in fishing wire line was back in 1978 while listening to a friend in a Spoonplugger Club in southern Ohio," Lyon told me. "He used a heavy Monel wire to 'map' a lake with a Spoonplug. I got to thinking about it and tried to find some wire. In a tackle shop in Geneva the owner brought out a dust-covered wooden box containing several spools of thin, single-strand, stainless steel wire made by the Williams Co. of Canada. I bought a spool and put it on a baitcasting reel."

Along with most Lake Erie anglers of the 1970s, Lyon was a devoted walleye fisherman. Erie walleyes were regarded as structure-oriented fish, caught during the summer near the bottom in 20- to 40-foot depths. Getting a lure down to the fish involved special rigs with very heavy lead sinkers and long trolling lines. The weights affected the action of lures, preventing the angler from knowing when lures were fouled and dulling the experience of fighting a hooked fish.

Lyon was looking for a different technique to get the bait down to the fish. Downrigging for Erie salmon was just starting to catch on in the area, but it was not considered a technique for deep structure or inshore walleye. Besides, Lyon and his friends were fishing from small boats. A simple and clean technique was needed. The wire, Lyon thought, had possibilities.

"I took it out on the lake, attached a $1/8$-ounce crankbait with no additional weight, and on the first trolling pass drove the bait into the bottom at 35 feet. That really got me excited because I had never used anything that could put a crankbait down so deep!"

That was the beginning of modern wire for walleyes on Lake Erie, and Lyon was on his way to becoming an expert in the field.

The Realities Of Wire-Lining

"Wire accomplishes three things for you," Lyon stressed. "First, it lets you fish a crankbait or spoon deeper than you ever thought possible, without the aid of a downrigger or a ton of extra lead. Second, it is more sensitive than the best graphite rod ever will be with monofilament line. Third, it provides unmatched control of the bait. You can actually jig a crankbait at any depth!"

If you are accustomed to long-line trolling with monofilament, wire-line fishing is not something you can jump right into

Anglers should hold the rod, when possible, rather than place it in a rod holder. Holding the rod permits better manipulation of the moving plug.

without some guidance. Although offering certain advantages, wire also has drawbacks.

Do not have any illusions about casting wire line. This is a trolling technique—you cannot cast wire line! Care must be taken not to get a bird's nest, or overrun, in the spool when threading the guides or letting line out. Wire must be kept under tension. Only the most experienced wire-line angler can pick out a moderate overrun without cutting the line. Until familiar with wire, Lyon recommends that beginners lighten the drag enough so that they must pull the line off the spool when feeding plugs into the water.

Kinks in the wire are the most common problem. When a twist in the wire is pulled tight creating a kink, the only solution is to cut the wire. Kinks reduce the strength of the line by at least two-thirds.

When Erie's deep-water, suspended walleye schools were "discovered" in the mid-1980s, the popularity of wire-line fishing really took off. As a pioneer in deep-water techniques, Lyon learned early that suspended walleye schools were easily spooked by a boat passing overhead. Planer boards that put lures far off to the side of

Walleyes On Wire

This Daiwa H27 reel is spooled with wire line on a fiberglass rod. The fine wire takes up about the same space on a reel as equivalent weight monofilament.

a boat's path became a necessity. Lyon was one of the first to successfully use wire line beneath planers.

But he is quick to point out that the fisherman who gains the greatest benefit from wire line is the small boat angler who does not have an elaborate planer board system or downriggers.

Proper Equipment For Wire-Lining

The proper rod is vital to the wire-line technique. Whether fishing wire in deep or relatively shallow water, straight out or with planer boards, rod recommendations are the same.

"When I started out with wire we were using $5^1/_2$-foot, pistol-grip, bass-action baitcasting rods," Lyon recalled. "We quickly discovered more fish were lost with this setup than were landed. Wire has no stretch, and when put on a stiff, fast-tip rod, baits were ripped out of the walleyes' mouths!"

Experimentation with rods followed. Now Lyon recommends a medium or medium-light downrigging rod in an 8- or $8^1/_2$-foot length. He emphasizes the rod does not need to be graphite. A fiberglass or graphite-composite rod with a softer action than all-graphite actually makes a better wire rod.

"This type of rod has the length to act as a shock absorber. Wire is not forgiving. A soft action means the upper half of the rod bends smoothly, which is necessary because the tip of the rod must always be pointed directly at the wire entering the water. You want to keep the wire from being turned at a right angle coming off the rodtip. Looking for the proper 'J'-curve in the rod is much more important than the material or what company makes the rod," Lyon explained.

The ceramic-lined guides found on most downrigging rods will hold up to wire line for years with only minor grooving. However, because of the chance of grooving, Lyon suggests NAFC members do not switch the rod from wire-line use to monofilament use without replacing the top guide.

Three Wire Line Riggings

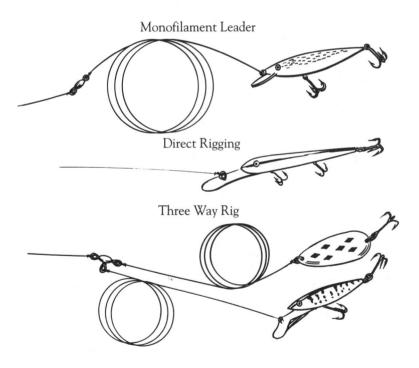

Monofilament Leader

Direct Rigging

Three Way Rig

Lure riggings for wire line fishing include swivel and monofilament leader (top), wire directly to the plug (middle) and a three-way swivel rigged with monofilament leaders to spoon and plug (bottom).

Walleyes On Wire

Reels for wire-lining should be levelwinds with large capacities and wide spools. They do not have to be elaborate, but they must have good drag with particular attention to smoothness at light settings.

His list of favorite wire line reels include: Daiwa's 27H or 47H; Penn's 10, 210MF or 320GTI; Shimano's TRN 100GT or 200GT. In a pinch an ordinary muskie-size or large-capacity bass free-spool reel such as Garcia's 5500 or 6500 will do the job. Anything smaller will not hold enough wire.

Because local demand for the wire was so great and retail sources limited, Lyon opened a tackle shop in Conneaut in order to obtain wire through wholesale distributors. His shop specializes in the reels, rods and baits used for Erie walleyes. In addition to the Williams Co., Lyon found another source for the stainless steel wire—American Wire out of West Chester, Pennsylvania.

When first starting out, Lyon used 10-pound test wire. With a .010 diameter, the wire was about the same thickness as 10-pound test monofilament. Today, Lyon spools his rods with 12-pound wire because it is a little more durable when used in planer-board fishing.

"Twelve-pound does not run quite as deep as 10, but it is very close," said Lyon. "I've gone to 12-pound as an all-around wire to save plugs from being lost. The 10-pound line is too flexible in a planer release and will eventually develop a weak spot. If you are going to run plugs straight—that is without using planers—you can get by with 10-pound test. However, 12-pound is the way to go for planer boards."

Crankbaits may be attached directly to the wire, or a snap may be used to facilitate changing. A snap swivel should be used for spoons. Many anglers prefer to use a 3- to 5-foot monofilament leader between the wire line and the lure, believing the action of the lure is enhanced. Lyon says a monofilament leader is okay when fishing deep water for suspended fish, but it should never be used when bottom bumping. The wire weighs the mono leader down, dragging it across bottom terrain, thereby fraying the leader in short order.

Tying the wire to a bait, swivel or snap is accomplished with a simple wrapping technique. Some anglers use a haywire twist, but Lyon has a slightly different wrap.

"I slide the snap or swivel on the wire, then form a $^3/_{16}$-inch eye

Attaching Snaps To Wire Line

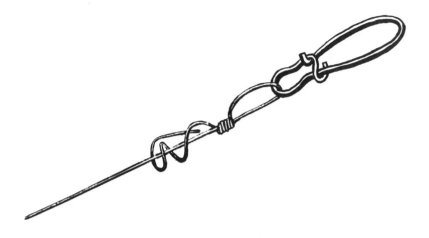

To attach snaps to wire line, bring the wire through the snap and back around itself five times, creating a $^3/_{16}$-inch eye in the wire. Then make a couple of loose twists with the tag end of the wire and fold the loose end back toward the lure.

in the wire by twisting the tag end five complete revolutions around the main wire fairly tight," he explained. "Next I make a couple of loose twists and fold the loose end back toward the lure so it doesn't pick up debris."

Fishing With Wire

With wire you can forget what the package says about the maximum depth of a crankbait. On wire, the depth of a diving crankbait is controlled by the amount of line out and the speed of the boat. Wire is heavier than monofilament. As the wire sinks it pulls the plug with it. It is possible to dig certain crankbaits into the bottom in 70 feet of water.

The accepted procedure is to count "wraps" to determine how much wire line is out. One "wrap" is a movement of the line guide across the levelwind mechanism. Using a Penn 320 reel, Lyon can place a Bomber 9A down 55 feet with just 45 wraps of line out.

The actual amount of line out will vary from reel to reel depending on the width of the spool. As a guideline for the large capacity trolling reels, Lyon says one wrap equals about one foot of depth when using a big-billed diving bait with a boat speed of 2 to 4 mph. Slower trolling speeds increase depth while faster speeds reduce the depth of the bait.

When starting out it is important to use a depthfinder to determine the exact number of "wraps" needed to achieve a particular depth with a particular bait.

Small crankbaits and shallow-lip baits will not run as deep as big lip plugs. When heavy trolling spoons are used alone, the depth is unpredictable, ranging from six to 20 feet. For best depth control, spoons should be used on a three-way rig in conjunction with a diving plug.

A three-way rig may be purchased ready-made at Lake Erie tackle shops. It consists of a three-way swivel and two leaders of plastic coated wire. With a three-way rig, the diving bait placed on the lower leader pulls the spoon down.

"I like a four-foot leader connected to the spoon, while the crankbait leader is one foot shorter," Lyon emphasized. "That way if you end up with a double—a fish on each bait—you are able to net both of them without too much difficulty."

While many anglers are initially drawn to wire line because lures can be run very deep, Lyon believes the greatest asset of wire is that it allows the angler the ability to jig or twitch a crankbait.

"With wire I can make the lure accelerate or stall simply by moving the rodtip forward and then dropping it back," he said. "This is particularly important in cold water situations when walleyes are lethargic.

"Wire does not stretch," said Lyon. "What you do with the rod creates an immediate response in the bait. You move the rod ahead, the bait speeds up. You drop the rodtip back, the lure stops. If the boat speed is slow enough, you can even twitch that crankbait sitting in 40 feet of water. This is why I say if an angler holds the rod and manipulates the bait, that angler will catch more walleyes than the one who simply sticks the rod in a rod holder!"

Of course rod manipulation is not possible when using side planers. But Lyon points out that planers impart their own jigging action on the bait. By steering the boat along a course that weaves in a big "S" pattern, planers slow down and speed up, providing erratic bait movement.

When anglers are unable to pick up fish by flatlining wire, but they know schools of walleye are in the immediate vicinity of the boat, the fish are probably being spooked to the left and right as the outboard passes overhead. In this situation, side planers should be considered. Anglers with limited resources may utilize one of the small on-line planers such as Yellow Birds or the one made by Wille.

"When you don't have a big boat or a crew to handle a big planer system, I like to use the Yellow Birds," Lyon says. "These are better in shallow water and in a small boat because you can do everything from a seated position. You let out enough wraps on the reel to have the bait running the depth you desire, then attach the Yellow Bird to the line. Put the Bird out wide when fishing shallow, and keep it in closer when fishing deeper water. When a fish triggers the release on a Bird, the planer slips down the line as the fish is fought to the boat."

Lyon goes through special instructions about drags and hooksets for newcomers.

"At the time of a strike, anyone not familiar with wire will automatically set the hook. Wrong!" Lyon said. "Just a firm lift of the rod is all that is needed. If you jerk the rod, you will tear the walleye's mouth, creating a large hole for the hook to fall out, or perhaps even ripping the lips right off the fish!

"Wire does not have the ability to absorb shock like monofilament," continued Lyon. "The automatic hooksetting ability with wire is unreal. Even with 100 yards of wire out, a hit rattles your equipment. That is why I instruct people to set the drag very light so it will barely slip when a fish hits."

Lure Recommendations

With more than 18 years of walleye fishing experience on Lake Erie, Lyon has accumulated considerable information on seasonal patterns and bait preferences. During the early season Lyon concentrates on the inshore walleye fishery, 40 feet or shallower.

"These walleyes are feeding primarily on emerald shiners," he said. "I like the smaller spoons this time of year, particularly those with green on them. Pro King, Hi-Tec and Northern King all make nice spoons about $2^1/4$ inches long. My early season plugs include Rebel's Fastrac, Bagley's Mighty Minnow, Rapala's Shad Rap and the Bomber No. 24 Long A. The fish are feeding on shiners and will bite the smaller lures better than the bigger stuff."

During the 1970s, Lyon fished the near-shore structure throughout the summer for walleyes using his favorite Norman Deep-N crankbaits. Today the inshore fishery still remains available, but with knowledge of Erie's deep-water walleyes, many anglers abandon the near-shore fish in early summer.

About mid-June, Lyon makes the move to offshore waters in search of suspended walleye schools. Through summer and early fall he will be fishing over bottoms 60 to 150 feet deep. The deep-water walleyes are gorging themselves on smelt, alewives and gizzard shad. Depending on the location of the forage, walleyes may be suspended 20 to 80 feet deep. The size of the natural forage increases, and so does the size of the plugs.

"Probably my favorite deep-water lure has been Bomber's No. 25 Long A," said Lyon. "Another one I like if I'm looking for really big walleyes is Heddon's Magnum TadPolly. Bomber's No. 9A is an excellent choice for going real deep late in the season. Other summer baits include Storm's Mag Wiggle Wart or any of the long minnow plugs with big diving lips. And in the deeper water we shift to bigger spoons run on a three-way rig.

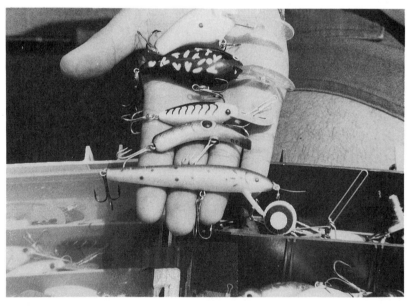

A wide variety of plugs can be used with wire line. For maximum depth, big-billed plugs can be used.

Complete Angler's Library

Walleyes you might have never reached with monofilament line and sinkers are there for the taking with wire line. And the thin wire may be spooled on conventional free-spool reels.

"Chartreuse and lime greens are real good producers in deep water," said Lyon. "The most consistent color is probably the pearl blue with a gray or black back and orange belly. It's a color you can fish any depth, any time, and it always produces. Firetiger is very good when the water is discolored from silt or algae. One of our hottest spoons last year was an orange metal flake with gold on the reverse; we couldn't keep it in the water without getting a hit!"

Art Lyon's techniques were fine-tuned on Lake Erie. They can, however, be easily adapted to large inland lakes. The ability to manipulate crankbait action in deep water with wire line may revolutionize your early spring and late fall walleye tactics. At the very least, they can be added to your bag of fish-catching tricks.

17

Slow Boat To Walleyes

by Gary Clancy

When Keith Kavajecz (pronounced Ko-vy-as) pulls into the ramp area with his sleek Dodge van towing a shining Skeeter boat, you know you are looking at an outfit built for getting places in a hurry. When the 135-horsepower Mariner on the transom kicks to life and man and machine bolt out of the hole, the feeling that speed is all-important is confirmed. But, once Kavajecz pulls back the throttle and shuts down the big motor, it soon becomes obvious that you are fishing aboard a slow boat to walleyes.

When Kavajecz and his fishing partner Gary Parsons won the Manufacturers Walleye Council (now Masters Walleye Circuit) team of the year honors and followed up with an impressive win at the MWC 1988 National Championships, their rise to the top among a fleet of the finest walleye anglers ever assembled was described as meteoric. Perhaps, but they got there by practicing precision boat control. To this team, that means slow with a capital "S."

With its sleek, bass-boat lines, metal flake finish and ritzy interior, the Skeeter System 135 walleye boat would, at first glance, seem an odd choice for a man who dotes on slow and precise presentations. But as Kavajecz explained, "We helped design the Skeeter 135 so that we would not only have a boat that could carry plenty of weight at a pretty good clip across big water, but one that would also allow us to employ any technique needed to catch walleyes." The big main engine isn't there for speed, as much as it

Walleye angler Keith Kavajecz feels boat control can help any angler account for more walleyes. He practices a number of different bait presentations based on a slow approach.

Slow Boat To Walleyes

is for getting a big load up and moving. By the time we add a pair of electric trolling motors, a half-dozen heavy batteries, a kicker outboard, enough gas for all-day running and all of our other gear, we are talking a lot of weight. It takes a big engine to move all of that weight at a speed that makes runs of 40 miles or so feasible. Today's best walleye fishing is on big water. Tournament anglers and recreational anglers alike need big, safe boats to make fishing that size of water safe, productive and enjoyable," according to Kavajecz. "But once we get where we are going, we depend on our three 'control' engines."

Backtrolling: Slowly And Precisely

"For backtrolling slip-sinker rigs on breaklines and weedlines for instance, we depend mostly on our 15-horsepower kicker. Gary Parsons convinced the folks at Mariner that their high-reverse thrust prop, which has long been a favorite with sailors attempting to dock sailboats, was ideally suited to backtrolling for walleyes. That prop, which allows you to gain extra thrust at lower rpms, is now available on all Mariner outboards from 4 to 15 horsepower.

"If it is dead-calm, or if the fish are shallow and spooky, we will backtroll with our 45-pound-thrust stern-mounted electric motor. We have reversed the head on the electric for added backtrolling power. Either way, by employing one of these two engines, and keeping an eye on our Lowrance X-16 graph or LMS 200, we can not only maintain the speed we want but keep our baits on the fish-holding structure."

While not claiming to be the best among walleye pros who make their living backtrolling a slip-sinker rig, Kavajecz has learned a couple of tricks to catch more fish while dragging live bait.

"The moment you feel a bite, mentally pick a spot on the surface of the water that you feel is right over the fish. That sounds hard," said Kavajecz, "but with a little practice you will become very accurate. As soon as you feel the fish pick up the bait, let line spill from the reel so that the fish does not feel any resistance. At the same time, throw the engine into forward and motor to the spot where you've calculated the fish to be. What this does is put you over the fish and provide you with a vertical, or near-vertical hookset; a much higher percentage hookset than the fish-behind-

Kavajecz nets a walleye that fell to a slow-drift presentation. Before setting the hook, he uses his bow-mount electric motor to pull the boat back over a fish that has picked up the bait.

the-boat-hookset commonly used by backtrollers fishing slip-sinker rigs.

Kavajecz also increases his hooking percentage by reeling line up until he knows he has just about all of the slack out of the line. Then, instead of lifting and "feeling" for the weight of the fish as is common practice, he reels like crazy and gets the fish coming before setting the hook with a quick snap of the wrist.

Naturally Kavajecz has very specific requirements when it comes to the rod and terminal tackle he uses for slip-sinker fishing.

His favorite rod for backtrolling with slip sinkers is one he helped design, the Team Daiwa Series for slip-sinkering. This specialty rod is long, flexible and limber, just what you want in a rod that acts as a shock absorber between you and the fish.

Kavajecz uses $^1/_8$- and $^1/_4$-ounce walking-sinkers for most back-trolling situations. "If you can't feel bottom with a $^1/_4$-ounce sinker in 20 feet of water, you are either using a poor rod or moving too fast," he said.

For minnows, Kavajecz likes a No. 2 hook and often fishes the big hook with leeches as well. He prefers two or three small

Kavajecz's Slip-Sinker Rig For Nightcrawlers

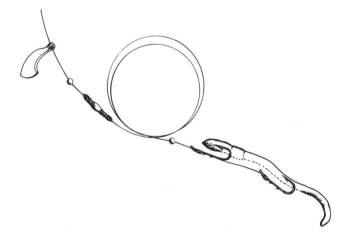

Kavajecz rigs a worm with a walking sinker, bead, small barrel swivel, another bead and two baitholder hooks. His snell, from swivel to hooks, varies from 2 to 8 feet in length depending on what the fish seem to prefer.

leeches on the hook as opposed to one large leech. Nightcrawlers are his favorite bait for slip-sinker fishing, and he fishes them on a two-hook snell, which he ties himself using 6-pound test leader material, two No. 6 Eagle Claw baitholder hooks and a small bead, just to make the homemade rig legal in all states. Kavajecz adds a puff of air to the crawler near each hook, not enough air to float the crawler, but enough to offset the weight of the hook.

The rest of his live-bait trolling rig consists of the sinker, a small bead below the weight and the smallest barrel swivel he can find. The length of the snell varies according to conditions, with short snells often working best when fish are tight to the bottom and long snells getting the nod when fish are slightly suspended or very spooky.

Kavajecz is so convinced that going slow is the right speed for catching walleyes, that he and Parsons tend to move at a snail's pace even when using techniques commonly associated with speed. These include tactics like trolling with crankbaits or using bottom-bouncers with spinners, both of which are techniques commonly described as excellent for covering a lot of water in a hurry, though they have proven effective at slow speeds.

Slow Trolling Bottom-Bouncers And Spinners

Drifting with bottom-bouncer sinkers and spinners baited with crawlers, minnows or leeches is standard fare on the big walleye reservoirs of the Dakotas. Few fishermen, however, put the planning and effort into a drift that Kavajecz does, and the practices aren't as popular elsewhere as perhaps they should be, given Kavajecz's success.

"We like to maintain a sideways drift along whatever break or contour line we are trying to follow," said Kavajecz. "This way, with four rods spread out the length of the boat and the two end rods pointed over the transom and over the bow respectively, we can cover a swath nearly 30 feet wide on each pass.

"Bottom-bouncers are ideal for this kind of fishing because they rarely snag up and the fish usually hook themselves," Kavajecz continued. "Most fishermen simply allow the wind to dictate how fast they drift. We use our electric motors and in some cases driftsocks to drift at the precise speed we find most conducive to the technique, and this has improved our success.

Fishing With A Bottom-Bouncer Rig

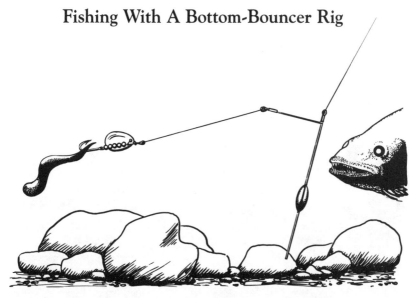

For slow trolling on rocky bottoms, Kavajecz uses smaller size spinners to help keep the bait from sailing up, away from bottom. A bottom bouncer rig should move almost upright and spinner blades should barely turn, when fishing at the right speed.

"When we won the Saginaw Bay Tournament," Kavacejz said, "we did it out of a Skeeter bass boat. That was before Skeeter had developed a walleye boat. Driftsocks or sea anchors, whatever you want to call them, helped us slow our drift down enough to catch fish during that tournament. We still carry four driftsocks in the boat with us, but we tend to use them only when our electric motors can't do the job. When we do use them, we like the smaller sizes, the 2- and 3-footers instead of the big bags. The big socks create a tremendous amount of turbulence, and in shallow water especially, that can spook fish.

"One of the most effective driftsock applications is backtrolling with console steering," continued Kavacejz, "or with a big tiller outboard. Not only will a driftsock slow down the speed of the boat, but it acts as kind of a "pivot-point," which makes quick, sharp turns possible.

"Gary and I tend to fish bottom-bouncers and spinners much slower than most anglers," Kavacejz said. "Size 4 and 5 Colorado blades are common on spinners used for fishing with bottom-bouncers, but Gary and I like sizes 0, 1 and 2 because they have less resistance in the water and are easier to keep near bottom. We try

Using a small, stern-mounted kicker motor in the 10- to 15-horsepower class is helpful for maintaining slow trolling speeds on boats with powerful power plants.

Complete Angler's Library

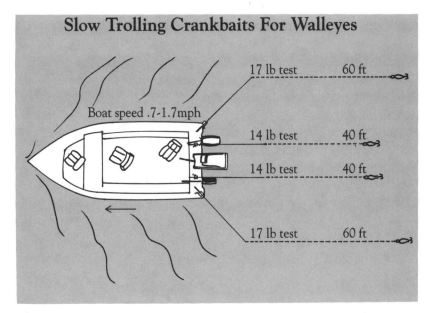

Slow Trolling Crankbaits For Walleyes

17 lb test   60 ft

Boat speed .7-1.7mph

14 lb test   40 ft

14 lb test   40 ft

17 lb test   60 ft

Setting inside lines for crankbaits shorter than outside lines prevents tangled lines. Heavier monofilament makes it easier to jerk snags free. A slow and consistent speed is the key to catching walleyes with this technique.

to troll at a speed where the spinner just gets twirling. We have found that this is also the speed at which the bottom-bouncers will remain upright."

Trolling Crankbaits At A Snail's Pace

Even when it comes to this "speedy" tactic for walleyes, Kavajecz maintains his slow but winning ways.

"We like to troll crankbaits somewhere between .7 and 1.7 mph," he said. "Compared with what most of the guys are running, that is like standing still. But we like to appeal to a walleye's feeding instinct, and to do that we maintain a slow trolling speed.

"The whole key to success when trolling crankbaits for walleyes is reproducibility," Kavacejz said. "You must be able to match exactly what you were doing when you caught a fish to be able to consistently catch more. That means not only do you need to know your trolling speed, but you have to know how far behind the boat and how deep your lure was running when the fish struck. We use Wille's Crankbait 'n line because it is color coded and lets us know exactly how much line we have out on each reel. Wille's

To catch walleyes like this, Kavajecz depends on electric trolling motors, a small, kicker outboard and driftsocks for boat control, as well as a variety of slowed-down lure presentations.

Complete Angler's Library

Crankbait Guide indicates how deep each lure we are using is running based on the amount of line out. Those two factors, and a trolling speed indicator, give us the reproducibility we are looking for.

"Crankbaits are great for fishing composition transitions, places where sand meets mud, for example," continued Kavacejz. "We used that technique to place fourth and sixth during the last two Lake Winnebago (Wisconsin) tournaments.

"One key to our slow-troll system is to use heavy line. We use 14-pound test monofilament on the two inside lines and 17-pound test on the outside lines. By running the lures on the outside lines farther back than those on the inside, we can get them just as deep, even though the line is heavier. Keeping them spaced this way prevents most tangles, and with the heavy line we can usually just jerk a snag free instead of breaking up our whole pattern to go back to retrieve a snagged lure.

"Lots of fishermen think you have to troll fast to allow a crankbait to reach its maximum depth. That is not true. It takes longer for the lure to achieve its maximum depth on a slow-troll, but it will get there, and once it does that slow wobble will trigger plenty of walleyes."

If Keith Kavajecz can ride a slow boat to walleyes right to the pinnacle of tournament walleye fishing, every angler should be able to follow his lead to find better walleye fishing—the slow and easy way.

18

Turn Weeds
Into Walleyes

by James Churchill

reg Bohn is a full-time guide from Hazelhurst, Wisconsin. Most of his endeavors have something to do with catching walleyes. And Bohn is very successful. He and his clients boat more then 3,000 walleyes each year, and they accomplish this on small lakes.

It's a treat, and a revelation, to fish with a man as skillful as Bohn. You sense his intensity as soon as he unloads his 16-foot Tuffy walleye boat, flips on his flasher and heads out onto the lake.

"I always fish small, shallow lakes early in the season," Bohn told me on this spring day. "They warm up the fastest and the fish bite better!" Bohn is a weed specialist, so he heads all around the small lake looking for newly emerging weed growth. Along the northwest shoreline in a shallow bay, he finds what he is looking for and drops a marker buoy. At the other end of the weedbed, he drops another. The weeds are an emerging patch of short, green "broadleaf cabbage," less than 10 inches tall.

The weedbed is located in a broad, six-foot-deep bay adjacent to a drop-off, which steps down to 20 feet. He marks the outer edge of the weedbed with two more buoys.

Bohn continues around the lake and marks two more beds. This particular lake is a favorite of his because it contains three shallow bays located on the north and northwest edges. Bays on the north side receive the most sunlight and warm up faster. Weeds start growing earliest here too, attracting baitfish and, in turn, walleyes.

Guide Greg Bohn connects his customers with hundreds of walleyes each year by fishing in, over and around weeds. He has developed his own jigs especially for these tactics.

Turn Weeds Into Walleyes

We headed back to the first marked weedbed. "By now the walleyes that may have spooked on out first pass should have settled down," said Bohn. "The first time you fish a lake you almost have to run right over the weeds to see them. That's why we have to give them a little time to recover. Of course, if we had landed here later in the day with the right sun, we could have spotted the weeds with Polaroid sunglasses without running over them. But then we would have missed the morning bite." Bohn punctuates his speech with expressive hand gestures.

Learn To Use Jigs Around Weedbeds

Bohn cut the big engine about 200 feet from the weedbed and used the transom-mount electric to move slowly closer. He rigged his rod with a $^1/_{16}$-ounce, round-head chartreuse and orange jig, cast with an oversize No. 2 hook and tipped with a head-hooked, $2^1/_2$-inch fathead minnow.

Bohn uses 7-foot, one-piece 100 percent graphite rods with an extra-fast tip for this type of fishing. He believes you need the sensitivity of a graphite rod, and he designs and markets his own brand of Stinger Rods that are rated for $^1/_{32}$-ounce to $^1/_4$-ounce lures and 4- to 10-pound test line. Today he uses open-face spinning reels, set up with 6-pound test line.

He casts well into the weedbed. Later in the season, after the weeds get thick, it will be impossible to work jigs through this bed. Now the jig can be worked between the plants and back to the boat with ease. He retrieves the jig with a smooth, swimming motion perfected by years of practice. "Try to hop a jig in the weeds and you will hang up," he explained.

Bohn switches to a weedless jig if he starts getting too many snags. He uses a self-designed model called a "Timber Jig," which has a frayed-cable weedguard. This guard is extremely flexible, but he recommends that the hookset be vigorous. "Hit 'em as hard as you can," he said. "You won't break 6-pound test line!"

The bites came. By the time we had worked all three weedbeds we had landed a two-man limit of walleyes.

The guide offered an explanation for our early spring success. "I settled for cabbage weed, but I was looking for a weed named elodea. Called walleye weed or waterweed, elodea comes up first and is often found near inlets of streams. Walleyes love this sparse, submergent weed. Find it and you have found walleyes. Other pre-

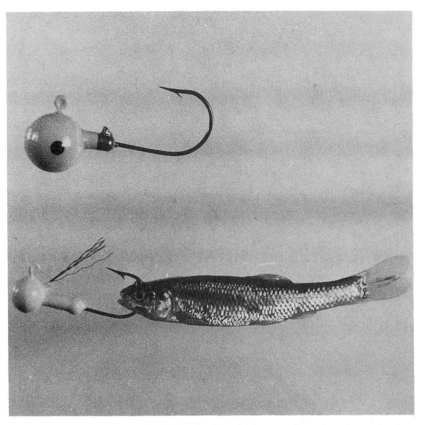

Compare a standard, wide-gap jig (top) and Bohn's Timber Jig with weedguard, tipped with a minnow. The stiff, wire weedguards of the Timber Jig repel most, but not all weeds.

ferred weeds are coontail and cabbage, of course, and sand grass. Bulrushes, pond lilies and cattails will sometimes hold walleyes when their favorite weeds are scarce."

Search For Submerged Weed Islands

The next recorded trip was in midsummer. By this time the weeds were well developed on all the lakes in the area. In fact, the small lake that we had fished earlier in the spring was so choked with weeds it couldn't be fished. Bohn headed for a 1,000-acre lake containing several varieties of weeds.

He steered us toward two mid-lake weedbeds. They were hard to see and were bypassed by most anglers. All that showed above the surface were a few seedpods from the broadleaf cabbage patch.

"In midsummer, walleyes will almost always go to an offshore

Bohn's favorite jigs and hooks include (l to r) leadhead jigs, weighted and unweighted weedguard hooks and floating jigheads with weedguards.

weedbed to feed," the expert explained. "On this lake the submergent weeds grow only about three feet tall because the water clarity is low. So wherever you see them sticking above the surface in mid-lake, it is sure to be a reef hump!"

"A glance at the hydrographic map for this lake showed this weedbed growing on top of a flat-topped hump, surrounded by deep water. I can guarantee that walleyes will work this weedbed. Let's try it out," he said.

A brisk wind was blowing white-capped waves across the top of the hump as Bohn explained our approach. "Most of the time in this situation, we could drift across the top of the hump and throw jigs. But this particular hump is too shallow, and we would spook the fish. We could also anchor or hold upwind and cast jigs across the top of the hump. This might catch some fish, but I would rather go downwind of the hump and anchor, then cast into the wind. This will result in fewer snags since you will be pulling the jig in the same direction the weeds are lying after being pushed downwind by the waves. Also, a current will be flowing across the top of the hump. Feeding fish will have their nose pointing into the current the same way they do on a river," Bohn explained.

Complete Angler's Library

"The jig will come at them from the direction they expect food!"

Bohn told me a good rule of thumb is to use as light a jig as possible. A $^1/_8$-ounce jig is about the lightest jig you can cast into a stiff breeze, and sometimes it takes $^1/_4$-ounce. Even so, you often have to side-cast to keep the lure low enough to make headway against the wind.

The jig should also be heavy enough to carry the line down the sides of the hump to entice fish that are holding deep. Bohn uses a weedless jig that can be worked slowly without snagging weeds. Leeches are the optimum bait for midsummer. They stay on the hook, keep well in a baitbox and walleyes relish them.

Bohn told me that a mid-lake weedbed can be fished with slip bobbers very effectively You use enough weight to sink the slip bobber almost to the stem, so it is less affected by wind and current. Bohn uses split shot and No. 6 Aberdeen gold hooks, or $^1/_8$-ounce jig tipped by a lively leech. He casts into the wind or anchors on the side of the hump and casts across wind to set up the drift of the bait. The bobber is set to a depth where it will carry the bait right over the tops of the weeds.

"Other hotspots for the midsummer weed-walleye fisherman

Bohn concentrates on a mid-lake weedbed with scattered openings that typically hold walleyes in early summer. Later in the season, he looks for wind to bring fish up to similar areas.

are very deep weedbeds, or what I call the lake carpet," Bohn said. "This is primarily made up of short sand grass. It might grow in 25 to 30 feet of water. Walleyes, especially the bigger, nonaggressive walleyes, often suspend right over the top of this lake carpet or burrow into it if it is thick enough."

Bohn also told me that the carpet layer is often completely un-fished. The weeds don't show up on most locators and fishermen don't realize where the fish are located. He works these sand-grass beds with a jig tipped with a leech drifting the jig on and through the weeds.

Another of Bohn's classic weed-walleye haunts are the cab-bage-weed patches. He showed me how the tops of the weeds come up to within two to six feet of the surface and how to look for holes in the weeds by boating over the top of them while watching with a pair of Polaroid glasses.

Rock piles or clean sand will not support tall weeds, and holes, or large openings, are found whenever such poor soil occurs. Bohn fishes these spots by holding nearby or right over the holes and jig-ging vertically.

At other times, Bohn may work the holes with slip bobbers, setting the bobber so it will dangle the bait just above the bottom. After he fishes the holes he resets the bobber and fishes the tops of the weeds. He casts to one side of the boat to avoid crossing over the fish. The wind will drift the bobber across the tops of the weeds.

Weeds less then six feet high are fished by using a floating jig and slip sinker, or egg sinker. Bohn sets the length of the snell so that the floating jig works through the upper layer of weeds. Drift fishing, or trolling, as slowly as possible with the lure at least 50 feet behind the boat, seems to be the best way to cover this type of weedbed.

His techniques work again. We are back at the landing at noon with our limit.

The next trip was in the fall.

Green Weeds Can Offer Fall Action

We left the landing on a fine October day and motored toward the center of a clear lake. On the way out he explained the unique aspects of fall walleye fishing around weeds.

"October is a fine month to fish, but the weed walleye fishing

Float A Jig For Walleyes In Weeds

Bohn attaches a sliding egg sinker and swivel to his main line and adds a 3- to 8-foot snell with floating jig tipped with a leech. The length of the snell depends on the height of the weeds he is fishing in.

is different from spring and summer," he pointed out. "Most weeds have died. When they die, the fish leave the weeds and move out to deep water. In deep lakes some weedbeds stay alive right 'til freeze up!"

We fished the deep-water beds by vertically jigging and caught one walleye. Then we couldn't buy another strike. "Walleyes are in and out of the weeds on a lake like this in the fall. Apparently they are out. Let's change lakes," Bohn declared.

The next lake we tried was fairly shallow, covering about 500 acres. We ran the whole lakeshore looking down into the water. "I'm looking for green weeds," he said. "Almost all the weeds in this lake are dead already, but if there are any live ones there are sure to be walleyes holding nearby."

Few walleye anglers go looking for weeds. Greg Bohn does, and that habit earns him fat walleyes like this time after time.

We worked the lake without seeing any green weeds, but spotted some on the Bottomline Locator, standing erect in 15 feet of water. "I think those weeds are alive, but the only way to tell for sure is to get a piece of one," Bohn explained.

He quickly tied a 1-ounce jig on his line and dropped it to the bottom. When the jig became snagged, he ripped it loose and pulled it to the top. It was a section of coontail weeds, still bright green. A broad smile spread across his face. "These are nice weeds," he said. "We just found us some walleyes!"

He reversed the motor to hold the boat well away from the weedbed and eased the anchor quietly to the bottom. "We should be able to catch these fish by dragging jigs right through the weeds," he explained.

Bohn had a game plan. We each tied on a $^1/_{16}$-ounce chartreuse and green weedless jig, lip-hooked a 3-inch redtail chub and cast as far as we could, letting the offerings fall to the bottom. Then we worked the jigs slowly back to the boat. We were immediately into fish. But, the action didn't last long. After three bites the action quit.

"Let's change to slip bobbers," Bohn told me. "The fish are very neutral fish and want plenty of time to look over the bait." We hooked the minnows lightly under the dorsal fin this time, on the same jigs. This technique worked so well that we soon had our limits of walleyes and were headed back to the landing.

Bohn told me he didn't work the shoreline weeds on this trip because it was the wrong time of the year. Shoreline weeds can offer excellent fishing in early summer, however.

To fish shoreline weeds, he advises keeping the boat well away from the outer edge of the weeds while casting to them. Anchoring at the weedline and casting perpendicular to the edge will also draw strikes. "Don't forget to work the inside weedline also," he said. "Walleyes are sometimes holding between the weeds and the shore."

Bohn also night fishes in the weeds. He locates the weedbeds during the day and returns after dark. He uses a medium/heavy rod, 15-pound test line and casts crankbaits along the edge or over the weeds. When crankbaits aren't successful, he often uses lighted slip bobbers and live-bait rigs utilizing minnows or leeches for this after-dark walleye fishing.

I learned more in three trips with Greg Bohn than in three decades of fishing on my own. With a little practice around weeds, you, too, can be catching walleyes in places most fishermen overlook.

19

Parsons On Planing For Walleyes

by Dave Mull

Gary Parsons of Chilton, Wisconsin, divides his time between professional fishing and a thriving dental practice. He's one doctor of dental science who knows how to use planer boards to help put lures in the mouths of walleyes. When Parsons puts together his planer board system, the fish have little chance of escape.

"It's all a matter of cutting your odds," said Parsons of his planer board approach. "It's a search-and-destroy mission. Basically, you set up a grid to locate the depth and the type of presentation the walleyes want. Then you simply fine-tune your whole setup until you're concentrating the lures the fish want around as many fish as possible."

Sounds simple, but it's not. Whoever thinks trolling is for guys who hang onto the tiller with one hand and a cold "brewski" with the other, hasn't fished with Parsons and his tournament partner (and brother-in-law) Keith Kavajecz. This duo won Manufacturers Walleye Council (now Masters Walleye Circuit) Team of the Year honors and the end-of-year championship tourney in 1988. Watching them troll is like watching a well-oiled machine, constantly adjusting boat speed, changing lures and watching the electronics.

"Trolling is a great way to fish because, among other reasons, your lure is in the water 100 percent of the time," Parsons said. "Planer boards help you put more lures in the water and probe more area."

Gary Parsons covers more water and more depths for walleyes by using planer boards. He has developed his system into a science that strains the water until he catches fish.

Parsons On Planing For Walleyes

Basic Types Of Planer Boards

Planer boards use water pressure to "plane" away from the boat. The first planer boards on the market were "skis" that used their own reels with separate line tethers. The reels attached to masts mounted somewhere near the middle of the boat.

Parsons generally opts for the more highly evolved "in-line" planer. These lightweight arrangements attach directly to the fishing line. They're small and easily stored. Some designs will pop off the line when a fish hits, then float until the fish is landed. Other planers stay attached to the line when the fish strikes, but turn in such a way that they don't provide much resistance between you and the fish. You reel the board to the rodtip, detach it and land the fish.

"If I'm fishing alone, I'll use one of the Wille Side Liners," said Parsons, referring to a new kind of in-liner he helped design. "If I'm fishing with a partner or using lead core line then I'll use a ski and mast; especially if I plan to spend all day fishing huge mud flats or suspended fish. If it's a day when I might be fishing structure as well as flats, using the boards just part of the time, then I'll rely on the Side Liners. They're always in my boat."

Parsons breaks out the planer boards when he suspects the fish are suspended and he needs to find out where and at what depth. Boards help you put more lines in the water and increase percentages for fish contact. Boards also hit the water when fish are scattered up and down a gradual slope and when the fish are too shallow to troll without spooking.

Parsons learned to use planer boards on Wisconsin's massive Lake Winnebago. Throughout the year, the walleyes often hang over big mud flats and are susceptible to well-presented crankbaits. Parsons believes these fish relate to mayfly and other insect hatches, feeding on the baitfish that follow the bugs.

Standardizing Gear Important To Success

"Filling a trolling grid is easier if you use the same kind of reels and the same line," Parsons said. "Identical line on each rod creates the same amount of drag in the water. Your only variables with six different lures are the lures themselves."

Standardized line is critical. "Different test lines have different diameters," Parsons explained. "Thicker diameters cause more resistance in the water, which impedes lures from diving.

Parsons likes trolling with planers because it keeps his lures in the water, and spread, at depths where they have the best chance of catching walleyes.

That's important when you want to get two identical lures to the same depth. If you have two reels with 8-pound test, just let out the same amount of line. With one of 8-pound and one of 10-pound test, you'll need to compensate by adding weight to the 10-pound test or by letting out less of the 8-pound test. It just becomes more complicated."

Parsons uses the new Wille Crankbait'n line, which is marked every 10 feet. For reels, he opts for Daiwa Mag Force MA15-3B baitcasters, but any reel with a large capacity spool, anti-reverse for backreeling, flippin' switch for push-button line release and a reliable drag will work.

Parsons has a number of systems for depth control, employing deep-diving crankbaits, lead core line and sinkers. Before using metered line, he counts passes on the reel. Experience has taught him how many passes allow specific lures to achieve certain depth ranges. He doesn't get too hung up on exact depths, however, declaring that the grid tells him what to do.

"There are just too many variables to say that if you let out 80 yards of line with, say, a No. 7 Shad Rap, you'll be fishing 12 feet deep," said Parsons. "Such a setup will be close to 12 feet, but it

Straining With Planer Boards

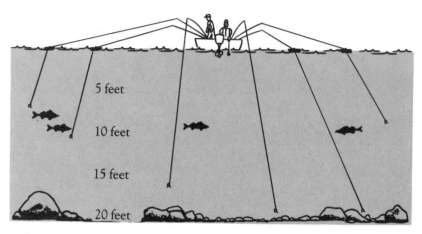

With a partner, Parsons will set planers to cover as many depths as he has rods. The longest lines go to the inside to prevent tangles. When he catches a fish, he concentrates the spread around that depth.

might be 11 and it might be 13. What matters to me is that the grid is covered. When we think fish may be suspended, we want a lure right on the bottom, a lure in the top four feet and other lures evenly spread at different depths in between."

Parsons recommends using a new chart compiled by walleye pro Mike McClelland for Wille Manufacturing, which lists depth ranges of 200 crankbaits.

Strategies For Covering The Water

For suspended fish, Parsons covers as much water and as many depths as possible. He places at least one reliable lure in the bottom zone and a dependable lure in the top four feet of water. From there, he spaces the other four lures to cover the rest of the water column at regular intervals.

Since crankbaits are reliable and allow a faster troll, Parsons and his fishing partner start with six cranks (in states where that many lines are legal). Shallow-running Rapalas and Bombers go on the outside lines while the inside lines take deep- or medium-running lures. Two lines are fished as much as 150 yards directly behind the boat and get medium or deep-running crankbaits. Occasionally, Parsons prefers the wider wobble of floating, shallow-running minnow baits placed in deeper water. That's when he uses lead core on the inside lines or directly behind the boat.

Once set up, he lets the spread go for 10 minutes or so, then starts changing lures. When one line catches a fish, he resets it, same bait, same depth. If it catches another fish within a short time, he'll duplicate the presentation with two other rods.

"Before long, you might be running six identical baits," said Parsons.

Parsons always wants to match his lures with other lures that work well at the same speeds.

"Normally I'll start with all cranks," Parsons said. "I don't start using live bait until I've established a pattern with cranks. Then I'll fool around with spinners and stuff on a line to see if the fish might want live bait more than a crankbait. Usually when I'm running live bait for suspended fish, it's with spinner rigs, and all my lines will have them. It's hard to get optimum performance from most crankbaits at spinner speed."

Small planer board models attach in line, so they do not require elaborate masts or other hardware. Some release from the line when a fish strikes; others stay in line but can be reeled back with the fish.

Occasionally, along with baited spinners, he runs Shad Raps, floating Rapalas and a few other lures that work well at slow speeds. This type of multiple presentation emphasizes the critical relationship between boat speed, proper depths and lure actions.

"Always make sure all your lures run well at the same speed or have about the same speed range," Parsons said. "When the spread is set, I troll in 'S' curves. That makes the lures on the outside of the turn run faster, while those on the inside of the turn run slower. Sometimes the fish will show a preference to a specific speed, providing you with more information to fine-tune your presentation."

When a fish hits, it usually hooks itself. The key is sharp hooks. All the crankbaits in Parson's arsenal get zapped with the Pointmatic Hook-Hone-R.

"We have a 95 percent hookup rate," Parsons said.

Parsons believes that often the boat herds fish right into the path of lures and baits trailing behind planer boards.

Although herding is most common in shallower water, the phenomenon occurs with suspended fish, too—usually on calm days.

"Sometimes we catch fish on the inside lines with nothing coming on the outside lines," Parsons said. "The boat seems to move fish out of its pathway, and the nearest baits get hit. When this happens, I duplicate the depth and presentation with the outside lines and move them to within three feet of the inside lines."

Using Planers On Slopes

Although planers are used mostly in the wide open spaces, a couple of conditions call for using them on slopes. First, when fish are at a precise depth and the boat might spook them. Second, when they're scattered up and down the slope.

In the first case, the fish are often shallow, relating to a specific depth along the shoreline. Parsons wants to cover the whole horizontal length of the slope at that depth without spooking the fish. He uses crankbaits and keeps his boat the same distance from shore. Running the lines close together puts at least one bait in the fish zone.

When the fish scatter at different depths along a slope, Parsons uses live bait rigs with a bottom bouncer to maintain bottom contact and avoid snags that might grab a crank.

Complete Angler's Library

Covering Slopes With Planer Boards

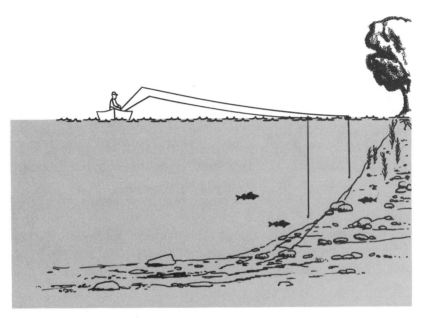

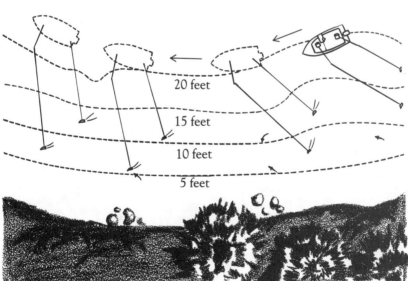

Planer boards can be used to cover breaklines by setting the line on the outside board shallower than the inside board. A curving, or "s," path gives the lures varying speeds.

Marking Suspended Schools

Parsons claims a Loran-C unit is indispensable on big flats—especially when he can't see markers on shore. A loran not only lets him find the place he caught fish the day before; it lets him pinpoint a school while fishing.

"Suspended fish are moving constantly," Parsons said. "A loran will help you stay with that moving school of fish."

When he hits the first fish, Parsons immediately enters the precise coordinates on the loran; second fish, same program. He then turns his boat around and trolls from one setting to the next, in the shape of a football.

"Each loran setting is on the tip of a football," Parsons said. "In effect, you're trying to find out how large the school is. Hit a third fish, set the loran, and start going in something of a triangle except you're not going in a straight line between loran settings. You're arcing.

"If you get into a big enough school, you might have five or six different loran settings for different fish that you caught in an area," Parsons continued. "It's like throwing out multiple buoys."

An obvious advantage of planer boards is the wide swath of water they cover. These boards are connected to masts. The line from the angler's rod releases from the board at the time of a strike, so there is no interference when fighting the fish.

One of the keys to using planer boards and crankbaits to catch walleyes like this is knowing how deep the crankbait will run, and knowing the water depth you are fishing in.

Planer boards surely are not necessary in most walleye fishing situations. But when walleyes suspend, lie up on long flats or become boat shy, planers will help you catch more fish. Take a tip from Parsons and give them a try.

So there you have it, a course on fishing planer boards from a man who has no peers with the gear. Increase your chances with planers, and odds are good you'll increase your walleye numbers.

20

Homing In On The Overlooked Sauger

by Jay Strangis

The sauger, or sand pike as some call it, may swim in the shadow of its popular cousin the walleye, but its aggressive nature leaves it little time to brood. A school of these bottom dwellers can snatch an entire school of minnows with little wasted effort. And even when in a less-than-active mood, a sauger will fin out of its way to sink its short, sharp teeth into a wavering baitfish—or an angler's lure.

Steve Pennaz learned these things about saugers years ago, and the knowledge draws him to riverways many times each winter to match his jigging skills with these underrated "sand sharks."

Saugers begin their springtime move in rivers across the country as soon as days start to lengthen and temperatures start to moderate. In the Southeast, that can be as early as January 1, likewise in the Northeast and Midwest if the winter is mild enough. Saugers begin their midwinter push upstream following early runs of baitfish—and their natural urge to move toward spawning areas, both feeder creeks and shallow gravel bars.

Saugers tend to travel in schools and are seldom found roaming in rogue fashion. In other words, where you find one sauger, you likely have found a bunch. That may be the sauger's biggest drawing card. That, and its irascible nature.

The sauger's personality hasn't escaped Pennaz's notice. "What impresses me most about the fish is how aggressive they are," the managing editor of *North American Fisherman* magazine declared. "We occasionally use jigs up to ³/4 ounce to reach bottom

Steve Pennaz likes the sauger's aggressive nature. That, and the fact that this great-tasting fish has a habit of being found in crowded company.

Homing In On The Overlooked Sauger

in a heavy current, but the big jigs don't seem to stop the saugers, even small ones. We have caught fish in the 6- to 7-inch range on these big jigs."

Pennaz took the opportunity to explain the characteristics of the walleye's smaller cousin as we fished the Mississippi River in central Minnesota in late February. We launched his 17-foot Tracker boat and ran downstream for about a half-mile, where Pennaz showed me there's more than one way to hook a sauger, and some ways are much better than others.

I lucked into a hapless walleye immediately, but the 3-pound fish barely drew a rise from my guide. He simply plucked the fish out of the water with the landing net and resumed fishing. Pennaz's mind was focused on catching saugers, and as I dropped the jig again, I noticed we were over deeper water. As soon as we had cleared the shallow walleye zone Pennaz nailed our first sauger of the day.

Searching Common Sauger Haunts

Pennaz had fished in this area the week before, so he had a general idea where to begin our search for sauger. When he's on unfamiliar water, he prefers to follow a system to search for schools of the fish. "If there's a dam, it's real easy to run up to it and fish the tail end of the deep pool below the gates," he said. "I try to stay on or near the breaks but have on rare occasions fished the bottom of the hole itself. My younger brother Bob hooked a sauger in 70 feet of water a few weeks back, and we had consistent action along a drop that went from 40 to 50 feet. Generally, however, we have our best luck along the top of the hole in 30 feet of water."

If the pool does not produce quickly, Pennaz immediately moves to the edge of the shallow "feeding flats" located at the corners of the dam. "The top of the flats hold a lot of walleyes, but they are shallow so try not to get too close or you'll spook the fish," he advised. "When you fish there, use long casts and keep the noise down."

Sauger, on the other hand, tend to hold on the bottom of the first break—in 30 feet of water in the area we fished.

The next likely locations Pennaz probes are wing dams. These small, wall-like structures built perpendicular to the bank along the main river channel can hold numbers of fish. "You want to check out the front, or up-current side first," Pennaz emphasized.

River saugers favor deeper water than their cousin, the walleye. The main river channel often holds the greatest concentrations of saugers.

"A lot of people fish the downstream side, but the active fish most often hold on the upstream side." Wing dams, he admitted, are not his favorite places to fish. "Boat control can be a real problem here," he said. "The fish are concentrated in a small area and consistent success requires a precise presentation. I don't have the patience required to fish these areas often."

Perhaps Pennaz's favorite sauger haunt, the kind of area we focused our attention on that crisp February day, is the main river channel. "Deep holes in the main channel almost always hold sauger. It's just a matter of finding an area where a school is concentrated," he said. "Sometimes they are holding along the drop or the upper end of a deep hole, but you'll often find them right in the middle of the main channel. Sauger school tightly, so focus your energies on areas where you hit fish."

Control The Drift To Catch More Fish

After catching a few small saugers in the main channel, Pennaz again cranked up the boat's main engine for a run downstream to an outside bend of the river. We were still in the main channel, but the current was a bit stronger in this location. As we drifted with the current, I noticed how Pennaz used the bow-mounted electric trolling motor to control our drift in the strong wind. Even with the current, we were able to work our $1/4$-ounce jigs almost straight up and down, giving us much greater control of our baits. Instead of dragging the jig, we were able to work them up and down slowly, keeping in constant contact with the bottom.

"You have to be able to maintain your position with the current," Pennaz said. "I like to follow the edges of the channel. It's easier to do that if I'm in control of the boat, not the current." Pennaz kept the bow pointed into the wind for better control, despite the fact that this placed it at an angle to the current. An eye on the depthfinder constantly confirmed our position.

"A lot of guys drift a certain area, then run back upstream and drift down again. They'll catch a fish, too, but the guys who can control their boat in the current are the ones who really pound the fish, because they'll sit right over an active school and keep their baits in front of the fish. The guys who merely drift fish a lot more dead water."

Pennaz's prediction came true. As we paralleled the shoreline in our methodical way, his rodtip bounced suddenly and he set the hook into a sauger—a fat fish weighing close to 4 pounds. Just as quickly, I felt a knock at the end of my line, set the hook and fought another scrappy river fish up to the side of the boat. Over the next couple of hours we boated more than 30 fish, including a couple more than 4 pounds, releasing all but a few for the table.

Jigs, Rigs And Bait For River Sauger

Thinking back on what Pennaz had said about $3/4$-ounce jigs, I asked him if he thought lure size was not important for such an aggressive-biting fish. "Having said what I did about heavy jigs, I'd still recommend going as light as you can," he told me. "In shallow, slower moving current, you can sometimes get down to bottom with a $1/16$-ounce jig."

I had missed a pair of hard strikes before Pennaz explained his philosophy about jigs. "I try to go with a jig that's got a good, wide hook gap," he said. He also favors lighter-wire hooks for their manageability around snags and because minnows stay on them longer. "With a thicker hook you aren't going to straighten the hook. I'd rather straighten the hook than break the line. You're going to get a lot of snags in the river, even if you're doing things

Bow-mounted electric trolling motors with foot control work well for maintaining a controlled drift in current. Drift speed should never exceed that which allows the angler to work a jig in contact with the bottom.

Homing In On The Overlooked Sauger

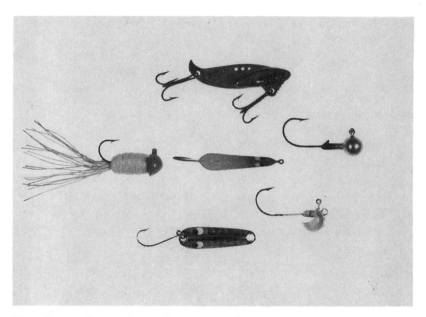

Here is Pennaz's favorite selection of jigging lures and jigs for river sauger. Note the wide hook gap and light wire on the leadhead jigs.

right, so it's best to start with the best tools available."

Pennaz also believes in stinger hooks trailing from his jigs to catch short-striking fish. They must help because nearly every fish we caught was hooked on the stinger. He showed me the subtlety of a properly rigged stinger. "Most commercial stingers are tied with stiff wire or heavy mono," he said. "I like to tie my stingers with 6- or 8-pound monofilament and a bit longer lead, about 3 inches." Pennaz buries one barb of the stinger's treble hook in the top of the minnow "as close to the tail as you can get it," leaving two exposed hooks turned straight ahead. "You have to get the stinger back as far as you can if you want better hooking percentages," he said.

We had little trouble getting our sharp hooks set in the jaws of feisty saugers. Pennaz attributed our success to more than the proper jig and stinger. He is a fan of shorter rods for this type of fishing. I happened to be using my Fenwick HMG GS963, a 5-foot, 3-inch stick I normally use when fishing live bait for walleyes. The rod performed classically. "Most people I see on the river use rods that are too long and much too limber," Pennaz said. "I prefer a 5 ¹/₂- to 6-foot, stiff-action rod because it is extremely sensitive and very fast. A short rod allows you to set the hook much quicker!"

Pennaz also places importance on his line. "Stretch is bad when you are trying to set the hook," he said. "I'm really impressed with Magna Thin line from Stren. It's super thin, very strong and doesn't stretch much. Berkley's Tri Max is also good."

As jigs go, Pennaz likes to have a variety on hand to see what the fish prefer on a particular body of water, on a particular day. "In areas where you can fish two lines, I like to start out with a jig on one line and a jigging spoon on the other," he said. The two-fisted approach often gets him tuned in more quickly to what the fish are looking for. "Different colors can have a dramatic effect on your success," he noted. "I've had tremendous success with chartreuse, fluorescent orange and combinations of the two. White and the new phosphorescent jigs also have their good days."

When Pennaz finds a productive pattern for the day, he rigs both rods with what's hot. "I find myself turning to jigging spoons more and more lately," he said. "Some days, they'll flat out outfish jigs. On a trip down here last week I kept track just for the fun of it.

For best hooking ability, lip hook a live minnow (top), then run one point of the treble stinger into the minnow just above and forward of the tail. Rigging the stinger underneath the minnow may result in more snags and less strikes.

Homing In On The Overlooked Sauger

A jigging lure, and properly rigged stinger with at least a 3- to 4-inch leader, will result in fat saugers like this.

Complete Angler's Library

In one hour, I caught 17 saugers and one small walleye—13 of them came on the jigging spoon. That's not to say jigging spoons are a magic bait. Some days they won't produce at all. All you can do is experiment with both and switch when the fish tell you what they want."

When it comes to minnows, Pennaz works in a manner opposite what most anglers who fish live bait might practice. "Because river fish are so aggressive, I like to use the largest fatheads I can get my hands on," he told me. "I believe river fish can locate the larger minnows more quickly and from farther away. They don't seem to shy away from a big bait. When I get out on the river with a bucket of minnows, I grab the biggest minnows in the bucket first and work my way down, rather than the other way around!"

And while some fishermen might kill the minnow by driving the jig hook through the minnow's head, Pennaz likes to keep it alive. He hooks it through the lips with the jig hook and attaches the stinger near the tail.

River fishing isn't easy. It requires excellent boat control skills and a bit of experimenting for consistent success, especially for those anglers who spend most of their time on lakes. But be careful. The abundance and eagerness of the fish you find there could get you hooked on it in a hurry.

Trout And Salmon

21

Drop-Back Technique
For River Steelhead

by Dave Richey

Some people live their entire lives seeking love, money or prestige. It's a much different story for steelhead guide Emil Dean.

His love affair is with steelhead, and his prestige comes from teaching people how to catch these silvery gamefish from Lake Michigan's tributaries. To say he is successful in producing fish is like saying that Henry Ford made money making cars.

If Henry obtained fame, fortune and prestige from his early automobiles, Emil Dean of Bear Lake, Michigan, has accomplished much the same thing with his hard-nosed attitude about studying rivers and developing fish-catching techniques that work. Dean—who is often called the Dean of Charterboat Skippers—personally devised and perfected a method of fishing large steelhead rivers from a boat, and his techniques can be duplicated by anyone, in any river where steelhead are found.

Seasonal Movements

"Steelhead move upstream from Lake Michigan in fall, winter and spring," Dean told me on a recent fishing trip. "Fall and winter fish spend all winter in the stream and spawn in late March or April. When fall steelies winter over in the stream they become darker in color than their fresh-run, mint-silver cousins that run in the spring."

Dean said male fish often move upstream first. As spawning

Knowing the timing of fall, winter and spring steelhead runs helps Emil Dean catch these gamefish. But what sets him apart from other fishermen is his ability to put a wobbling plug in a steelhead's path.

Drop-Back Technique For River Steelhead

time nears, their physical characteristics begin to change as their body metabolism undergoes dramatic alterations. Males develop a broad red sash along the lateral line, brilliant red or orange-red gill covers and cheeks, and an enormous, hooked jaw. The kype, or hooked, lower jaw is a spawning characteristic of salmon and trout.

Dean said females usually arrive just before spawning time, and are often fresh from Lake Michigan and cloaked in a coat of silvery scales as bright as a newly minted dime. The courtship is brief, and once spawning begins on shallow gravel bars, a hen steelhead will lay her eggs in one or two days while attended by two to six male fish.

"An important thing for river fishermen to remember is that all steelies—like all people—do not mature at the same time," Dean said. "The trout often begin their pre-spawn staging routine in Lake Michigan off the Manistee River mouth and trickle up-stream a few fish at a time. They don't run all at once, and that's why good fishing can be found over a period of several weeks during the fall, winter and spring periods."

Dean believes ripening males and females will hold in deep holes, runs and pockets of quiet water near any obstruction that breaks the current flow. He pointed out one such spot as we motored upstream under marine jet power in his customized, heated riverboat.

Boat Positioning Is Important

The skipper nosed the bow of his boat into a logjam 25 yards above a long, slick run that paralleled the riverbank. The run was about 75 yards long, 10 yards wide and about 12 feet deep.

"This looks about right for anchoring," Dean said as the boat's bow eased up to the jumble of logs. He hit an electrical switch and a 50-pound ball of heavy chain eased to the bottom from his bow-mounted anchor winch. "It takes 50 pounds of weight on heavy anchor-cable to hold the boat in the proper position to fish this run," he said.

He explained how the drop-back method works when fishing a hole, run or long slick. Chosen lures are FlatFish for slow currents. Tadpollys, Wiggle Warts, Wee Warts, Wee Steelie Warts or Hot 'n Tots are used when the water is deeper and faster.

Steelhead may hold anywhere in a slick run like the one we

Big, tackle-busting steelhead often strike a wobbling plug out of sheer annoyance. On the other hand, a plug in a steelhead's lair may drive the fish away.

were fishing, Dean explained. He has found that runs of 75 yards in length can be fished from one anchored position. Longer runs mean picking up the anchor, drifting downstream and anchoring again to fish the bottom half of the run.

He rigged three outfits by adding an Ambassadeur 5000 bait-casting reel to an 8-foot, light-action baitcasting rod. Each reel is stocked with 20-pound braided Dacron line, and an 8-foot length of 12-pound clear monofilament is attached to the Dacron to serve as a leader. A tiny snap attaches the line to the lure.

"The reason this technique works is because of boat placement and how the lure is presented to steelhead," Dean said. "You must properly position the boat directly upstream from the fish, and then literally drop the lure back to where you feel steelhead are holding. A fish will do one of three things when it sees a plug wiggling downstream toward it. It may strike the lure as it comes near, move away from the lure while dropping back downstream or, in a worst-case scenario, flee the hole and move to a completely differ-ent stretch of river."

Dean says drop-back steelheading is simple to master, and judging from the length of time it took for me to grasp the funda-

Fishing Wobblers For Steelhead

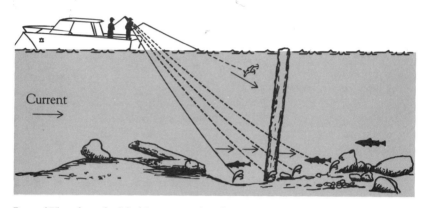

Runs of 75 yards can be fished from one anchored position. For longer runs, a second anchorage should be taken downstream. Dean allows his wobbling plug to hold in the current for 15 to 30 seconds before letting out another three feet of line.

mentals, it appears that anyone with normal hand-eye coordination can learn in just a few minutes.

The rod and reel is held in the left hand with the free-spool button pushed in as if preparing to cast. Thumb pressure is used against the reel arbor for control, and 25 feet of line is released into the current.

"That's it," Dean coaxed. "Let the lure wiggle in the current for 15 to 30 seconds (longer during very cold weather), and then ease off the thumb pressure to allow another three feet of line to slip off the arbor. That causes the lure to move downstream three feet at a time. Good, now add thumb pressure again."

I allowed another three feet of line to slip out from under my thumb, and then added thumb pressure to the spool. The rodtip danced from the action of the Hot 'n Tot, and the lure wiggled in place for 30 seconds before I released another three feet of line.

I could just feel a steelhead watching the approaching lure and waiting for it to get closer before striking.

My thumb had just tightened on the spool when a lightning jolt shot up my arm as the rodtip slammed down to the water. A

Complete Angler's Library

When a steelhead is hooked, Dean advises bringing in all lines to avoid tangles, and possible break offs. Many times, it is necessary to pull anchor and follow the fish downstream.

Drop-Back Technique For River Steelhead   227

steelie had grabbed the lure, instantly rampaged to the surface and twisted head-over-tail across the water before slipping below again.

"It's a bright fish," Dean said. "Looks like a fresh hen, and I'd guess her weight at 12 pounds. Just keep light pressure on her and I'll clear these other two lines."

Michigan's law allows the use of two lines per angler, and we were fishing with a total of three lines when my fish hit. It bored across the river current, twisted into the air on a belly-smacking leap that made my guts hurt, and then sounded for bottom.

Dean raised the 50-pound ball of anchor chain, and we slowly began drifting downstream toward the fish as it wallowed on the surface. We closed to within 20 yards before the steelie lit out on a sizzling downstream run like its tail was on fire.

Slowly, firm rod pressure and a delicately adjusted drag began sapping strength from the steelhead whose sides were the color of a new chrome bumper. Five minutes of bulldogging rushes and bare-knuckle scrapping took place before Dean could slide the meshes of his large landing net under the fish.

"Want her?" Dean asked. I shook my head negatively after taking a few quick pictures, and the guide lowered the hen steelie over the side and slowly released her.

She darted out of sight into the dark water, and we moved back up to our original location. Dean dropped his anchor chains over the logjam again, and we began fishing the run that had just produced a fish.

"Normally, if we'd had a strike farther down in the hole we wouldn't have returned to fish it again," he said. "But that fish struck right at the top of the hole, and where there is one fish we usually find more. Let's keep fishing this spot until we cover both drops, and we should hit the best of the rising water."

The majority of the holes and runs that Dean fished below Tippy dam can be fished in one drop, but some, like the one we were running our plugs through, had to be covered in two stages. Dean explained that if a fish doesn't hit or his clients don't hook a fish on the top end of the hole, he'll raise the anchor and move down to fish the bottom end after anchoring again.

Keep An Eye On Current And Water Levels

Rising water means that water is being released through the

Dean claims one of the best times to draw strikes from steelhead is when the sun breaks through a cloudy sky. He will fish especially hard during those periods of the day.

Drop-Back Technique For River Steelhead   229

turbines of Tippy Dam and Dean has learned that as the current increases and the water level rises, they wash food and debris into the stream. The surge in current and water level seem to trigger steelies into striking, and the same holds true when the water begins to recede.

From the time the water starts to rise, reaches flood stage and begins falling again, between two and three hours will pass. This critical time period usually produces some of the day's best fishing.

We had one other strike as we dropped our lures back down through the hole, but the fish was on and off in less than a heartbeat. The fish hit 60 yards downstream from the anchored boat, and Dean felt it might hit again after dropping farther downstream. He voted to raise the anchor and make our second stop.

The boat was anchored in midstream to catch the downstream end of the long hole. The current flowed strong and hard down the middle, then raced through a shallow run. Then it sliced hard against the riverbank before turning through a stretch dotted with deadheads (log ends) left over from the timbering era 100 years ago.

Dean's Favorite Lure Colors

Dean explained his lure color choices as he rigged up our lines for the second drop. He said silver- or chrome-plated lures are good under almost all water conditions, but he feels yellow with black stripes and gray pearl are deadly colors. White lures with red heads are good, too. Gold-colored lures have been very productive in recent years, and he uses gold plugs every day.

"Snap this gold Hot 'n Tot on and see what happens," Dean said. "We've got plenty of current here, and deep water, and this lure should be scratching bottom in 12 to 14 feet of water. That's the trick, getting the lure down so it digs its bill into the gravel as it wiggles downstream. Steelhead usually can't resist smacking the lure."

Rigged up, we began our drop-back procedures again. We'd release 25 feet of line, let the lure wiggle, and then release just three feet of line at a time with at least a 15-second pause. Drop the lure back another three feet, pause with thumb firmly planted on the reel arbor, let it shimmy in place and drop it back another three feet.

My mind was wandering as I watched a bald eagle soaring high over the river. Dean, attuned to the river's moods, felt a tiny pluck at his lure. He kept the plug digging for several more seconds, then dropped it back three feet. A silvery fish slammed into the lure with a savagery unknown to many other gamefish.

"Here, take this rod and I'll bring the other lines in," he hollered. "This fish is really wild so play him nice and easy until I clear the lines and raise the anchor."

Cashing In On A Doubleheader

His hands were whirling like a dervish as he tried to hurry the other lines to the boat. One lure came in, and at the precise instant he grabbed the second rod, another steelhead hit it like a runaway freight train.

"A doubleheader," he yelled. "Two steelheads at once doesn't happen often."

A twin bill on steelheads is a handful, and landing both fish becomes a grim task when trying to cope with headstrong rushes of big steelies in the Manistee River's heavy current. Dean's fish would streak toward mine and jump, and my steelhead would belligerently try to cross the border into his fish's territory.

We threaded our lines over, under and around each other as first one fish would vault from the water and crash down, only to have the other steelhead try to duplicate or exceed the effort. Somehow, and I'm not sure how, the guide managed to play his fish from the cabin of his riverboat while raising the anchor so we could drift downstream closer to the rampaging steelhead.

Fifteen anxious minutes passed before my buck steelhead, all 15 pounds of him, came rolling to the surface near the boat. The broad crimson stripe along the sides and the fiery glow of cheeks and gill covers were a gaudy contrast to the long torpedo shape and silver coloration of Dean's fish.

We managed to tuck both fish into the net, and suddenly the guide's drop-back technique for taking steelhead seemed to be the answer to a big-river steelhead fisherman's dreams.

Timing—as with falling in love, hitting the Lotto or getting a substantial pay raise at work—is everything, even with the drop-back method. Steelhead often hit best during the morning when the water level starts to rise and again when it falls.

Dean has learned at least one important fact during his 23 years of guiding fishermen. If the day is cloudy, cold, raining or

This 12-pound steelhead fell for a T4 Flatfish in a silver pattern. Some of Dean's favorite lures are the Flatfish, Tadpolly and Wiggle Wart.

Complete Angler's Library

snowing, and the sky suddenly clears and the sun peeks out, that is the best time of all to catch fish.

"I've seen it happen hundreds of times down through the years," he said. "Fishing may be slow, and then the sun comes out. It may shine for only a few minutes but if a steelhead is going to hit, the strikes almost always occur when the sun shines. I caution my clients to fish hard whenever the sun is out."

Dean's drop-back steelheading technique is the cure-all for many fishing ills, particularly for those anglers who have difficulty telling when a fish hits. There's no doubt when a steelhead hits a drop-backed lure; it's a wrist-spraining jolt that often jerks a rod out of the hands of unsuspecting anglers. There's only one word to describe these strikes: savage.

Drop-back steelhead fishing can be adapted to large or small rivers. If the stream is large enough to accommodate a boat, and the angler can read the water to determine where fish should hold, this method will take fish.

This technique doesn't guarantee large numbers of fish, but it does produce some of the biggest steelhead taken each year. If the thought of tangling with a 15-pound buck steelhead is what is needed to light a fire under jaded anglers, try the experience of an arm-wrenching strike from a big fish on no-stretch Dacron line.

Dean's drop-back method of fishing is the most exciting brand of steelhead action developed in years, and if big trout and hard strikes are needed to rekindle a desire to fish, try this method. You'll never be the same again.

22

Best Nymphing Method

by John Holt

Limit me to just one method of fishing for trout for the rest of my angling life, and I would choose nymphing with a tight line presented with a tuck cast. For taking big trout in tough water under trying conditions, nymphing is tops in my experience. Period.

For many of us who consider fly fishing a way of life, the words "nymphing" and "trout" are not often found in the same sentence, especially if the word "fun" is also going to be a part of this piscatorial syntax.

Well, I flailed away, unsuccessfully all too often, with the zealousness of a dry-fly purist. Then one day Tim Tollett, a very good angler on Montana's Beaverhead River, said, "John, if you want to catch big fish, and I don't mean just once every 10 years, pay attention to what I'm doing!"

Tim operates Frontier Anglers in Dillon, a central location for fishing some of the best trout waters in North America. He knows the intricacies of the Beaverhead as well as anyone, spending more than 100 days a year on the water using a variety of techniques and tactics to take the river's big browns and rainbows, trout that see a good deal of pressure from serious and skilled fly fishers.

These are not easy fish to take. When there is no specific hatch to match, nymphing is a proven, consistently successful method for fooling trophy fish.

There have been days on the river when none of my friends,

Mastering methods for presenting a nymph imitation with a fly rod is not an easy task. But when there is no hatch to match, this method will outfish all others.

Best Nymphing Method

Tim Tollett fishes a point fly and dropper through several deep runs on Montana's Beaverhead River following a tuck cast and mend of his line.

who are top-notch anglers in their own right, have raised a trout. Then I've watched Tim work the same run and take not one but two or more good trout.

Now when the fishing turns difficult, I shift to Tim's approach with much greater success in a score of formerly discouraging conditions and usually take at least a couple of nice trout. But mastering this approach taught by someone I consider one of the best big trout anglers in the West has not been easy. Many elaborate facets inherent in the technique reveal themselves over the course of stream-borne experience.

One day Tim was making what appeared to be awkward casts tight to a willow-choked bank we were cruising past, then throwing a quick upstream mend in his line.

Then he hand-stripped the setup reasonably taut and fished the cast through by following the course of the line with the tip of the rod as it eventually moved ahead of him with the force of the current.

A 9- or $9^1/_2$-foot, 6- or 7-weight graphite rod and leaders of $7^1/_2$ feet or less tapered to no smaller than 3X were the standard tools of madness here.

Complete Angler's Library

Tollett works the tuck cast and drift by leaning into the run. Once the fly has passed the run, he picks the line up smartly to initiate another tuck cast.

Best Nymphing Method

Driving The Fly With The Tuck Cast

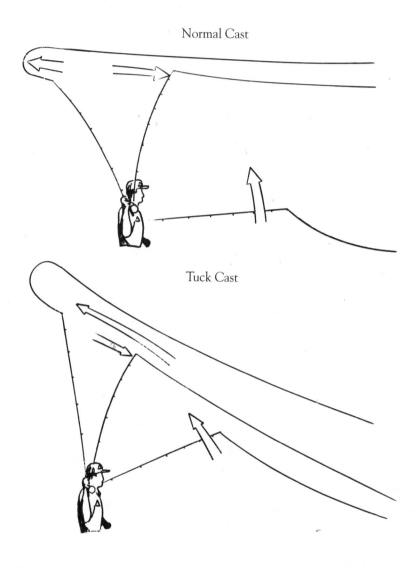

Normal Cast

Tuck Cast

In a normal cast (top) the line is dragged off the water, then brought back in the back and forward casts on a plane parallel with the water. Using the tuck cast (bottom), the angler lifts the line smartly off the water, then uses a shorter backcast to bring the line to a 30-degree angle in both the back and forward casts, driving the fly into the water.

Complete Angler's Library

On a day when others were taking few if any trout, Tim fought and released a dozen or more, with two more than 20 inches.

The Keys To Tollett's Nymphing Technique

What follows is the method as revealed to me in the course of some serious fishing with Tim on the Beaverhead and Big Hole rivers.

Big trout do the majority of their feeding on aquatic nymphs along the bottom of a river in the calmer (benthic) currents. To take these fish, you have to sink your pattern down deep and then keep the furry thing at depth.

This is accomplished through casting and fishing technique, weighted nymphs and the judicious use of lead weight.

To make a tuck cast you must first pick the line up smartly off the water. The path of the line will be up on approximately a 30-degree angle from the water. To insure this flight plan, follow the backcast with the tip of your rod (instead of the more common level cast that stops at one o'clock behind your shoulder).

When you feel the rod load with the weight of the line, cast forward much as you would when using a spinning setup. A proper cast will feel like you are tugging on a small, pliant tree limb behind you, simultaneously offering give and resistance.

As soon as the line is out before you, check (or tuck) the cast by pulling up on the grip with your third and fourth fingers—sort of like hitching your arm when you pull a door shut. This will drive the nymph down into the water.

When you first practice this you will be using a good deal of arm and wrist motion, but as you gain experience the cast will be controlled with a surprisingly small amount of wrist action.

As soon as you tuck the cast, preferably while the line is still in the air, throw a quick upstream mend by flicking the rodtip in this direction. This swift move will put a belly or slack into your line and buy you a few precious feet or even inches of lifelike float for your nymph that should now be bouncing along the rocks and gravel—the difference between connecting and going fishless.

Don't worry if you get hung up and lose a fly or two. That goes with the territory.

The tucking motion offers a good deal of accuracy, and when made bank-tight, it will drop the nymph to the bottom with minimal drift back toward your casting position, which also would be away from the trout hiding near shore.

In fast current you will need to add one, two or even three lead twist-ons to facilitate the sinking action. I prefer twist-ons to lead shot because they seem to sink faster, drift more naturally and, most importantly, don't hurt as much when they hit you in the back of the head (just kidding).

While almost any nymph can be tied with weight added to facilitate sinking, a pattern tied without weight will have a more lifelike drift along the bottom. Using lead twist-ons attached from three to six inches above the fly will provide sufficient sinking capability and produce more fish.

The distance of six inches seems to work best, allowing sufficient free tippet to work naturally in the current, but if you fail to take fish at six inches, experiment and drop down (or even increase the length) until you are successful.

So much of any form of successful angling is based on the willingness of an angler to experiment and modify proven techniques to match current conditions. Nothing in fishing is carved in stone.

Once you've made the cast, control the line with the index finger of your rod hand while stripping the slack with your free hand. Do anything necessary to maintain contact with the nymph and extend the drift. This includes leaning, reaching, stretching and, in general, looking like a circus contortionist.

Detecting the trout's take is a combination of experience and an acquired sixth sense, but be careful not to concentrate so hard that when a big boy hits your nymph you clamp down on the line and break off the trout.

Leader Is Critical For Current And Depth Control

In this type of fishing the leader is critical. This tapering monofilament mixture of varying diameters of line connected by blood knots is your communication network with the river bottom and the trout themselves. By adjusting the amount of weight and, to a lesser extent, the length of the leader you can control the depth of your nymph.

Depth is the ultimate factor in taking fish. The best cast and drift on the planet will not move a trout if the fly drifts harmlessly out of its line of sight and feeding lane.

On fast flows where you expect to tie into big trout you will

Nymphing:

Point Fly And Dropper

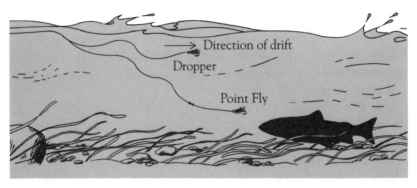

Point fly and dropper: twice the chance a trout will see your fly. To attach, leave 12 to 15 inches of tail from the blood knot when you tie on a tippet. Use this tail to attach the dropper. Use a weight sleeve about 6 inches above the point fly to achieve the proper depth of drift.

want to use a 7-foot leader tapering to no more than 3X and more likely 2X and lX. You'll need this strength of line to hang onto a hefty trout gone berserk with the bite of a hook in a narrow, fast-cruising river. And even with this heavy-duty setup, you will lose your share of fish: frustration and challenge all in one.

Rigging The Point Fly And "Dropper"

The most effective method of fishing nymphs is with a point fly and a "dropper." The dropper is another fly pattern attached above the point and off the main stem of the leader.

When you tie in your tippet section, which will be about 18 inches on a 7¹/₂-foot leader and 2 feet on a 9-footer, you leave anywhere from a foot or so of tail from the blood knot to tie on this dropper.

Over the years I resisted using the two-fly rig, but Tim finally convinced me with brutally simple logic: "Two flies mean twice the chance that a big boy will see the bait!"

Time again has proven the veracity of his words and now that I examine fly fishing literature with a critical eye cast to nymphing,

I am amazed at how little writing is devoted to this device. The British have been taking crafty trout with a point and dropper for a long time.

Probably the best two-nymph selection includes: a point-fly pattern that imitates the aquatic insect during the phase of its life in which it crawls along the bottom and an emerger pattern for the dropper.

The selection will depend on where you are fishing and either your on-river experience or that of a guide or fly shop operator. The choice of patterns is dictated by aquatic insect life present in the water you are to fish, time of year and to a certain degree the type of water you will be working.

For example, fast, slightly off-color conditions could indicate nymph patterns tied with bright materials and perhaps several wraps of gold or silver tinsel to help reflect the little light available beneath the surface and in turn catch the attention of the trout.

I tied into and lost a very large (more than two feet) brown on the Beaverhead using a Partridge & Peacock on the point and an Antron emerger as a dropper. The trout rose up from the bottom through the shifting currents to take the dropper. Tim took a

Tollett casts the weighted point fly and dropper upstream, then fishes the setup through the bottom of a run on Montana's Big Hole River. Note how he extends his arm to cover as much of the run as possible.

Complete Angler's Library

Tollett caught this Beaverhead River brown trout on a nymph in a deep run. His drift technique is so effective that it seems to produce in seemingly "dead" runs.

number of 16- to 20-inch browns and rainbows with the same setup drifting right through the gut of bruising, deep runs formed at the tails of chutes and long riffles.

Watching someone as skilled as Tim in this method is a revelation. He took fish whenever he beached our raft on a gravel bar or bank and fished holding water.

At the end of the day when I discussed this with other anglers who had not been fishing with nymphs, but rather dries, their success ratio was not even in Tim's ballpark.

Putting The Technique To The Test

Another time and in another place, a local expert took four fish in a run of 50 feet or so and then looked at me as if to say, "Let's see what you can do, fella!"

Using the tuck and mend cast with a point and dropper fished with a tight line that was drifted right at the bottom through the run, I took three rainbows, all more than 15 inches. Not bad for second man through. Thanks, Tim.

I guess in a way I was saying, "That's what this technique and a little practice can do, fella!"

23

Titans On
Gossamer Line

by Ottie M. Snyder

Dick Swan of Clare, Michigan, is an innovator and a fine fisherman. His noodle rod, light-line fishing system for stream salmon and trout has helped many anglers tackle and land record-sized fish on line as light as 2-pound test. Like the species he pursues, Dick's system has also become anadromous, spawned in the stream and migrated to the lake.

Actually it was the distance from Michigan to the Pacific Northwest that caused Swan to start experimenting with big lake trolling utilizing his light-line techniques. In pursuit of summer-run steelhead he made the trip out West for years to tackle the gamesters. At that time of the year there were no fish available in streams close to home.

A dozen or so years ago he simply tired of making the long trip and decided to purchase a boat and try trolling for salmon and steelhead on the Great Lakes. But he would try it with his own system rather than fish like most of the other anglers. Just as they had done when he first started fishing the streams, anglers quickly informed Swan that it was impossible to tackle chinook or steelhead by trolling with 2- or 4-pound test line. But as he'd done in Midwest and Pacific Northwest steelhead streams, Swan proved them wrong.

Any troller seeing the *Lite Liner*, Swan's 24-foot Starcraft, quickly knows it is not the typical Great Lakes fishing boat. It does not look like a porcupine with six, eight or a dozen rods set in

Dick Swan admires a fine chinook, or king salmon, taken while fishing with ultra-light line in Lake Michigan.

downriggers. It carries only two rods set at any one time—rods of up to 14 feet in length! And it clips along at $3^1/2$ mph.

Swan's unique setup doesn't end there. When a fish hits one of his two baits, the boat ceases to be anything more than a platform from which the angler fights the fish. The boat goes into neutral and the other trolled line and downrigger balls are cleared immediately, permitting the angler to fight the hooked fish one-on-one. The accepted method aboard most Great Lakes boats would be to continue the troll. This naturally puts the fish being fought at the stern of the boat and keeps additional baits in the water for the possibility of more strikes—a practice you won't see aboard the *Lite Liner*.

The result, according to Swan, is that the angler gets to enjoy a direct fight with each and every fish hooked. "If the fish decides to take them around the boat two or three times or make four or five long runs it's up to the angler to follow and fight. The boat does not help to wear down the fish," he said. "Perhaps (light-line fishing) is not for everyone, but my customers would not enjoy catching salmon and trout any other way.

"On most big boats trolling for salmon and trout, the person fighting the fish does not really celebrate much in landing it," said Swan. "They've done little more than crank the fish in while the boat continues to move forward. That isn't much of a challenge when the reel is spooled full of 17- to 20-plus-pound test line. When my anglers land a 20-pound chinook or steelhead they definitely enjoy a sense of accomplishment," Swan said.

Special Rods Allow Light-Line Presentations

So just what is this system that permits fighting a fish as strong and powerful as the king salmon on line that closely resembles a spider's web? Swan, both a stream guide and lake charter operator, is primarily a custom rod builder who specializes in light-line rods for both stream and lake applications.

His rods are all built on ultra-light blanks, in both glass and graphite, and most measure at least 10 feet. All of Swan's custom-made rods are built from blanks designed by West Coast salmon and trout expert Gary Loomis. Other than the Dip Stick, a custom Dipsey Diver rod made to troll 15- to 20-pound test line, the rest of the rods offered by Swan—he lists at least 38 models standard and makes some to order above that number—are designed to fish

Light line and long noodle rods to absorb some of the shock of the powerful runs of Great Lakes trout and salmon are a trademark of Dick Swan's boat.

nothing heavier than 8-pound test line. Most (24 models) are made to handle nothing heavier than 4-pound test.

Called noodle rods by their developer, these rods are designed to act as a shock absorber for fishing line small enough in diameter to permit presenting a bait to salmon and trout in clear water streams without spooking them. Swan insists that anglers utilizing light line (2- or 4-pound test) can entice many times the strikes of an angler fishing even 8-pound test. Many who've questioned the effectiveness of the noodle rod system have been proven wrong at streamside.

Swan said that when he first took the rods to the West Coast, traditional steelheaders there stood by insisting that he'd never land a fish on such light line. Then they watched him hook and land five fish to their one. It is this same proven stream system that he has modified and taken to the Great Lakes for trolling, and his success catching big salmon and trout is impressive.

Modified Lures Improve Hooking Success

Utilizing only two rods and altered J-Plugs (primarily), Swan runs leads back 50 to 60 feet behind No. 16 rubber-band releases at the cannonball. He trolls along at what most consider searching speeds of $3^{1}/_{2}$ mph. When he first started trolling with J-plugs and 2- to 4-pound test line he quickly discovered that the popular salmon plugs would have to be altered slightly. First, the hook harness provided with each bait had large, plated hooks that Swan simply could not get sharp enough to permit a good hookset.

He quickly developed his own harness, which consists of a No.1 VMC, round bend treble hook at the front and a No. 6 or No. 8 treble of the same type, at the back of an 8- to 12-inch-long piece of 12-pound monofilament line. Swan insists that this harness rig permits him to hook up solidly with fish, utilizing 2- or 4-pound test line on the rod and the rubber-band release system. He says that the small trailing treble is usually embedded in the

How To Rig A J-Plug For Light-Line Trolling

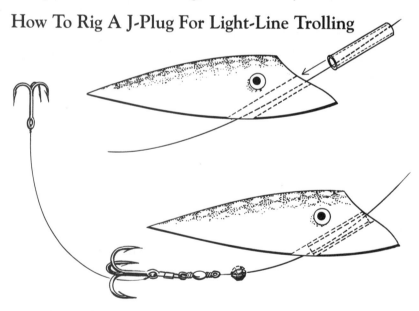

Swan modifies a J-Plug by replacing the factory hook harness with his own, including a No. 7 or 9 VMC round bend trailer hook, tied with 12-pound test monofilament from a No. 2 or 3 VMC round bend. The main line is run through a cut and smoothed piece of glass pipette, glued into place inside the plug. A glass bead is threaded on the line before tying on a snap swivel.

outside cheek of a fish hooked on the front treble.

After changing to the custom harness on the J-Plug, Swan discovered another problem when fighting a fish hooked on the small diameter line. The plug, designed to slide up the line when a fish hits, lessening the fish's ability to use the plug as a lever to dislodge the hooks, was being ruined. So, too, were long sections of the light line. The line was literally sawing into the body of the plug!

After experimenting with many different materials to line the plug, he finally settled on a glass pipette, which is nothing more than a glass straw commonly found in chemistry labs. He has pipettes the same diameter as the hole in a J-Plug cut down to the same width of the plug and smoothed on the ends. The pipette is then glued into the hole eliminating the slicing effect.

Swan uses just a few other trolling-lure designs to supplement his selection of J-plugs: Hot 'N Tots, Yakima Hawg Boss, Super Toads, Rebel Fastracs, Luhr-Jensen's Diamond King and Eppinger Flutter Chucks. His terminal tackle needs are few because the speeds he normally trolls preclude the use of many baits.

Light Line Has Special Advantages In Shallow Water

When Swan first started his charter business he utilized some 6- and 8-pound test monofilament. After a couple of seasons and catches averaging 90-plus percent of all hooked fish, he decided the heavy line was too easy. He now uses nothing heavier than 6-pound test. He fishes $11^1/2$-, 13- and 14-foot rods while trolling, each equipped with Penn Mag 10 reels spooled with Berkley XT monofilament on each.

Swan does not put his boat in the water until after the spring steelhead fishing in streams has ended, usually around May 1. He believes that his light-line trolling system has an advantage both early and late in the season when fish are in close to shore, especially where the number of hits is concerned.

"During the middle of summer, when we are running baits down 60 feet or deeper, there's not much advantage in the smaller-diameter line when it comes to hits," said Swan. "The only benefit really is the increased enjoyment of the fight, because even the heavy stuff disappears at those depths. But my system really shines during the spring and fall when the fish are shallow and there's heavy boat traffic. The fish are spooky in these situations and tend to stay away from the heavier lines."

My wife and I can attest to Swan's belief. Several years ago Swan joined us at Rogers City, Michigan, for a couple of days of fall chinook trolling in, of all places, Swan Bay. The fish concentrate there in the fall, staging to make sporadic spawning runs up the creek of the same name. Boat traffic is heavy and most fish come from water with bottom depths of less than 40 feet.

I had been fishing Swan stream steelhead rods for years, but this meeting was to be the first time I'd be able to test his trolling rods. Breaking from his tradition, I rigged up four rods—two flatlines and two to be set just five to seven feet down and run well back off downriggers. I hooked Rebel Fastracs to all four lines.

In just two and a half hours of fishing, with 4-pound test line, we landed our 15-fish limit of king salmon. We missed only four fish strikes and didn't lose or break off a single fish that was well hooked. The action was fast and furious and included a quartet of kings at one time, with only three anglers on board, as well as a couple of doubles.

As the first fish of the four hit a rigger-trolled bait set at seven feet, my wife Vicki took the rod and Swan and I moved to clear the flatlines. As each of us cranked furiously to retrieve flats set back 150 and 200 feet behind the boat, both took slamming hits from kings—three fish on and one line still in the water. I had no choice but to put my rod back in the rod holder, fish still attached and clicking off line against the drag, as I attempted to clear the other rigger-set rod and both cannonballs. I jerked the rod to break the rubber band and started to retrieve the 60-foot lead just as a chinook slammed that bait, too. It was truly Chinese fire drill time. I held the long rod high with one hand while working frantically to clear both cannonballs from the water.

Swan, meanwhile, was doing the same with his rod, holding it high, letting the fish work against the big fighting "C" of the noodle rod while trying to work the net under Vicki's fish with his free hand. Once her fish was landed, Vicki moved to the rod in the rod holder expecting to clear it, thinking the fish that was hooked had long since gotten off. Wrong! It was still there, with the sharpened wire hooks on the bait buried in its mouth.

Four fish on, three anglers in the boat and all four fish landed. Our smallest fish during that one-and-a-half-hour trip was 22 pounds and the largest was 27—all taken on 4-pound test

Swan custom builds his own noodle rods. These fish-fighting sticks are built in different sizes, but none are less than 10 feet in length. Most are made to accommodate line of 4-pound test and lighter.

Titans On Gossamer Line 251

Besides the altered J-plug he likes to use, Swan's lure selection is simple: (top to bottom) Yakima Hawg Boss, Rebel Fastrac Minnow, Fat Rap, Hot 'N Tot and trolling spoons.

monofilament, and not a single break-off! Back at the dock we talked to several fishermen who came in well after we had returned. The next best catch from the same waters was nine kings, split among five anglers who had been fishing eight rods with 17- to 20-pound monofilament.

Light Line Can Help You Catch More Steelhead

Another area in which light-line trolling shines is Great Lakes steelheading. Most anglers fish the thermal bars (a band of warmer water squeezed between colder waters) that are easily identifiable by a "scum line" that collects on top of the water. The scum line is nothing more than terrestrials (insects), grass and other surface debris that collects on top of the warmer water. In water as deep as 750 feet, 15 to 20 miles offshore, steelhead congregate under the thermal bars to feed on the insects that collect here.

Anglers pursuing these fish over the past several years have had tremendous success. Those opting for light-line tactics enjoy even more hookups. Again, because fish hold as shallow as 10 feet or less under the surface, the smaller diameter line generates more hits.

In those areas of the Great Lakes where summer-run

Skamania steelhead have been planted, trollers find close-in action that is unrivaled in terms of fishing excitement. The original home of the Skamania in the Great Lakes is the 45-mile-long shoreline of Indiana. Each year many anglers from all over the country who've been introduced to "Skamania Mania" make the trip to Michigan City or Burns Waterway, Indiana, in pursuit of Skamania.

Swan, too, is there each year from the end of June through the month of July—which is normally considered the best time.

The Skamania steelhead is an explosive, acrobatic salmonid that leaves many saying that if anglers boat 50 percent of the fish hooked they've had a good day. With the light-line, noodle rod system it is not uncommon to land well above 70 percent of the fish hooked. The shock-absorbing action of the ultra-light long rod does not give the fish as much leverage as a shorter, stiffer rod. That leverage is what allows many steelhead to throw the hook when jumping.

A 20-pound steelhead is a trophy fish regardless of the method it is taken on, but add to the trophy the knowledge that it was taken on 4-pound test or even 2-pound test line and the thrill is increased tremendously. Those baits outlined earlier for salmon fishing all work well for steelhead, too.

Light-line trolling need not be done exclusively with a custom-made rod. Many manufacturers now offer longer, lighter-action trolling rods in their lines. I've fished 8-, 10- and 12-pound test exclusively for years on Daiwa Strike rods, $8^1/_2$-feet long in medium/light tips. The only time I go heavier than 12-pound test line on any trolling gear is on a rod rigged with a Dipsey Diver.

Light-Line Trolling Catches Walleyes Too

Salmon and trout trolling is not the only method where light line can increase angler hookups and enjoyment in the fight. In the central and eastern basins of Lake Erie, trolling for walleyes is the practiced method. Even out in the western basin where drifting and casting is the norm, more and more anglers are going to trolling during the summer doldrums. Again, dropping down to 2-, 4- or 6-pound test line with a light-action rod, a rubber-band release and normal walleye trolling baits, anglers will see more hits and increase the fight of the sometimes lethargic walleye. It too, like salmon and trout, is a sight feeder and extremely line-shy.

A lady angler hefts her first Skamania steelhead, an 18-pound fish taken on 4-pound test line and a Swan noodle rod.

Complete Angler's Library

Practice Means Changing Tactics

Light-line trolling does bring with it some change of tactics for the angler. Since the boat is placed into neutral and all lines are cleared while the fish is fought, it's only natural that fewer lines are set. It is also only natural to accept that the light-line troller cannot join a group of boats that continue to troll when fighting fish. Light-line trollers must accept that the difference in their tactics will create a hardship for others in a pattern. Light-liners must fish away from the packs and establish their own territory.

This isn't quite the handicap one might think. With a pack of boats fishing a pattern, there are bound to be fish spooked off to the side by boat noise and the number of baits being trolled through the water. The light-liner, set up to one side or the other, offers baits to these fish on line that is invisible in the water.

I've found that by utilizing Swan's light-line trolling methods and his custom noodle rods I have increased my enjoyment in tangling with Great Lakes salmon and trout. The system works, as is attested by the 27-pound king salmon and the 24-pound Skamania steelhead on my trophy wall. Both fish were taken on IGFA 2-pound test monofilament.

I've also found that I can increase my enjoyment without the big investment of custom rods by picking light-action trolling rods offered by most manufacturers and fishing line that is considered too light by most salmon trollers.

Besides the increased enjoyment, you'll find that by fighting fish on light line you also pick up more strikes in shallow-water situations. Give it a try on your next trolling excursion for Great Lakes trout and salmon. You'll double your fun.

Muskies And
Northern Pike

24

Muskies After Dark

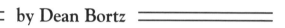

by Dean Bortz

D uring recent years, a new approach to muskie fishing has been developed, but the technique is just starting to filter its way out of the small fraternity of anglers who founded and refined it.

Night fishermen have broken muskie fishing myths perpetuated by fishermen who believe that muskies simply sulk their way through the hot, long summers. The discovery of night fishing success has changed the fishing patterns of its pioneers living in the muskie country of northern Wisconsin, as well as their thoughts on muskie feeding habits.

If anyone is creating a bulge on the night fishing learning curve, it has to be Joe Bucher of Eagle River, Wisconsin. Anyone talking to Bucher for 30 minutes will be convinced there is no better way to approach summer muskies than under a cloak of darkness.

Bucher Has Proven His Night Fishing Success

Considering his muskie fishing success in recent years, there is no reason to doubt him. How good is it? Consider this: In one three-night stand he and his clients caught 28 legal muskies, including a 50-incher. The catch was no fluke. A few weeks earlier, he and his clients caught 29. The high point of the week came one night when a man who had never caught a legal muskie in 35 years of fishing landed six, including two longer than 40 inches! Unbelievable? Not if you've fished muskies at night.

Pioneer of night fishing for muskies, Joe Bucher hoists a 48-inch fish estimated at more than 30 pounds, which he released.

Muskies After Dark

Discovering Night Fishing

Don't cuss out the water-skiers. They may be one reason that night fishing is so effective on most gamefish species, except, perhaps, northern pike. Bucher, a northern Wisconsin fishing guide, lure manufacturer, writer and fishing educator, discovered the benefits of night fishing during the early 1970s—even before he began guiding.

At that time, Bucher played lead guitar and sang for Raven Strait, a Milwaukee band. From 1970 to 1973, Bucher rocked until 2 or 3 a.m. in Milwaukee night clubs, then flew straight home to hit the lakes until daylight. After getting in a few hours of walleye or bass fishing, he hit the sack.

"The lake was full of water-skiers during the day. By the time I was finished playing, the boats had been off the water for about five hours and the fish were active.

"The fish had adapted to the pressure. It seemed like most of the gamefish, except pike, fed after dark because of the traffic," Bucher said.

That knowledge became useful once Bucher began guiding for muskies in the mid-1970s. At that time, northern Wisconsin guiding tradition dictated the format: Guides picked up their clients at 8 a.m., cooked them a shore lunch, then dropped them off at 4 p.m. Fishing wasn't bad during the spring and early summer, but once the dog days hit, nothing happened. Good guides brought in one muskellunge every three days.

Bucher didn't like the results and, because he began getting into the bait business about the same time, he switched his guiding to morning and evening outings.

"The mornings were okay, but the evenings were definitely better. Most anglers at that time did not believe muskies fed after dark. If they caught one, they thought the muskie was just getting in a late feed," he said.

Bucher stayed on the water later and later, and noticed that he caught more and bigger fish at twilight. His afternoon outings ran from 2 p.m. to dark for three years and, as time progressed, "dark" kept getting later and later. Bucher started noticing that the first seven hours, from 2 to 9 p.m., were not as hot as the one hour after 9 p.m. Checking back through his logs, it didn't take him long to figure out that more than 70 percent of his muskies came after sunset.

Bucher uses a mallet to flatten a Colorado-style blade on this spinnerbait. The flattened blade emits a thumping vibration that attracts muskies. He prefers black spinnerbaits at night

Muskies After Dark

Back into the dark water—a fine muskie is ready to be unhooked after a tag has been placed on its dorsal fin. The fish hit on a winged surface bait.

Then, in 1983, Bucher diverged from the norm even more, re-belled against tradition, and guided clients who were willing to fish from 5 p.m. to midnight. His success rate skyrocketed!

"That was my greatest year of muskie fishing to that point. We averaged two to three muskies per night and had nights when eight and nine fish were boated," Bucher said.

"It changed everything."

During the early years of night guiding, Bucher relied on wood surface baits and shallow-running lures such as spinnerbaits and bucktails. He made oversized bucktails and found that, with a cer-tain blade, those bucktails produced on windy nights. Those bucktails helped Bucher overcome some early mistakes.

"I started out with surface baits," he remembers. "I drove to the landings and, if it was windy, I didn't go out. What I didn't realize was that I was missing the best fishing of all—fishing wind-blown water with subsurface lures."

Bucher found that wind actually makes muskies less spooky. Instead of finding one fish on a spot, he found several. The big bucktails accounted for many fish on those windy nights.

One night the bucktails really busted open the lake for Bucher

Complete Angler's Library

and his clients. It was one of those evenings that night fishermen learn to anticipate—when humid heat blows in from the southwest to squeeze sweat beads from the skin.

The dark night forced Bucher and two clients to wipe the sweat from their brows, but the action before the storm was just as steamy. They caught eight muskies, nailing seven on big, black bucktails on one bar alone. The action continued past midnight.

Bucher knew he was onto something and as he learned more, the word spread.

"I won't say that I discovered night fishing. I think there might have been a couple of old pros out there who were doing it, but weren't saying anything to anyone. However, I will say that I popularized it by writing about it and talking about it at seminars. Before that, people did not talk about it," he said.

Why Night Fishing Works

Those big bucktails did more than catch eight muskies that hot night in 1983. They also unraveled another mystery about muskies that Bucher has been able to use to vary his night fishing methods and effectively increase his annual muskie catch.

Fishing Shadows For Muskies

As shadows fall, muskies become active, especially on waters busy with daytime activity. Concentrate your efforts on shadowed areas of the lake first, then work out as darkness falls.

Not only do muskies feed at night because of heavy daytime boat traffic, they also feed at night because they can see well. If they couldn't see well, they would be forced to feed during the day, regardless of traffic.

"After thinking back on that catch, I realized that those muskies were feeding heavily. And to do that, they had to be able to see well.

"The biggest difference between a muskie and a northern pike is vision. Northern pike simply have poorer sight, and that may be why muskies are more difficult to catch. Fishermen can trigger northerns into striking, and I have noticed that where both species are present, northerns will be caught in the clearer water.

"That difference may be why northerns aren't often caught at night and why muskies tend to follow; they see leaders. That may be why big muskies are often caught on light line. They can't see it. That's why night fishing is hot."

Muskies seem less wary and more aggressive after dark. That may be because the cover of darkness camouflages leaders, lines, boats and angler movement. Most fishermen believed muskies could see better than northerns, but no one knew what the degree of difference was until Bucher began experimenting with deep-running crankbaits during his night-fishing outings.

That experimentation eventually convinced Bucher to develop his own crankbait, the Depth Raider, which he has tested for five years before putting the finished design into production for 1990.

No matter how dark the night, no matter how deep a bait dives, a muskie can see it. Knowing that gives night fishermen a broad range of tools that doesn't vary much from what might be used during the day, except that crankbaits may be depended on more heavily at night than during the day.

There is also a theory that night fishing is effective because, besides pursuing daytime fish put down by boat traffic, night fishermen are working an entirely "untouched" family of fish. Avid night anglers have noticed that many muskies caught after dark are "clean," meaning they have not been hooked, netted and released by other fishermen. Their mouths and fins are not torn, their scales are not scraped. Telemetry research with other species, such as walleyes, has discovered the existence of fish "families" or groups of fish of the same species, in the same body of water, that display behavior patterns that vary from other fish, such as using different spawning areas and home ranges. Night fishermen believe the same is true with muskies.

When To Try Night Fishing

Bucher begins fishing different lakes at different times of the year, with the amount of boat traffic being the primary determinant of the day to night change. If boat traffic begins early on popular waters, such as Vilas County's Eagle chain or Oneida County's Minocqua chain, then it's time to begin night fishing.

However, in most cases, night fishing turns on by the end of June and continues through July, August and into mid-September. After September night fishing becomes iffy, but still occurs. The fall night feed resembles a cold-front feed in many respects and will be discussed later. Of course, cold fronts occur frequently late in the year. In 1989, Bucher caught a 28-pound muskie after dark on November 6, when the water temperature was 43 degrees. He was slow-trolling near a school of ciscoes at the time and that may be the key to catching late-season muskies on lakes containing ciscoes. The silvery members of the whitefish family spawn in shallow water after dark in November.

Lakes also have physical characteristics that can make one better than the other for night fishing. As already mentioned, boat traffic is one key ingredient.

A lake also needs a good amount of well-defined, shallow cover (weeds) that offers muskies a feeding area. In contrast, deep lakes with sparse shallow cover often make better trolling lakes than night fishing lakes, especially if the lack of cover is coupled with good oxygen levels at all depths. Even if such a lake has heavy boat traffic, fish will continue to feed during the day above the deep thermocline.

Night fishermen should also consider water clarity. Fish will be active in either type of lake; however, fish will be found shallower in stained water and deeper in clear water.

Of course, when choosing a lake, fishermen should select one with a good muskie population. Make a choice, get to know the lake and fish it under all weather conditions, including cold fronts. In fact, the night following a cold front may be the only time anglers can actually expect to catch a muskie—if they do their homework.

Bucher has discovered that muskies stick their noses to the weeds and rarely feed following post-frontal conditions on "bluebird days" with mile-high skies.

"During warm, stable conditions, muskies will feed for a long time day or night. But they stick close to the bottom after a clearout.

"On the night following a cold front, however, day muskies will feed during a short burst of activity. The feeding spree may last only minutes during the twilight hours (between dusk and darkness)."

That feeding spree relates directly to the fading light. As shadows fall across weed edges and rock bars, the fish become active. Knowing there is only a short time to capitalize on the cold front behavior, anglers who know the lake's active spots plan a precise route, hoping to encounter fish as they become active. Since shadows first cover a lake's west side, the western weed edges are the first place to hit. Similar shadows fall on the east side of points and islands. Muskies on rock bars will normally feed later than "weed fish" in the same area, perhaps because the rock bar lacks cover and the muskies aren't comfortable on the open area until it gets darker.

"That's how I unlocked the secret to cold front fishing," Bucher said.

"I had a milk run set up. I would hit the best spots at the key time period. Someone would catch a fish, then it would be over. The key was the changing light."

Deep-running crankbaits are useful on cold front nights. The fish feed in the same spots that are used during more active periods, but they stick closer to the bottom.

"During an active period, fishermen can be successful using surface baits or bucktails above weeds, but I found that, during cold fronts, deep-diving crankbaits caught more and bigger fish because the bait gets down to where the fish are," Bucher said.

The biggest secret to night fishing success is learning one lake well enough to predict feeding times. On one, Bucher discovered a weed ledge on the lake's west end that turned on regularly at 8:45 p.m. Another spot, a rock bar out in the lake, did not turn on until 10:10 p.m. during July. In both cases, fish activity was triggered by changing light conditions.

Fishermen can use any of four bait types for night fishing:

Bucher attaches a split ring to the front eye of a diving plug. The ring allows better action at very slow retrieval speeds, tempting strikes from wary muskies.

winged surface baits, spinnerbaits, bucktails or crankbaits. Surface baits can be retrieved very slowly above weeds. The plopping noise, wake and silhouette give muskies something to aim at. Spinnerbaits and bucktails can be used between the surface and weed tops. When using spinnerbaits at night, Bucher prefers single blades that are flattened with a hammer. Flat blades create more vibration. Spinnerbaits are also useful because the blade always spins, even when dropped into weed pockets. Bucktails should be oversized with large blades. Both bucktails and spinnerbaits can be dropped along weed edges, but no bait works the weed edges like a crankbait.

Bucher often turns to crankbaits for night fishing, especially now that he has perfected his Depth Raider, a jointed crankbait made from the same plastic that is used to make bulletproof car windows. He developed the Depth Raider after using wooden crankbaits for several years. Bucher said a plastic bait is more durable than wood and allows for better hookset because the fish can't sink their teeth into it. The lure also makes a clacking noise when the jointed segments hit together during the retrieve. Bucher still has the original prototype, and though he has caught more than

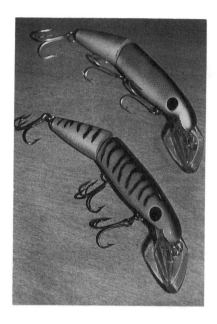

The Depth Raider, a jointed crankbait developed by Bucher specifically for night fishing, is made of hard plastic and measures 7¹/₂ inches in length.

100 muskies on it, the bait is barely scratched. The bait runs at 10 feet when casting with 20-pound line; double that when trolled. Crankbaits run shallower when using heavy line and deeper when using lighter line. When night fishing, select a line weight based on the depth of the weed edge.

Boat control is just as important as proper bait selection. Knowing one lake well not only allows fishermen to find active fish, it will help them stay on the weed edges. Following an edge is difficult enough during the day; it's even more difficult at night.

"Fishermen must know the lake intimately to effectively fish at night. They must also have good fundamental techniques. A 'bad' crankbait fishermen during the day will be real 'bad' at night. The same goes with boat control. Fishermen have to have good boat control during the day, but they need great boat control at night.

"It takes precise movement along a weed edge to be successful. The better fishermen are good at the fundamentals, such as casting, retrieving and boat control, the more fish they will catch," Bucher said.

Equipment And Night Fishing Safety

Sonar equipment is a must for finding weed edges in the dark.

Many LCRs, however, are next to useless unless they are back-lit. Flasher units just may be the night fisherman's best friend. The bright, flashing light tells a night owl everything he needs to know, without turning on a light.

Headlamps are the next most valuable piece of equipment. Unlike flashlights, headlamps are rarely misplaced, can be turned on quickly once a fish is hooked and they never fall in the lake. Coon hunters discovered the usefulness of headlamps years ago, and now night fishermen are catching on.

As far as equipment goes, Bucher uses 7- to $7^1/_2$-foot, heavy action rods and baitcasting reels smaller than normal muskie reels.

"The smaller reels have internal parts identical to the larger reels, but they are easier to hold on to. The only difference is line

Night Fishing Safety

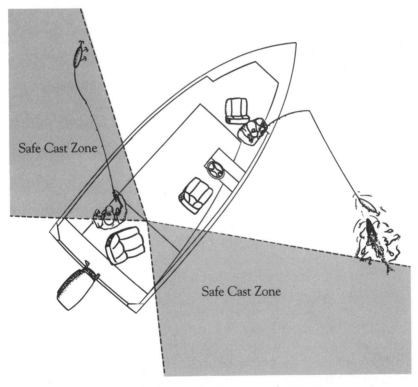

Use caution when fishing at night. Designate casting zones to avoid hooking your partner on a backcast. Never set the hook until you feel the strike of a fish. A missed set could send a big plug flying toward you or your partner.

Alan Grischke caught his largest muskie, a 33¹/₂-pound fish measuring 50 inches, at 1:30 a.m. while fishing with Bucher.

capacity, but fishermen will be making shorter casts at night."

If baits don't have hooks on split rings, they do after Bucher gets through modifying them. When hooks are on split rings, muskies cannot "torque" against the bait. That means fewer fish get away. Of course, all hooks should be sharpened.

When using surface baits after dark, steel those nerves so the hooksetting action comes after the fish's weight is felt on the line. Muskies have a habit of surfacing behind a bait and tracking it for several feet before striking. That can unnerve a fisherman in the dark, causing an early hookset. That action, lacking the weight of a fish, often brings the bait right back at the angler's face. To avoid that, set the hooks by sweeping the rod down and to the side.

The boat should be clear of all gear other than what's being used at the time. Nets or gaffs should be handy, but out of the way.

Leave the front running lights on while fishing and carry a spot-light that can be used to scan the lake while motoring.

Night Fishing: A Different World

There is nothing quite like chasing muskellunge under the stars. Having a fishing partner who is an amateur astronomer makes the night even more interesting.

However, just about the time an angler is trying to determine which way the Big Dipper is pointing, the night's first hungry muskie will slash the bait at boatside bringing the fisherman back to reality. That's the exciting thing about night fishing—no one knows when those fish are going to strike because no one can see a follow after dark. A boatside strike has a way of stopping the heart for a second or two. That's what makes night fishing exciting.

Joe Bucher's years of studying muskie behavior has paid big dividends. His technique is so effective that he is positive it will work on lakes with heavy boat traffic—and muskies.

"It was through a quirk of fate that I started fishing late at night. Now I'm a night owl because of it," he said, adding that he will continue fishing muskies after dark until he has completely figured out the secretive creature.

"We know a lot about night fishing now, but, just like any other fishing technique, there is always more to learn. We haven't learned everything there is to know about night fishing—yet."

25

Trolling: Route To Trophy Muskies

by George W. Sandell

There is a solemn truth that muskie fishermen are different, different from any other type of angler on the water. The reason for this difference is the fish itself. The muskie is a resolute rebel—cantankerous, defiant, gutsy and muscular. It is a mean fish.

No fish has attracted such an incensed, dedicated group of hunters as the muskie, and it doesn't take a social psychologist to figure out why. These resolute anglers, like helpless lemmings, plunge ever onward in pursuit of the muskie, which dares them to catch it. It does this by playing games with their lures, by following them, snorting at them and then ignoring them. It gets the angler's pulse racing in expectation by surging toward the bait—and then leaves the angler screaming and defeated by turning away at the last instant.

This heartbreak game is played out mostly in the shallows, the weedbeds, the surfacing rocks, the sandy reefs. But casting for muskies seldom takes place where the biggest muskies are found—and that is deep.

Almost all of the really notable (that means 55 pounds or more) muskie catches that have been recorded during the past 20 years have come as the product of trolling. They were caught by anglers who didn't really care if they saw the fish that hit their bait—or saw any of the chase at all. They plain just wanted to catch muskies, and preferably big ones.

Some will say that these trolling fisherfolk attack that exercise

Len Hartman, who may have caught more muskies than any man alive, displays a 50-plus-pound fish. Hartman believes trolling to be the best way to catch the biggest muskies.

Trolling: Route To Trophy Muskies

with considerably less skill than that required of a consummate caster. They come with a dramatically smaller arsenal of baits, rods, reels, lines and leaders. Drama is less important to them than fulfillment. And they have caught some big ones. The biggest muskies in all of North America, in point of fact.

Records Of Biggest Muskies Favor Trollers

We can begin by considering the 65-pounder caught by young Ken O'Brien of Toronto in October of 1988. And then there was the almost 57-pound giant caught by Gene Borucki of Northbrook, Illinois, in the waters of Upper Manitou in northwestern Ontario, in July of 1984.

The purists, of course, will discredit O'Brien's catch because it came to him while he and a friend were out trolling "to catch anything." And, to be sure, he was not a bona fide muskie angler at work. He was a classic example of a weekend fisherman, armed only with a tiny Countdown Rapala, a 4-inch leader and 8-pound test line. Borucki, on the other hand, was a true muskie addict, a veteran of the muskie wars in many of the most challenging waters on the continent.

The most important fact in both of these notable catches, of course, is that they were made while trolling. O'Brien was fishing in 35 feet of water in Canada's muskie-rich Georgian Bay when the giant that measured 58 inches in length and $30^1/_2$ inches in girth struck. The fish bested a 26-year-old Canadian muskie record by 3 pounds! Borucki's catch took top honors in the annual competition of the International Game Fish Association for 1984, plus first prize in Canada's popular Molson Big Fish Contest.

A Lifetime Hooked On Muskies

By far the best-known disciple of trolling today is Len Hartman, who with his wife Betty has caught more than 3,696 muskies in 50 years of hunting for these fish. They have caught more big muskies in more places than any angler in the history of the sport. And they have caught most of them (more than 90 percent, Len will tell you) while trolling.

As a young man in Pennsylvania, Len found that his winter trapping earnings provided enough spare cash to spend much of the rest of the year fishing. He loved to fish for trout, bass, and the

Len Hartman, seen while fishing the waters of Ontario's Rowan Lake for its giant muskies. Hartman is a consummate troller with intense concentration.

occasional pike. Then one day he caught a muskie—by mistake. The challenge and excitement of that single catch changed his entire perspective on fishing. He and Betty decided to learn more about these energetic fish.

After an odyssey that took them to many of the better-known lakes of Ohio, Pennsylvania, New York and Ontario, they ultimately gravitated to the St. Lawrence River. There, they discovered, big muskies were relatively easy to come by—by trolling.

It was 1950 before Len and Betty began to work the river in earnest. Their first year produced only six fish, but all were more than 30 pounds, and they had also seen some of those bigger bruisers.

The next year, they began fishing the river "full-time" and harvested a total of 89 muskies between them, two more than 40 pounds. They were fishing deep, trolling big artificials. Though successful, Len was not satisfied with the commercial baits available. He wanted a lure that would get down 35 feet or more, into the deep holes and channels the muskies were calling home. He spent much of the next winter developing lures that he believed would do just that.

He called his creation the "Muskie Bug," and it was little more than a lathe-turned, wooden lure with a large metal lip that would

Trolling: Route To Trophy Muskies

take it down, and keep it down, where the true giants of the river were feeding. His hunch paid off. The Hartmans increased their catch totals almost every year, hitting a monstrous 254 in 1962!

In the late '60s, the Hartman's fishing time decreased substantially as the result of health problems. But Len is still an active member of the muskie-chasing fraternity of American fishermen and continues to guide many groups in popular Canadian waters, as well as on the St. Lawrence.

What Len has learned over his half-century of tracking, testing and teasing muskies is that the big ones spend most of their time in deep water, where schools of larger forage fishes abound and life is a lot more peaceful. To get the fish in those depths to come to the hook, he has developed a keen talent for getting his lures down, keeping them down and running them by his quarry at a speed they can't resist.

Al Skaar, one of the pioneers in the formation of Muskies, Inc., and publisher of *Muskie* magazine, tells of fishing with Len on Upper Manitou, Lake Ontario.

"He is an amazing individual," said Skaar. "He has no need for a depthfinder or bottom charts. He lets his lure out, senses its sink

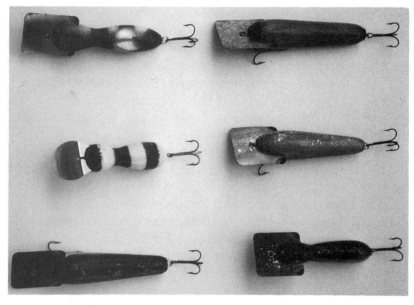

Here are six representative samples of the Hartman family of handmade "muskie bugs." The big lips are the plugs' most notable feature, a design that takes the lures deep.

Homer LeBlanc, inventor of the Swim Whizz muskie lure, with which Hartman caught his largest muskie, returns the favor by using one of Hartman's muskie bugs to catch this giant.

rate with his hand, and knows instantly when it hits the bottom.

"He pulls the lure up just a little, sets the motor for a speed that produces just the right amount of lure action, and moves on, steady as a rock!"

All the while, Len has his rod pointed straight at the lure. When the lure hits bottom, he quickly adjusts the line to bring it up to a level where it can perform its enticing task. "He has an incredible knack for matching motor speed to depth levels to keep the bait working at full efficiency at all times," Al added.

Don Pursch, operator of Nielsen's Fly-In Camp on Ontario's Rowan Lake wanted to see this skill for himself—over the deep waters of this lake which has become a kind of muskie fishermen's "mecca."

"I couldn't believe it," he told me. "Len is all business in the boat, and all he thinks about when he is on the water is where that bait is and how it is acting. He means to catch a fish, and nothing distracts him from that objective...not even a depthfinder!"

It is this type of concentration and single-mindedness that differentiate Len from his fellow sportsmen who live by the casting rod, reel and carnival of lures. The action is sparse, but the dedica-

Deep Trolling For Muskies

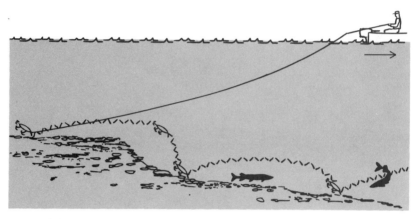

Hartman holds his rod at all times when trolling, using feel to tell him where and how fast his lure is running. He trolls as slowly as he can, while still keeping the lure just off bottom.

tion is complete. Not the sort of excitement that hangs a case of muskie fever on the practitioner, until the big one strikes.

Statistics Show How Most Muskies Sought

Bill Davis of Lake Forest, Illinois, is a past president of Muskies, Inc., and its resident statistician. For more than 10 years, Bill and his wife Rita have fed their computer with all of the catch statistics from the organization's 6,000-plus members. Each catch report contains 13 separate details, including length, weight, lure type, lure color, water depth, time of day, sky conditions, body of water, and whether the angler was casting or trolling.

At this writing, Bill and Rita have a file on almost 45,000 muskie catches, and more than a half-million facts associated with those catches. The most arresting number in that file is that which documents the average muskie angler's disdain for trolling. Less than 5 percent of those fish were caught while trolling. It is the visible action at the surface that captivates today's breed of muskie hunter.

But things are beginning to change. Seasoned muskie guides are dedicating more and more hours to the quest for the new world's record, and increased attention is being given to trolling. There are even a few practitioners who have taken to the use of downriggers and diver-type attachments to achieve greater depth and, they hope, bigger fish.

A number of lure manufacturers have responded to this interest by making larger, heavier baits, many with larger lips to bring them down faster. Len's own "Muskie Bugs" are still being made by the Smith Bait Manufacturing Company of Minocqua, Wisconsin. Famous for its "Smity" line of lures, this company reports that the interest in Len's "Bugs" has peaked dramatically, and the deep-diving business is booming.

Up in New York, trollers are still enjoying the sport of landing big muskies, many of them more than 40 pounds. Steve LaPan, a research technician now with the state's Department of Environmental Conservation, reports that most of these catches are the result of trolling at a depth of 35 feet or more.

"We know that there are even bigger muskies to be had at depths of 50 to 60 feet," said LaPan, "but few fishermen have developed the skill to get their baits down to them. Our bigger muskies congregate in these deep holes and are difficult to pull out. But those who succeed are going home with some great trophies!"

Trolling may not be the most exciting way to spend time on the water, but it can be the most productive. Let out enough line so the lure just skirts bottom, set the drag properly, point the rod straight out and wait.

Trolling: Route To Trophy Muskies

"A fish that I will never forget," is how Hartman described the 67-pound, 15-ounce giant he caught on August 10, 1961, in the St. Lawrence River—one of some 3,700 muskies he and his wife have boated.

We asked Steve if there was a 100-pound muskie out there somewhere as reported in a recent magazine article.

"Probably not," Steve told us. "That sighting was of a large muskie that came up to strip a 15-pound lake trout from the line of a charter boat angler. Actually, most any 40-pound muskie could do that—and we have plenty of those around here today. All it takes to get them is trolling with the right tackle and the right amount of patience— a muskie angler's greatest ally."

The right tackle? Any of those new larger, big-lipped lures, such as the Cisco Kid, Swim Whizz, Believer—or a Hartman-designed Muskie Bug. Hook them onto a 4-foot leader. Keep the line tight. Test the action constantly, and match your boat speed to the optimum action of the bait. If you observe those few rules, you will be capitalizing on the 50-plus years of experience of the greatest living muskie fisherman of our time.

Hartman also offers these tips:

First, develop confidence. Deep-water trolling will produce more 40-pound-plus fish than the total casting efforts of muskie fishermen everywhere. Get yourself in good muskie waters and be patient. Trolling will produce.

Second, avoid areas that traditionally produce smaller muskies, those less than 30 pounds. If you are on a body of water where there are deep holes or channels, you can bet your best bucktail that the big fish you are seeking is more apt to be down there than cruising near the surface with his younger relatives.

Third, use a stiff, but fairly light, monofilament line for minimum stretch but maximum lure action. Hartman prefers 14-pound Berkley Trilene.

Fourth, remember, you are attempting to make your lure appear the same way an injured or disoriented forage fish might. To imitate those fish, your lure does not have to move at high speeds. The muskie will hit your bait when he sees it—but you must get it to him without moving it too quickly.

This catechism of trolling is so brief and simple that the preponderant majority of muskie anglers will continue to doubt its promise.

But when a troller pulls the next world's record muskie out of a lake or a river near you, the rate of conversions to this practice will skyrocket. At least for a while. By giving trolling a fair trial the next time you are out on the water, you can greatly increase your chances of catching the biggest fish of your lifetime...maybe even the record-breaker!

26

Deep-Water Casting
For Muskies

by Steve Heiting

Peter Haupt's date with destiny—October 27, 1982, to be exact—came on an unusual day. Haupt, then a Hayward, Wisconsin, plumber, had turned the water off at a client's home and knew he wouldn't be able to turn the pipes back on unless he worked well into the night. That bothered him.

"I just had to get out muskie fishing. It was one of those days when your inner senses tell you to go fishing," he smiled.

Haupt, whose boat and trailer were attached to his truck, left the house to get a tool and never returned. He listened to his inner senses. It paid off in a huge way.

When Haupt returned to Hayward that evening, he brought with him a $54^3/4$-inch, 47-pound muskellunge, the largest taken in Wisconsin during the 1982 season. It's also one of the largest muskies ever caught in the Hayward area, which bills itself as the "Home of World Record Muskies." The late Louis Spray caught a 69-pound, 11-ounce fish in 1949 that once stood as the all-tackle world record.

Haupt caught his fish using the technique for which he has become a Hayward-area legend—deep-water casting. He believes large muskies spend their days in deep water, and he fishes in a way most muskie anglers would deem unconventional.

Darkness comes early in northern Wisconsin in late October, and Haupt didn't sneak away from his plumbing job until about 3:30 in the afternoon. A strong south wind had melted the snow

Peter Haupt's 47-pound muskie drew plenty of attention, including that of 1982 Wisconsin gubernatorial candidate, Tony Earl.

Deep-Water Casting For Muskies

from a pre-winter storm the week before, and rain dripped from a leaden sky.

Considering the amount of daylight left and the wind's effect on a solo fisherman launching a boat, Haupt decided to fish Big Round Lake, northeast of Hayward; under the same weather conditions he had lost a monster muskie there the year before.

Haupt figured the big muskie he lost in 1981 weighed at least 45 pounds. He hooked it near the Penny Bar, a small hump in the middle of nowhere that doesn't show up on the lake map. "If it did, it would be the size of a penny," Haupt said. "You know, there are still some people who are trying to find that spot."

Haupt motored to the Penny Bar and snapped on the same bait with which he had lost the big muskie, a deep-diving lure of his own manufacture called the Ojibwa. He figured that the "same spot-same conditions-same lure" principle would work.

Haupt's Penny Bar tops at 13 feet, drops off to 50 feet on all sides and features rocks the size of watermelons and bushel baskets. He threw a marker float on top of the bar, and then he backed off to begin his drift. Some shoreline protection allowed him to start the drift in relatively calm water, but the gusts quickly snatched the boat as it drifted lakeward. As the wind blew Haupt's boat off course, away from the Penny Bar rather than toward it, he continued casting.

"The plug landed in more than 35 feet of water, and the bait was still in its dive when the big muskie hit it," said Haupt. "I knew it was a good one as soon as I set the hook."

Haupt initially feared the muskie would tangle with the marker buoy's anchor line, but the wind blew the boat clear. Then the fish began swimming back and forth along the side of the boat, but never circled it. Eventually, it was boatside.

"When it was six feet away, my mind was racing as I tried to figure out how to bring it in the boat. But just then a big wave lifted it up and brought it right alongside. I reached down and put my right hand in the gill and pulled it in," Haupt remembered. "That was the only fish that ever caused me to quit fishing and head for the scales."

Back in Hayward, the fish weighed in at 47 pounds. The next day, it weighed $47^3/_4$ pounds on a different scale. "That was after a lot of slime had been wiped off," Haupt said.

Haupt became an instant celebrity as word spread of the huge

Haupt's 47-pound muskie serves as a pleasing reminder of his catch, and of fish like the 40-pounder and other giants he has caught and released over the years.

muskie's capture. The next morning outdoor writers from Chicago were calling him for the story, and he was asked to pose with the fish for a photograph with then Democratic gubernatorial candidate Tony Earl who was at the Telemark Lodge near Cable for a debate with Republican candidate Terry Kohler.

"As we left, Tony said to me 'Catch a bigger fish,' and I said to him, 'Win the election,' " Haupt recalled.

Earl went on to serve four years as Wisconsin's governor, but Haupt has yet to top the 47-pounder. That's not to say his fame was gained on one fish, however.

Muskies Favor Deep Water

Over the years, Haupt caught another 40-pound muskie, which was released, and guided another angler to a 40-pound fish. And every year, he or his clients boat at least one muskie topping 30 pounds, a weight considered to be the true trophy standard of muskie fishing. Most muskie anglers fish a lifetime without ever catching one that big.

That's an even more impressive mark considering Haupt only fishes and guides for muskies in the fall, when he's free from his

Deep-diving plugs are Haupt's preferred baits. He modifies them to reach the deeply submerged structure where he likes to hunt big muskies.

summer occupation as a performer with Scheer's Lumberjack Shows of Hayward. He's also co-owner of The Ranch, a Hayward-area restaurant where the mounted 47-pounder now resides. In his free time, he's a muskie historian and lure collector.

"I start fishing around Labor Day and continue until freeze-up, when the tourists are gone and the fishing gets good," he said. "I consider the first full moon of August the start of the best time."

While many muskie fishermen pound shorelines and shallow weedbeds, Haupt aims his casts toward deeper water, seldom shallower than 10 feet. He said most large muskies will be found in the 10- to 20-foot range, although many will be suspended in deeper water.

"I've always been an advocate of casting toward deeper water, rather than toward the shore," he said. "If I'm working a shoreline, I'll float the boat near shore and cast outward, away from the cover."

Haupt said the answer to why the bigger muskies are found in deeper water is "one of the mysteries, the enigmas, of muskie fishing," but he thinks it's because better feed is found in the depths. Rather than panfish, the muskies are eating ciscoes, whitefish, suckers and even bullheads, which can all be found in deep water.

Bullheads? "Bullheads are pork chops. You see schools of baby bullheads swimming around, but nobody ever gets big bullheads," said Haupt. They don't get a chance to mature because muskies are gobbling them up. I once caught a 27-pounder that had a 2-pound bullhead in it," Haupt explained.

Another reason bigger muskies are found in deep water is that average muskie fishermen seldom pursue them there. "I truly believe the fish that live in deep water do not see that many muskie lures," Haupt said. "They probably see more walleye lures than anything else."

Getting Big Plugs Deep Is Critical

To get to these deep-water muskies, Haupt relies on large, wooden, deep-diving plugs. The bait he designed, which is now called the Phantom Ojibwa by the manufacturer who purchased its rights, is a jointed diver with a huge lip to carry it downward. He has modified a number of other plugs to enlarge the size of their lips and therefore make them dive deeper.

In regard to other muskie lures, Haupt calls bucktails boring.

Haupt designed the Ojibwa muskie lure. This battle-scarred specimen is the one that took the 47-pounder in 1982.

All you do is cast them out and reel them in." And jerkbaits "are aptly named," according to Haupt.

The deep divers are retrieved in an irregular and slow pattern, as slow as Haupt can fish them while still getting wobbling action.

"I really try to simulate a distressed baitfish," he said. "I want a lure to resemble a baitfish that has faltered, lost its school and is trying to get into cover. That's why I position the boat over cover and try to bring the bait back to the cover."

The remainder of Haupt's equipment isn't very complicated. He likes long fiberglass rods, about 7 feet. "I don't know anything about graphite yet. When fiberglass came along, I embraced it and had no other reason to change," he said.

However, these rods have guides that are larger in diameter than the normal muskie rods, since larger guides don't freeze up as quickly in the cold weather of October and November. The rods are also one piece through the butt to accommodate lures that weigh 2 to 4 ounces.

In reels, Haupt likes the Ambassadeur line "because they take the pounding of the heavy lures. They require no repair over the years." He spools the reels with 25-pound test monofilament be-

Haupt rarely aims his casts toward water less than 10 feet deep. He says big fish spend a lot of time in deep water.

Complete Angler's Library

Deep-Water Casting For Muskies

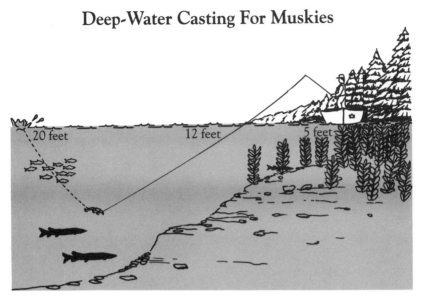

20 feet   12 feet   5 feet

Haupt's deep-water casting method often involves keeping his boat over shallow, shoreline cover and casting to deep water, preferably the 10- to 20-foot depths.

cause he seems to catch more and larger fish using mono instead of braided Dacron.

"I like everything about mono except its elasticity, although that hasn't affected me negatively," he said.

Haupt uses wire leaders with cross-lock snaps to join the monofilament and plug. He makes his own 12-inch leaders, which he admits are harder to cast. "But you get used to them," Haupt said.

Best Muskie Period Marked By Challenging Weather

Haupt considers his body to be a key element in his fishing success. "I'm still athletic because of my work as a lumberjack show performer. When I hit the fall my circulation is great. My hands stay warm, my feet stay warm, and they have to because it's cold out and I want to keep on fishing," he smiled.

Colder weather is a signal to big muskies to begin feeding heavily for the long winter months ahead. For some reason, maybe because of the changing air pressure, a snowstorm centered in the Rocky Mountains signals time to get out on the lake, Haupt said. "I don't know why, but in Wisconsin and Minnesota, that's a good

With the rodtip kept low during the retrieve, the angler maximizes the depth of any lure.

time to be muskie fishing. And you have to pay attention to the wind. It's uncomfortable, but big fish seem to bite best on windy days."

Finding Trophy Waters During Trophy Months

The months of September, October and November have long been known as the trophy months, and Haupt fishes lakes that have a reputation for producing trophy fish.

"To grow big fish, you first need good genetics. Many of our lakes in the Hayward area have the Lac Courte Oreilles strain of muskies, which can grow to be huge fish.

"The lakes I fish usually have a lower population of muskies than some of the more popular lakes. Most are not rated Class A (Wisconsin rates muskie lakes either Class A, B or C), but the way I look at it, this means there's more food to go around to the available muskies," Haupt said.

Trophy lakes generally receive less pressure than lakes known to produce lots of smaller muskies. "This preserves the muskies. These lakes either don't get fished as hard or there's lots of inaccessible or deep water," Haupt explained.

While the 10- to 20-foot range is Haupt's preferred depth, an angler hoping to follow his technique will soon realize that many lakes have hundreds of acres of this depth. Finding the best areas is often a system of trial and error. Haupt suggests looking for areas with vegetation that hasn't succumbed to the approaching winter.

Rocky points and humps are also good, Haupt said. But there's a time every October when the muskies prefer a plain, sandy bottom. The presence of sunken logs on the sand helps attract fish.

Log cribs, built by fishermen and sunk as a form of fish habitat, hold muskies.

Despite his years of deep-water fishing, Haupt will not claim to have seen a world-record muskie, as will some guides. The 47-pounder is the largest he's hooked, though he has seen two fish that were bigger—one in the Lac du Flambeau chain of lakes in north-central Wisconsin and one in Big Round Lake, within 200 yards of where he caught the 47-pounder.

He spotted the second big fish in late November 1983 in Round Lake and hasn't seen it since. "We had a stiff northeast wind with rain changing to freezing rain. It was starting to get slippery in the boat, and I was beginning to question my sanity for being out there. I reeled in a bait and had it out of the water ready to whip it out again when I saw the fish. It didn't have great length, but it did have tremendous depth. It was very light-colored and there's probably a 50-50 chance it was a hybrid. If so, it would be a world's record for hybrids.

"Without a question, it weighed more than 47 pounds. I would say it weighed 55 to 58 pounds."

It's hard to say whether Peter Haupt will ever catch a bigger muskie than his 47-pounder. But you can bet he won't catch it from shallow water.

27

Ice Pike Fever

by Otis Smith

ce pike fever has consumed me for so long that it has become a part of my life. Over the years I've been successful
at capturing my share of big "slough sharks," what I like to
call northern pike, and have always thought I could hold my
own against any wintertime pike angler.

Then I met Marlin Ormseth and the realities of life set in. It
was just like the professional boxer who ran into someone faster,
stronger and smarter. My first meeting with Ormseth was at his
place of business, Northview Bait & Tackle located in Sioux Falls,
South Dakota. We discussed the possibility of me doing some fishing seminars at the shop. Before I knew it, I had been invited to go
along on a hunt for ice pike in eastern South Dakota.

That first day on the ice with Ormseth proved to be a real eye-
opener. In one day of fishing, we caught more pike then most anglers catch in several seasons. Ormseth introduced me to a number of fishing methods, baiting systems and tip-up techniques that
I had never seen or heard of before. His expertise will revolutionize ice pike fishing.

When Ormseth goes into an area to set out his spread of tip-
ups he refers to the procedure as "laying out a mine field." His initial pattern covers shallow water, deep water and mid-range
depths where wandering, feeding northern pike may be found.
When a depth pattern is determined, which doesn't take long to
figure out, he relocates all tip-ups to the area producing the most
strikes.

It doesn't take Marlin Ormseth long to find big pike under the ice once he lays his "mine field."

Ice Pike Fever

Adding oversized flags, or flags of contrasting color to a tip-up ensures visibility, even under poor light conditions.

Ormseth's main fishing grounds are the prairie lakes of eastern South Dakota, where each ice angler is allowed four lines. Many states allow wintertime anglers to use two lines.

Ormseth said you never know from one day to the next which area will produce fish. A shallow water area might be hot for two or three days, then shut off. His favorite starting points are backs of bays, weed patches, weedlines or points leading into deep water. Each of these areas attracts baitfish that pike feed on. Ormseth advised me to set some of the tip-ups where there was only a foot or two of water below the ice. He noted that shallow water will often hold a lot of baitfish. Even large pike will cruise into the shallows in search of food.

Leapfrog To Locate Pike

When Ormseth encounters a very large bay or a long, good-looking shoreline he will begin setting tip-ups at one end of the bay or shore, staggering the tip-ups from shallow water into deeper water areas. By the time he has his last tip-up set, the area covered can be as long as 250 yards. Ormseth gives the first tip-ups about 90 minutes before resetting them 50 yards out in front of the spread.

The procedure of drilling new holes 50 yards in front of the spread of tip-ups and leap-frogging the rear tip-ups to the front of the pack is repeated every half hour. It does not take long to cover a lot of shoreline using this procedure.

Tip-ups in trouble-free conditions are a must for this type of fishing. Ormseth's favorite is the Polar tip-up. This virtually trouble-free model has a reel that rests below the water. The reel attaches to the tip-up base via a spindle inside a sealed tube, which prevents freeze-up. The tip-up has an adjusting nut, which allows the angler to tighten or loosen the tension on the reel, depending on the size of the bait and aggressiveness of the pike. For example, if smaller baits are used and the pike are not aggressive, tension can be loosened so the pike feels less resistance when taking the bait.

Polar tip-ups come with two different spool sizes. Ormseth prefers the large line-capacity spool because it accepts and feeds line most effectively. It also offers insurance against running out of line. A northern pike can strip yards of line from an unattended tip-up in a hurry.

Ormseth said a tip-up is no better than the line you put on it. He prefers Berkley's Polar tip-up line because it is designed just for tip-ups. The coated line resists waterlogging, comes off the reel smoothly and has an additive in its coating that prevents it from freezing and sticking to the ice, even when wet. Best of all, it does not tangle and is highly visible out of the water.

If a Polar tip-up has one fault, it may be the color of the flag, Ormseth noted. A fluorescent orange flag is not the easiest color to spot in some light conditions. To combat the problem, he increases the size of the orange flag and attaches a same-size black flag to it.

The increased flag dimensions with two contrasting colors aid in making a strike visible under most light conditions. Obviously this flag setup will be more visible at greater distances.

Another important item Ormseth adds to his tip-up rig is a button on the line. A standard shirt button can be used. The tip-up line is run through one of the button holes, then doubled back through another hole. Rigged this way, the button can be slid up or down the line, but will stay where you position it as a depth marker. This way, when you later get a strike, it's a simple matter to rebait and reel the line back onto the spool up to the button. This saves checking the depth each time the line is reset.

To complete Ormseth's modified tip-up, a Berkley Cross-Lok snap is tied to the end of the line. The snap allows easy attachment of pre-baited terminal rigs.

Northern pike can be caught through the ice on a variety of baits. Live suckers, shiners or chubs are good. Where legal, bluegills or crappies also make excellent baits. Generally speaking, a pike's metabolism is slower during the winter, which is one reason dead bait is so effective on ice pike.

One of the premier dead baits is frozen smelt, and it is the main bait Ormseth uses. He has designed a quick-strike rig that not only utilizes the smelt, but adds a touch of live bait. Ormseth calls his rig the Northview Pike Special Rig. The combination live/dead bait rig is a real pike catcher.

The special pike rig is made with uncoated seven-strand wire. He also uses smaller-than-mono-diameter line, which is less visible, but most importantly, resistant to the razor-sharp teeth of a pike. The finished rig has a total of three treble hooks.

To bait the rig, Ormseth runs a nail through the center of a

Complete Angler's Library

Ormseth's Quick-Strike Rig

Ormseth's Northview Pike Special Rig makes dead smelt look like live bait. A nail is used to make a passage through which the wire leader is passed. The hook assembly holds the smelt horizontally under the ice.

frozen smelt to create a pathway. He passes his 14-inch leader through the dead baitfish and slides the smelt down to the center treble; the other two trebles are placed at opposite ends. He then tail-hooks a live fathead minnow to the end trebles.

A quick-strike rig, be it a Northview Pike Special Rig or a European-style quick-strike rig, offers several advantages, including immediate hookset. Using a traditional single hook, it is necessary to wait for the pike to swallow the bait before setting the hook. With the quick-strike rig, as soon as a pike takes the bait the angler can set the hook, resulting in a higher hooking percentage. The rig also helps ensure that the pike will only be hooked in the mouth. This gives the fisherman the option of releasing the fish unharmed.

When pike sometimes need extra enticement, tail-hooking live minnows on the outside hook gives motion and adds flash to the Northview Pike Special Rig.

European Quick-Strike Rigs

A European quick-strike rig is also made up with seven-strand wire, either coated with black plastic or uncoated. Two "partridge" hooks rigged in tandem are used on this rig. A partridge hook consists of a large hook with a smaller hook welded to its shank. The bottom hook is stationary while the upper hook slides, making it adjustable to the size of the bait being used. The small hook is embedded in the baitfish, leaving the larger hook exposed. The exposed hook allows for quicker hooksets.

When Ormseth fishes with live bait, he uses the European-style quick-strike rig. If only very large dead bait is available, he also uses the European rig.

The first day I fished with Ormseth, we were accompanied by his employee Jeff Decker and my son John. We caught more than 100 northern pike using Ormseth's method. The pike we caught were not of trophy size, but many of them weighed more than 11 pounds. We kept a limit of 24 pike that averaged nearly 8 pounds each. Not bad fishing in anyone's book.

There are numerous little things that Ormseth does to refine his tip-up technique. In order to save time and cold fingers, he has

Complete Angler's Library

his quick-strike rig pre-baited so that when he gets to the lake all he has to do is snap the rig to the Cross-Lok snap and drop them in the hole.

Ormseth also supplied each of us with our own bait bucket. Each bait bucket held a half-dozen pre-baited rigs. Whenever we got a strike, the man handling it took a bait bucket with him. When the fish was landed the angler simply unsnapped the hooked pike from the Cross-Lok snap and snapped on a new, pre-baited rig. This method saved down time, enhancing the chances of more strikes. Once the tip-up was reset the angler could unhook his catch at his leisure. During slack periods we would rebait, keeping each bait bucket loaded with pre-baited rigs.

The bait buckets really paid off, especially when we were far away from some of the tip-ups. The pike would come into the bay

European Quick-Strike Rig

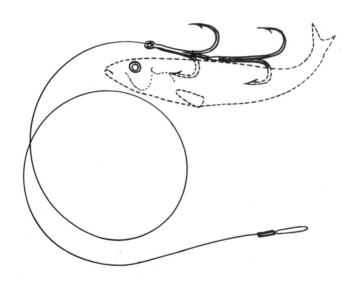

European quick-strike rigs leave hooks entirely exposed for extremely effective hooksetting ability. They also can be adjusted to fit the size of the bait..

The secret to Ormseth's success is that he covers territory quickly, leap-frogging tip-ups to new holes until he finds fish.

Complete Angler's Library

Pre-baited Northview Pike Special Rigs cut Ormseth's rebaitng time to a minimum. He simply attaches a pre-baited leader to the main line after each strike.

in schools. There were times when four of five flags would go up at once. We must have looked like Keystone cops as we grabbed bait buckets and scattered across the ice racing toward the tip-ups.

A couple of other important pieces of equipment for winter northern pike fishing include a gaff, a jaw spreader and a pair of needle-nosed pliers. They don't call northern pike toothy critters for nothing. A springed jaw-spreader will spread the pike's jaws with ease, making hook removal with needle-nosed pliers easy and lessen the likelihood of injuring fish you plan to release.

28

Jerking Big Summer Pike

by Steve Grooms

Everyone knows those old stories about northerns losing their teeth in summer are nonsense. Yet summer pike often act as if they had sore, toothless mouths.

Summer is the time of peak food abundance in natural lakes. A short feeding foray gives a summer pike all the food it can digest. In summertime the living is easy for pike, making things tough for the pike angler.

Yet summer pike fishing can be great, if you know how to go about it. And one man who knows how to go about it is Ron Kobes. Kobes, a guide who lives in Blackduck, Minnesota, has an unequalled record in northern pike tournaments. He won the 1989 Lake Bemidji Classic in Minnesota, and has a victory plus two second-place finishes in the biggest pike tournament, the World Northern Pike Championship, held on Gull Lake in Brainerd, Minnesota. And throughout the summer, he keeps clients happy with good pike.

Please note: Kobes does not specialize in catching aggressive, no-brainer pike in fly-in Canadian lakes. He has made his reputation catching big pike in heavily fished Minnesota lakes, often in the crunch of tournament fishing pressure. His biggest Minnesota northern was just under 21 pounds. He caught a pike in the World Championship that went 19 pounds, 14 ounces—still the biggest fish ever entered in that tournament.

You could say Ron knows summer pike.

So, what's his secret? As anyone who follows tournaments

Complete Angler's Library

Ron Kobes uses big stickbaits to catch big northern pike. He has mastered his art on lakes with heavy fishing pressure.

Jerking Big Summer Pike

knows, there is no single secret to winning. To place well consistently, an angler needs top equipment, hard work and highly polished angling skills. Secrets just won't take you very far.

And yet there is a sort of secret. Kobes takes just about all his summer pike on jerkbaits. Once in a great while, he'll prospect for fish with a muskie tandem spinnerbait or a Northland jig tipped with a minnow, but Kobes is a dedicated jerkbait specialist. He hates to use anything else because he is convinced jerkbaits are the top summer and fall pike bait. And he's earned the right to say so.

Jerkbait Imitates Big, Free Meal

Why are jerkbaits so deadly on summer pike? They give an action no other bait can match. "Baitfish dart around," said Kobes. "And with a jerkbait, you get an erratic darting action you can't get with any other bait. It looks like a distressed baitfish's last-ditch effort to get away."

Jerkbaits are big enough to look like a meaty mouthful to a pike. The combination of the size of the bait and the lunging action tells a pike this is a large meal that can't escape. That sends out a "come and get me" signal pike can hardly resist.

But standard out-of-the-box jerkbaits don't work the way Kobes wants them to. He modifies them in several ways, primarily by weighting them. These weighted jerkbaits are far superior to standard jerkbaits in two ways.

First, they are easier to work. The big rap against jerkbaits is that you have to be Arnold Schwarzenegger to use them for long periods. Manipulating a standard jerkbait is murder on those back muscles most people don't use often. But Kobes can fish a weighted jerkbait all day long in perfect comfort. And he insists anyone can do it. You simply have to weight the lure so you aren't fighting it so much.

A second problem with jerkbaits is that they usually run too shallow. But Kobes's weighted jerkbaits sink 50 percent deeper than standard jerkbaits. Weighted, shallow-running "stickbaits," such as the Teddie Bait or Windels Whaletail, run down to about three feet. The deeper diving Suick or Bobbie Bait, when weighted, get down to six feet for most people and eight feet for Kobes. Kobes can get the Windels Muskie Hunter down to 10 feet.

Kobes with a big "jack" that fell to one of his stickbaits. Kobes likes to fish at midday, if boat traffic is not heavy.

Those depths may sound shallow, but they're significantly deeper than ordinary jerkbait depths go. Unweighted jerkbaits are virtually surface baits. Like football, fishing can be a game of inches. Getting a few feet deeper makes all the difference.

Kobes throws just a few jerkbaits almost all the time. They fall into two classes. The "tailbaits" are deep-diving jerkbaits. The Bobbie Bait has a metal tail that helps it dive when jerked. The Suick has a similar tail and a similar motion. Though it lacks a tail, the Muskie Hunter has the same diving, bobbing action. When weighted, these baits run 8 to 10 feet deep and are therefore able to catch the attention of pike working deep weedlines.

"Stickbaits" are buoyant, tailless chunks of wood that dance left and right on the retrieve. In fact, they are the muskie-sized version of the Zara Spook lure, famous for its "walkin' the dog" action. Kobes likes two baits in this class, the Windels Whaletail and Lindy-Little Joe's Teddie Bait (which comes in two sizes: the Big Jerk and Little Jerk). These baits have vigorous side-to-side action that really grabs fish. They are great whenever their shallow running depth (about three feet) is appropriate.

Though muskie anglers use huge "pool cue" rods to throw

jerkbaits, Kobes has switched to the slightly lighter rods sold for bucktail use. He has two favorites. The Berkley M19, 6-foot, 4-inch rod is rated for lures from 1 to 4 ounces. The St. Croix 2401 Premier Graphite is $6^1/_2$ feet long and is rated for $^1/_2$- to 1-ounce baits. Kobes modifies his rods, usually by taking off a few inches of handle and wrapping the area in front of the reel in foam for more comfort.

Throwing jerkbaits for big pike is rugged fishing and requires rugged equipment. Kobes uses Garcia 7000 reels, which are famous for their strong gears. He uses 36- to 50-pound Dacron line and ties his own leaders, using ball-bearing swivels, strong Berkley Cross-Lok snaps and 18 inches of 104-pound test Sevenstrand wire.

Kobes runs a Ranger 680T boat. He fishes standing in front at the trolling motor. At the back he has a Bottom Line 310XT graph, while up front is a Si-Tex flasher mounted near the trolling motor. Kobes keeps his eyes on the Si-Tex as he prowls structure. He's careful to tune the Si-Tex's power setting until he gets the "second echo" that tells him he has plenty of signal power for showing underwater objects.

Follow The Weedline For Big Northern Pike

What Kobes is looking for with that sonar is the faint flickering signal that indicates weeds. "You want to fish so you are in and out of the weeds, which puts you on the weed breakline," he said. And that's the first key to finding summer pike. Kobes runs the boat right along the weed edge where northerns concentrate in summer to feed.

He emphasizes the need to stay at the weedline. "People think the breakline is the weedline, so they just put the boat at a certain depth and keep it there," said Kobes. "But that's not true. I know places on Gull Lake where the weedline is 150 yards from the breakline. Stick with the weedline." As he fishes, Kobes is always looking for clumps, pockets and points in the weeds. Summer pike concentrate in these features.

Mostly, Kobes fishes the weedlines on major flats, broad areas where the water level remains at a constant depth. These areas are full of forage fish. A flat might be a big region of 4- to 8-foot water on a major flat-topped point. Because flats hold baitfish, they concentrate food that attracts predators like pike.

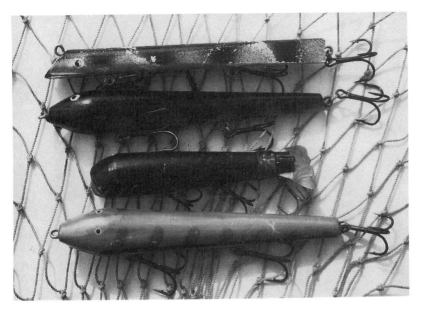

Kobes's favorite stickbaits (top to bottom): Windels Muskie Hunter, Windels Whaletail, Bobbie Bait, Lindy-Little Joe Big Jerk (Teddie Bait).

There are good flats and not-so-good flats. One key to a good one is having a nice drop to fairly deep water. So a flat in a shallow bay isn't worth much, while a flat that drops off to 12 or 15 feet could be a gold mine for pike. The second requirement of a good flat is it must have dense weeds, probably cabbage or coontail.

Here is Kobes's location system in a nutshell: fish right along the weedline of flats that break to deeper water. Then concentrate on little irregularities in the weeds.

At the start of each day, Kobes tries to get a pattern on the fish. He runs the boat with the electric motor up front, threading back and forth along the outer edge of the weeds. On many lakes, that puts the boat in about 14 feet of water. Kobes will throw a deep-running jerkbait out ahead of the boat, working the semi-deep water of the breakline. Meanwhile his partner is throwing a shallow-running jerkbait up over the flat to see if the fish are there.

By the time Kobes has checked out a few flats, he knows whether the pike are in the deeper water in front of the flats or in the weeds in shallow water. Then both anglers switch to the jerkbait and type of water that is producing. From that point on, fishing becomes a matter of running from spot to spot, covering

After finding out how much weight it takes to achieve a slight, nose-down float, Kobes drills into a stickbait and inserts lead weights with glue. His jerkbaits sink and run 50 percent deeper than standard jerkbaits.

water and slugging it out with the pike that charge these wounded-fish imitations.

Lure color isn't critical most of the time. "I try to stick with natural colors—yellow and green perch finish, silver and black—almost all the time," said Kobes. "Now and then I do better with something wild, like a neon green. But mostly it is natural colors."

Weather is a major variable. The ideal condition is a period of stable weather with a heavy overcast or chop to reduce light penetration. A heavy fog (the heavier and more persistent, the better) really pulls the pike in shallow. Bluebird weather and the passing of many fronts make fish hold deeper.

Time of day is not a big variable. Pike, in fact, probably hit better at midday than any fish. But midday boat traffic can be a negative factor, driving pike deeper. Sometimes Kobes has to choose spots to fish by working around nuisance fishing or water-ski traffic. He might then look for isolated, weedy rock piles, one of the places that gets overlooked by most anglers.

When selecting a jerkbait, consider the depth of the water you will actually be working, not the full depth of the water. There is

Complete Angler's Library

often a one- to five-foot zone of relatively open water above the weeds. The depth of that zone determines which bait can be used; it doesn't matter how deep the water is under the weeds. Fish as deep as you can without getting hung all the time.

Success Lies In Learning To Work Bait

Once you've chosen your jerkbait, Kobes recommends the following procedure for working your weighted lures. Stand with your rod pointed down, almost touching water. The retrieve is a series of downward pops or jerks of the rodtip. Each jerk travels about two feet. The bait will dive and glide as it moves forward. At the end of each glide (when a normal jerkbait would be floating to the surface), give it another pop. Between pulls, reel in the slack.

Casting Jerkbaits For Big Northern Pike

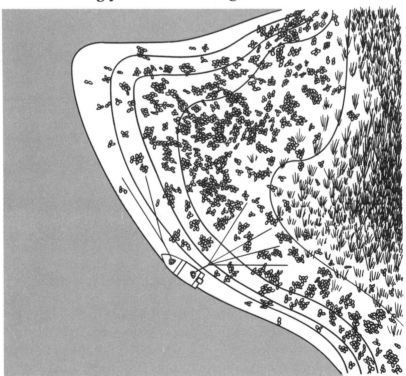

Kobes casts to weed-covered flats that drop to fairly deep water. He also prefers those with dense weeds to those with scattered weeds. With a partner, the pair can cover both the flat and the weed edge at the same time.

Working a jerkbait is something you have to learn by practice. "The key is to get into a good rhythm," said Kobes.

It isn't hard. Kobes guides fishermen of average skills all the time, and they pick it up. When the rhythm is right, the baits come to life. Tailbaits lunge up and down. Stickbaits whip side to side like dying minnows.

The strike of a pike is not subtle, which is a good thing. "It isn't the world's best hooking situation," said Kobes. "The fish get a fierce grip on the piece of wood, which makes hooksetting harder. And you have to suddenly whip the rod from tip-down to tip-up."

But since northerns really whack a bait and hang on, feeling strikes and setting hooks is not as difficult as it might be. One reason Kobes switched to slightly softer rods was he was hitting the fish so hard on the set he was opening large hook holes.

Northerns follow baits very much the way muskies do. Kobes milks the end of the retrieve for a little more action before making the next cast. With the deep-diving tailbaits, he teases the bait up in a "stair-step" fashion with a series of quick little rod pops that move it a foot at a time. With the tailless stickbaits, Kobes uses his reel handle to give the bait a series of light whacks that makes it go crazy without moving it in much.

Is it worth putting so much work into the end of a retrieve? Kobes knows it is. "If I catch ten fish," he said, "four will be in the first few feet of the retrieve and four in the last few feet of retrieve. The middle of the retrieve is the least productive."

Jigs Produce Smaller Fish

Now and then, Kobes gets a client who is not comfortable with jerkbaits. Then he switches to jigs and minnows. The best jig is the banana head Northland Stinger jig, usually the $1/2$-ounce size. "If I go to jigs, I know we'll catch fish, but I also know we aren't going to get the quality fish I get with jerkbaits," said Kobes.

This system truly produces. Kobes expects to take 25 or 30 pike in an average summer day. They'll run from 4 to 10 pounds. Try beating those numbers on Minnesota waters in summer!

As summer fades into fall, fish size moves up. Why? Kobes thinks the best pike spend summer suspended in deep water near deep cisco and whitefish schools. Late summer brings a shallow movement of these fish, and Kobes begins to notch more "teen" pike.

Complete Angler's Library

Northern pike are not subtle biters. Set the hook hard to ensure a solid hooket.

Kobes has seen several lakes lose their quality pike in recent years. Pike are aggressive and their populations can be hurt pretty easily. Kobes fishes almost exclusively catch and release. The big pike—the ones that are so thrilling to catch—aren't good in the pan anyway.

Kobes has many more tricks and tackle modifications, but his basic system is fairly simple. He clings to the best weedlines of the best flats, working modified jerkbaits both over weeds and along the deeper weed edge. If you do that, you'll be into the summer pike in a big way.

Striped Bass And
White Bass

29

Striking Silver With Bucktail Jigs

by Gerald Almy

A
rching a long cast across the wind-rumpled waters of a Virginia lake with his graphite rod, Dale Wilson engages the baitcast reel, turns the handle twice and suddenly stiffens, leaning back with his muscular body into what could easily be his 20,000th striper.

Wilson doesn't know for sure how many stripers he has caught. He releases virtually all the fish he catches and doesn't keep a running tally. But fishing virtually every day and connecting on anywhere from a handful to several dozen stripers during each session on the water surely has put him into tens of thousands of inland striped bass during his decades of guiding on Smith Mountain Lake in central Virginia. Amazingly, virtually all of these fish have been caught on a simple leadheaded jig with an unpainted head and white bucktail dressing.

Bucktails: The Key To Wilson's Success

Usually when an angler uses one lure almost exclusively you would consider it a narrow-minded approach; the fisherman is probably not very skilled or knowledgeable. That's not the case with Wilson and the bucktail jig. Wilson, a full-time guide, uses the jig for probably 90 to 95 percent of his striper fishing. Yet he is widely acknowledged as the most skilled and talented striped bass angler in the state, if not the entire Mid-Atlantic.

There are occasions when Wilson employs such standard striper lures as the Cordell Spot, Rebel Spoonbill, Bomber Long A

These stripers, totaling more than 50 pounds, were taken on $^1/_4$-ounce white bucktail jigs with unpainted heads. Striper guide Dale Wilson has lost count of the fish he's caught.

Striking Silver With Bucktail Jigs

and various topwater plugs. But for the vast majority of his fishing for this sleek, pin-striped true bass, Virginia's striper master goes with the leadhead jig dressed with white bucktail and either a saddle hackle tied along each side over the deer hair or a twister-type grub attached as a trailer.

And while Wilson uses this lure primarily on Smith Mountain and adjacent Leesville Lake where he guides full-time after giving up a career in teaching and coaching, he has also found this lure, and his methods for fishing it, produces on countless other striper lakes throughout the country.

Jigs' Action Drives Stripers Wild

"The bucktail jig imitates a striper's natural forage—shad—better than any lure made," Wilson said. "It has a subtle action, really no action at all. But when you fish it right, it duplicates the appearance of a shad. Put a slow-moving shad in front of a striper and he's going to hit!"

There is perhaps no better proving ground for finding out if a striper will indeed strike a lure than Smith Mountain, a 20,000-acre power company lake nestled in the foothills of the Blue Ridge Mountains east of Roanoke, Virginia. Smith was formed in the 1960s and has since established itself as the premier striped bass lake in the Mid-Atlantic.

Each year the clear mountain lake produces more stripers that qualify for citations as outstanding catches than any other body of water in the state. In fact, so many hundreds of fish were being entered for these awards a few years back that the state had to raise the minimum weight limit from 10 to 15 pounds. The fishing continued to get better and eventually there were 500 to 700 awards given out each year for fish weighing 15 pounds or more. In 1989 the state again raised the minimum weight for a citation award—this time to 20 pounds. So far, this move has only slightly stemmed the tide of entries.

Wilson personally turns in few of his fish for citations, preferring instead to release virtually all of his stripers unharmed. And that represents an enormous number of fish—virtually all caught on the bucktail jig. Wilson, who lived in the area when the lake was formed, knew every underwater contour when Smith Mountain was impounded, and he uses that knowledge to catch thousands of stripers every year.

Late winter and early spring are the best times to catch stripers. Jig fishing is hot when the water temperature hits 20 degrees F., and stays that way until it reaches the mid 60s.

On a few outstanding days he and his parties have taken 60 to 80 stripers; numerous trips have accounted for 30 to 40 fish. A typical day on the water during prime season in late winter and spring will yield 10 to 20 fish averaging 6 to 12 pounds, but running up to 30 pounds-plus on occasion.

Tough Gear Best For Powerful Fish

Although his intimate knowledge of the lake helps, Wilson says that anyone can catch stripers in the spring using the techniques he employs. "First off," he said, "it's important to start out with the right tackle." Although he's caught huge stripers on 6-pound line and ultra-light spinning rods, this is not the gear he recommends.

"A 6-foot, stiff-action baitcasting rod made of graphite is best. I like IM6 graphite because it's light, stiff and sensitive. You need a quality levelwind reel with a smooth drag filled with 14- to 20-pound line. I use 17-pound test, but some fish still break me off occasionally."

Spin gear and 10- to 14-pound line can be employed if you prefer, said Wilson, but baitcasting equipment is the most efficient

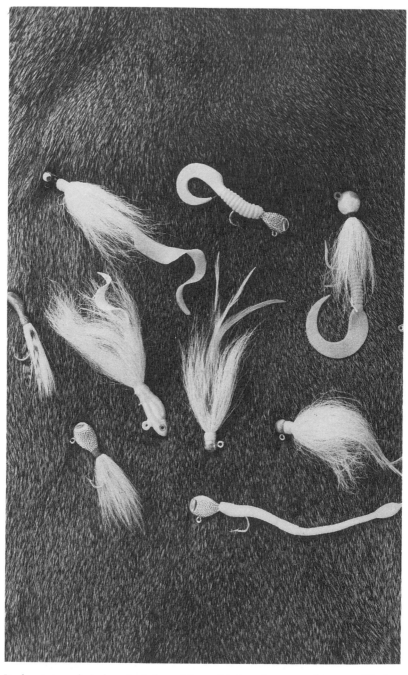

Jigs best imitate shad, the striper's favored forage fish throughout most of its range. The best colors include white, pearl, green and yellow.

for this form of fishing because it stands up to big fish.

One of the nice things about Wilson's striper system is its simplicity. For lures you will need a selection of $^3/_{16}$- and $^1/_4$-ounce leadhead jigs with thick white bucktail dressings measuring 3 to 4 inches in total length. You can use jigs with the heads painted white, but Wilson prefers unpainted leadheads because they have a more natural, dull metallic appearance that closely duplicates a live shad. Some of the jigs he stocks are tied with a single saddle hackle feature along each side in white, yellow, green, blue or red. Others have just the white deer hair dressing.

"The jig with the feather on the sides by itself is usually the best offering," Wilson said. "It's compact and most closely imitates a real shad swimming through the water. It's the top lure for most clear water situations."

If the water is stained or muddy, though, or if fish are feeding on larger shad, a 3- to 4-inch plastic twister-tail trailer sometimes increases strikes. This works best on a jig without saddle hackles along the sides. Top colors are pearl, chartreuse, green, white or yellow, and the twister part of the tail should be rigged pointing down for the best action.

Wilson mainly uses round-shaped leadheads, but sometimes employs oval ones. He insists on extra-strong hooks, because stripers up to 30 pounds and heavier are possible with this fishing technique.

Best Times For Bucktail Fishing

Fishing with jigs produces stripers for Wilson year-round on Smith Mountain, but late winter and early spring are the hot times of the year for this method. "In the dead of winter, vertical jigging with slab spoons is often the best technique," said Wilson. "Once the water temperature rises into the mid-40s, though, you'll start finding fish moving out of the deep areas and into shallower water where jigs produce best. Depending on what part of the country you're in, this can be anywhere from late January to sometime in April. In Virginia, the first week of March usually sees the first good jig fishing for stripers in shallow water. Sometimes things can heat up as early as February if we have a mild winter."

The very best fishing begins when the temperature climbs to 50 degrees. Action will continue strong until the shallows warm

Locating shad is the key to finding stripers. When you spot shad on your sonar unit in open water, drop a jig. Strikes come quickly.

into the 60s. Once the water temperature rises above that, jigs will still score, but they must be fished deeper, slower and farther off-shore. The exception is during surface feeding flurries in summer and fall when the fish crash into schools of shad on top. Then a jig can be cranked through the frothy whitewater where stripers are feeding just below the surface, eliciting thumping strikes from frenzied bass.

Stripers Are Predictable From Year To Year

For spring fishing, Wilson concentrates on flats and long, slowly sloping points, red clay banks, coves and creek arms. These are the areas that consistently produce action. Once you find an area that holds stripers, keep it in your memory bank or better yet, mark it on a topographic map and try it in subsequent years. Stripers will usually return at about the same time to that location for similar feeding binges.

While finding this prime type of water is important, it's also vital that it has shad occupying it. If you don't see shad skipping or jumping occasionally or mark them on your depthfinder, you will not likely find stripers in good numbers no matter how choice the habitat appears. And even if an area held stripers a week before, if the shad leave, the stripers will follow them.

"You have to be flexible and mobile to score best with this method in the spring," Wilson admonished. "The fish move a lot, following concentrations of baitfish. Hit a good-looking spot with a few casts, then move on to the next one. I might fish 15 to 20 different points in an afternoon searching for fish."

When stripers first move into the shallows in spring, their only interest is in feeding. As days grow longer and warmer, however, many fish begin concentrating in the major tributaries of the lake, led there by their spawning. These are good areas to check in April and May, as the fish make mating runs up rivers and feeder arms of lakes. Spawning is not successful in most lakes, but the fish still make the effort and concentrate in these locations in good

Where To Catch Stripers On Bucktails

Primary (A) and secondary (B) points, as well as back bays (C) are good places to start looking for springtime stripers. But if you don't see shad, visually or on sonar, move to another spot.

Striking Silver With Bucktail Jigs

Water clarity dictates jig size. Twister tails give jigs more bulk, making them easier to see in stained water.

numbers. Jigs score exceptionally well here because they imitate the shad stripers feed on throughout most of their range.

Tight-Line Jig Presentations Work

The problem many anglers have when fishing jigs, according to Wilson, is that because the lure is called a "jig" they think they should bounce or hop it along. "You'll catch some fish that way," said the guide, "but you'll take a whole lot more if you simply reel it in very slowly and smoothly, without any movement at all. The slow swimming appearance of a jig retrieved like this looks just like a shad, and the stripers can't resist it!"

The only manipulation Wilson makes, on occasion, is to stop his retrieve and simply allow the jig to drop back down slowly on a tight line. He simply stops and lets it sink like a wounded shad that has lost its gas and is fluttering down helplessly.

Best Retrieve Targets Upper Layer Of Water

The depth to retrieve the jig varies with the depth of the water you're fishing and where the fish seem to be holding. Usually you'll be probing areas from five to 15 feet deep at this time, and the jig should run anywhere from two to 12 feet down. Stripers rarely hang out right on the bottom, and if you find you're getting

While light tackle has certainly taken big stripers, the best rig is a medium/heavy baitcaster, and a good levelwind reel strung with 14- to 20-pound monofilament.

Striking Silver With Bucktail Jigs

Stripers, like the average-sized fish Wilson holds, fall for white bucktail jigs when they are presented properly.

Complete Angler's Library

hung up, you're reeling too slowly. Sometimes the fish may be just below the surface and hit the bucktail virtually as soon as it touches down. If this happens, take your cue and start reeling as soon as the lure plunks into the water, so it swims just a few feet below the surface. In most cases, retrieving the offering five to eight feet down will be the best payoff zone for late winter and spring fishing. During summer, allow the jig to drop 12 to 24 feet before crawling it back in the same smooth, steady retrieve, interspersed with occasional pauses.

Evening is settling over the calming waters of Smith Mountain Lake now as Wilson works in one last striper, releases the fish and cranks up the big outboard to head back for the marina. In just three short hours he and his partner have put 10 stripers in the boat, keeping one to eat, releasing the other nine—a typical afternoon on the lake.

Whether the fish was his 20,000th, Wilson doesn't know for sure. One thing he does know is that casting bucktails in spring for stripers is about as surefire a technique as there is for this sleek, pinstriped transplant from the sea now found throughout so many lakes in North America. Give it a try on your local striper lakes this spring and chances are you'll agree.

30

Balloons Are For Kids...And Hybrids

by Chris Altman

"**B**allooning is not really a new technique," said Jim Curtis, "but rather a modification, a better way to present live bait under a variety of conditions." Curtis, a full-time hybrid and largemouth guide from LaGrange, Georgia, plies his trade on West Point Lake, a relatively young impoundment on the Georgia/Alabama border that is considered one of the finest hybrid and largemouth bass lakes in the country.

While guiding in excess of 200 days each year, Curtis has developed numerous angling techniques that have helped him and his clients catch more fish. Ballooning live bait is just one of those techniques, and he uses this method to boat hundreds of fat hybrid bass each year.

Hybrids are a genetic cross between the striped bass and the white bass and, like their genetic parents, they are voracious open-water predators. As a result, most hybrid experts believe that fishing live baits, specifically live shad, is the most productive technique to catch these fish.

Balloons Carry Live Bait To Skittish Fish

"When live bait fishing was legalized here on West Point," Curtis related, "I began experimenting with a variety of presentations. When the fish are holding in deep water, as they tend to do in the summer, it is quite easy to present the bait without spooking the fish. But hybrids are a skittish bunch in shallow water and you

Bass guide Jim Curtis has used the "ballooning" method to catch hundreds of nice bass like this one.

Balloons Are For Kids...And Hybrids

can pretty much destroy your chances of catching them if you spook the school of fish. It's rather difficult to present live bait to them when they are holding or feeding in the shallows."

When the hybrids are cruising the shallows, most anglers resort to artificial lures. By positioning the boat well away from the structure, anglers can toss heavy artificials such as jigging spoons, Rooster Tails and Little Georges to the fish without scaring them. But Jim Curtis knows that nothing looks more like a shad than a shad, so he devised a way to get his live bait to the fish without having to run his boat over the structure and risk spooking the school of feeding hybrids.

"I originally began using large, cork or Styrofoam floats, and that worked fairly well. But I soon discovered that balloons were even better," Curtis said. "Since balloons float on top of the water, rather than riding partially submerged like a cork, they offer very little resistance to the bait. The shad can swim around at a natural pace, towing the balloon with very little effort." On windy days, ballooning is used to float a bait to the shallows, and Curtis notes that balloons catch the wind much better than a cork, thus simplifying the presentation.

Tricks To Rigging With Balloons

Regardless of the area being fished, Curtis' balloon rig is unchanged. "Most of the time, I will position the balloon on the line so that it holds the shad about halfway between the surface and the bottom, resulting in a lead of 3 to 8 feet of line between the balloon and shad," said Curtis. "You really don't need to worry all that much about depth if you give the shad a long enough tether, because the shad will swim and change depths constantly. I never use a weight of any kind on the line because I want the shad to swim freely, even up to the surface. "A 6- to 7-foot, heavy-action casting rod is preferred. Curtis opts for a good baitcasting reel equipped with a clicker, and spooled with 17- to 20-pound test. A 2/0 Kahle or side-bend hook completes the rig. Jim always uses freshly netted shad and tries to match the size on which the fish have been feeding.

Curtis recommends inflating the balloon to about the size of a large orange and then tying it to the line with an overhand knot. "One of the keys to the technique is tying the balloon loosely so that the line can slip through the knot," he said. "But the knot

Balloons are superior to cork floats because they ride on top of the water. The live shad used for bait can swim naturally because the balloon creates so little resistance.

must be tight enough so that the air will not leak.

"I also like to use balloons of different colors on each rod so that I don't get them confused. When you are fishing with several people in the boat, for example, one can watch the green balloon, another will watch the red, and another will watch the yellow. Everyone is responsible for their assigned rod and balloon, and it saves a lot of confusion when the hybrids move in and start chasing the shad."

Confusion? While that may seem a bit far-fetched to the uninitiated, hybrid fishing is a roller coaster ride of angling thrills. Anglers often probe and search for hours on end without seeing a sign of fish. Then, suddenly, the calm surface will turn to a frothy boil and there will be a bruiser hybrid on every line.

"Ballooning is possibly the most exciting way to catch hybrids that I've ever seen," said Curtis. "When a hybrid moves in and starts looking at the bait, the shad will get excited and try to swim away, dragging your balloon with it. Then, when the hybrid moves in for the kill, the shad will usually dart to the surface, often leaping completely out of the water while the hybrid slaps and strikes at him. It really is one of the most exciting moments in fishing, bar none!"

When a hybrid finally grabs a shad, Curtis says that it will usually drag the balloon rapidly across the surface for several feet before pulling it down. "Sometimes, the balloon will disappear under the surface, but I'd say 75 percent of the time the line slides through the balloon's knot until the friction breaks the balloon. After the fish has run with the bait for a few feet, take up any slack in the line and set the hook. Be sure to remove the broken balloon from the line and dispose of it properly."

Curtis points out that ballooning shad is not actually a technique in and of itself, but rather a means of presenting live bait to the fish. As a result, he utilizes his balloon rig throughout the year, whenever the hybrids are shallow. "It is best suited for relatively shallow water, say, two to 15 feet, where the presence of a boat would spook the fish," he said. "Hybrids tend to feed in shallower waters during the cooler months of spring, so I use a balloon pres-

Ballooning Live Bait

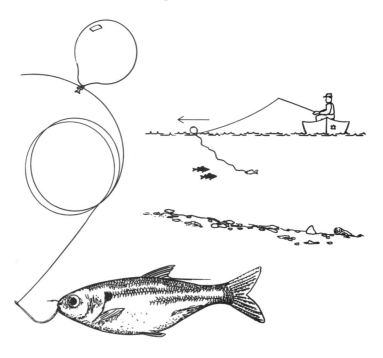

Wind, or current, can be used to take full advantage of ballooning. Tie the balloon directly to the unweighted line so that the live baitfish swims freely. Let the rig drift into likely habitat.

Balloons allow anglers to position their bait over feeding fish without spooking them.

entation most often at that time. Hybrids are low-light feeders, and even though they will hold in deep water during the days of summer, they will move shallow to feed in the mornings and evenings, and on cloudy, overcast days." In other words, while you may find ballooning applicable most often during the spring, do not overlook its potential throughout the year.

One of Curtis' favorite techniques is to use the wind to present his ballooned shad. "When the wind has been blowing onto a shallow flat, long point or underwater bar for several hours, hybrids will often move in to feed on the schools of shad that have followed drifting plankton to the downwind side of the reservoir," he said. "The balloon rig is one of the best ways to catch hybrids in this situation.

"I like to anchor the boat with the bow facing into the wind just upwind of the structure," Curtis continued. "Then, after rigging the shad on balloons, I'll drop them over the back of the boat and feed line while the wind carries the balloons onto the structure. This way, I never have to drive the boat over the structure and risk spooking the fish."

Curtis also uses the balloons when slow-trolling live bait. "When you need to cover a lot of water, trolling offers your best chance of hooking up with the fish," he said. "Often, you will find

the hybrids feeding along riprap below dams and under bridges
and trestles. These long expanses are difficult to cover thoroughly, so I prefer to slow-troll a live bait down the length of the
structure. Basically, I simply put the balloons out, place the rods in
rod holders on the side of the boat, let out 40 to 60 feet of line and
then start easing down the structure with my trolling motor."

Drift fishing is another approach in which balloons shine. In
the spring, when hybrids make their false spawning run upstream
from the lake into the river, Curtis will follow. "I like to find a section of the river along a well-defined channel where the lip is littered with stumps and debris," he said. "I will let out my balloons
30 to 60 feet and drift downstream using the trolling motor to
keep me over the top of the channel lip while the balloons trail
along behind the boat."

Bank Anglers Greatly Benefit From Ballooning

While bank-bound anglers are often handicapped in their
quest for hybrids, Curtis notes that ballooning can greatly improve their odds of catching fish. "Anglers fishing from the bank
(or even a bridge) can use a balloon to carry a live shad or minnow
well beyond casting distance," said Curtis. "The key is using the
wind or current to carry your balloon and bait to a productive
structure."

Though Curtis utilizes his balloon rig most often in his quest
for trophy hybrids, he is quick to point out that it is applicable to
live-bait fishing for virtually every species of fish. The same tactics
discussed in this chapter are suitable for striped bass as well as hybrids.

Ballooning golden shiners is a technique rapidly gaining favor
among Florida's trophy largemouth fishermen. Traditionally,
shiner anglers have used corks to suspend their offerings in and
around the thick mats of vegetation common in Florida's lakes
and ponds. But many have discovered that windblown balloons
enable them to present the shiner without damaging the bait
(casting dislodges scales) or spooking the fish. Balloons will also
pull through thick vegetation rather than hanging up like a cork
bobber. That is a big plus when a trophy largemouth swims off
with your shiner.

Jim Altman, a chemical engineer for Toyota Motor Manufacturing and a resident of Lexington, Kentucky, uses balloons to

This big hybrid bass fell to a live shad suspended under a balloon.

present small bluegills when searching for bass in farm ponds through the South. "Most of the time I am fishing from the shore," he said, "and by utilizing the wind, I can use balloons to present bluegills to weedbeds and brush piles beyond my casting range. And when a bass takes off with my bait, the balloon will either slide on the line or break, so the bass feels little or no resistance, which might otherwise prompt him to drop my bait!"

Ballooning is a creative live-bait presentation that can be applied in fishing situations from coast to coast. Use your imagination. The possibilities are endless!

31

Spot And Chase Summer Schools

by Soc Clay

T hey wait in the evening, scattered along wide places in the lake. Silent, they keep a constant vigil, ever watching for signs of schooling shad—dark splotches riffling the calm surface of the water.

Their boats range from sleek and fast to squat and slow. The outboards idle, sending out streamers of steam, even into the sultry air of midsummer. The gatherers consist of some of the best fishermen on the lake. There are rank amateurs among them as well. It requires no special skill to experience the excitement that occurs when 100, or perhaps 300, aggressive, hungry fish herd hapless minnows into a tight wad on the surface and then attack. One just has to be there, close-in, ready with waiting rod, cocked bail and a flashy lure that will travel some distance. It is summertime, and in many lakes and rivers across the country, white bass numbers are up and growing.

The white bass, a member of the true sea bass family and close relative to the ocean-going striped bass, were once native only to Lake Erie and several large river systems found in the upper South and much of the Midwest. Over the years, the species has also been widely stocked in many of the nation's largest reservoirs. Some argue that the very best fishing for the species occurs in Lake Erie during early summer when it is possible to catch hundreds of these hard-fighting fish in a single day. River fishermen often do equally well in the mid and upper reaches of the Mississippi and Ohio rivers. In all, the National Fresh Water Fishing

Charley Taylor's favorite times for chasing hungry, schooling white bass are the hours of early morning or late afternoon.

Spot And Chase Summer Schools

Hall of Fame lists a total of 35 states that keep records for the largest of the species, which grows to more than 5 pounds.

One thing is certain, however. Regardless of where the species is found, the most exciting time to fish for this gamester is during midsummer when they collect in huge numbers and prowl surface regions looking for schools of spring-hatched baitfish.

Following The Constant Movements Of White Bass

White bass, also known as silver bass, sand bass and streakers, are movers. They swim ceaselessly during the day, searching for schools of small shad or other baitfish. Like wolves, they hunt in packs of as many as 300 fish. They literally surround hapless baitfish and herd them to the surface before a vicious, slashing attack begins. The white bass' objective is to eat or injure as many baitfish during the assault as possible.

During the summer, when shad or other spring-hatched baitfish reach desirable size (between $1^{1}/_{2}$ and 2 inches in length), great schools of hunting whites prowl the near-surface area of large creek arms and main lake bodies searching for schooling baitfish that are drawn to the surface to feed on zooplankton. One such school observed on Iowa's Spirit Lake during the 1940s was estimated to cover 40 acres. The attacks normally occur in the morning hours or late afternoon when the sun drops near the horizon, allowing light-sensitive phytoplankton (the principal food supply for zooplankton) to float to the surface to feed on nutrients in the water.

A Guide Talks About White Bass

Charley Taylor, a 53-year-old fishing guide, school teacher and President of T's Lure Company in Somerset, Kentucky, has been spotting and chasing the "jumps" on lakes spread out across the middle belt of the U.S. for the past 30 years.

For Taylor, the two best times of the day to cash in on the aggressive feeding behavior of white bass is from 7 to 9 a.m. and from 7 p.m. until dark.

The size of baitfish in a river or reservoir will determine the start of the jump-fishing season. White bass have a smaller mouth than largemouth bass and favor smaller minnows to feed upon. Once spring-hatched baitfish reach the $1^{1}/_{2}$- to $2^{1}/_{2}$-inch size and begin schooling on the surface, white bass go into action. This can

Complete Angler's Library

occur as early as late May in some southern reservoirs and as late as early August in the species' northernmost range.

Where the jumps occur in lakes, reservoirs or rivers will often be determined by the clarity of the water. If there is the slightest bit of color to the main lake body or major creek arms, Taylor targets these places first. Most times, he looks for jumps to begin in big bend areas in the main lake or the largest coves found in the big creek arms, since both white bass and shad prefer open water during this period. The idea, he says, is to first spot the schools of shad and follow the heaviest concentrations at a distance, waiting for the attack to begin. Gulls and other fish-eating birds will often reveal the location of the next jump during heavy activity. Once the attack begins, however, it churns the surface into a foaming froth that can be seen from a mile away.

Spotting And Chasing Gets You Within Casting Range

When the jump starts, the guide cranks the outboard and runs the boat at full speed to within a long casting distance, targeting the leading edge of the fleeing shad before shutting down. The guide's choice is a $6^1/2$- to 7-foot, light-action rod balanced with an open-faced spinning reel (preferably the new models that feature elongated spools for longer casting distance). It should be spooled with 6-pound test clear monofilament. This setup is ideal for making long, accurate casts with a variety of lures, including the $^1/2$-ounce Mr. Champ, Kastmaster spoon, $^1/4$-ounce leadhead jig dressed with 2-inch plastic grub or a heavy chugger-type plug with an 18-inch length of leader attached to the back hook eyelet and a white, single-hook hair streamer fly tied to the end of the trailing line. Small tube-jigs are also deadly for white bass at any depth. For jump-fishing, a $^1/2$-ounce wooden float (the long, slender kind) should be attached to the line a foot above the lure to give added casting distance.

When selecting lures, Taylor believes it is important to choose a design that is similar in shape, length and color to the baitfish on which the white bass are feeding; the chugger and trailer fly is a good example. The guide looks for long, hair-hackle streamers that he can clip to match the size of the baitfish. To rig the trailer fly, he selects a $^5/8$-ounce topwater plug such as the Heddon Chugger or the old Lucky 13 and ties an 18-inch length of leader with the fly attached to the back hook eye (the hook should be re-

Erie Rig For White Bass

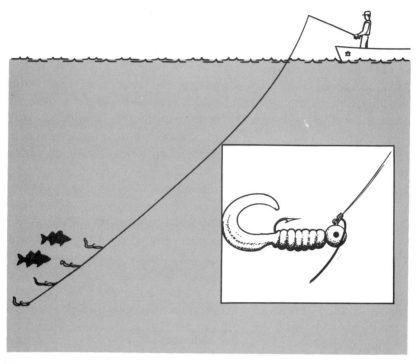

Rig multiple jigs by tying the first lure with an improved clinch knot, leaving the tag end long. Space, and tie, the second lure on the tag end and repeat. When bass are schooling, it is not uncommon to catch more than one on a single cast.

moved to prevent tangling). This rig can be cast long distances and the chugging action will often attract feeding white bass when a straight retrieve fails. In most instances the fish will strike the fly, but sometimes they pounce on the plug as well.

Rarely, Taylor notes, do schools of feeding white bass refuse to take artificial lures. When that happens, he suggests you look for a new school of breaking fish rather than spend time trying to figure out this sometimes moody species.

Another trick Taylor uses when fishing the jumps is to bend the barbs on the hook(s) down with a pair of pliers so that when a white bass takes the bait it can be reeled to the boat, lifted in and allowed to flop free of the lure on the bottom of the boat. Using this technique, Taylor has time to get in several more casts before the school leaves the surface. He also keeps two or more rods rigged with various lures in case his first choice fails to attract an immediate strike. Also, if a fish is hooked too deeply to come off easily, he can lay the first rod down and begin casting with another while the school is still feeding on the surface.

Dealing With Spooky Fish

Sometimes the attacking school of white bass is easily spooked. When this occurs, Taylor shuts his big motor down a good distance away and closes in with the trolling motor on high, approaching the feeding fish on a 45-degree angle, aiming the boat ahead of the fleeing minnows.

When the lake is extremely clear a school of white bass will often surface for only a short time before sounding. This makes for tough fishing, but Taylor says fish can still be caught by allowing a spoon such as a Blade Runner, manufactured by Hogeye Lures or a blade-type like Cordell's Gay Blade or Heddon's Sonar lure to flutter down to the 10- to 20-foot depths before beginning the retrieve. Watch the line, though, because many bites come while the lure is dropping.

Chugger And Fly Rig

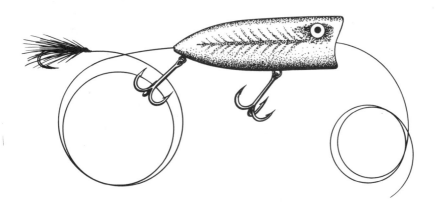

Rig a trailer fly to a chugger to catch white bass. The large, floating plug attracts attention, often followed by a strike on the fly.

Any small jig will catch white bass when they begin chasing shad. Lighter colors are preferred.

The easiest white bass to catch, the Kentucky fishing guide believes, are the ones that attack schooling baitfish near shore or when the water is stained (not muddy), which causes shad to move more slowly.

When the attack begins near shore, white bass are able to herd the shad and prevent them from escaping quickly into open water. As long as the baitfish are on the surface, the attack will continue. In stained or cloudy water, shad can't see well and move more slowly, again causing the attack on the surface to last longer. In both of these instances, white bass don't appear to be very selective in what they bite, thus allowing anglers a wider choice of lures.

As darkness falls, Taylor continues to capitalize on the white's schooling tendency by marking the spot nearest shore where the last school appeared. Then, by running a long tie-off line from the bank and laying out an anchor in deep water, he is able to position the boat well offshore, over drop-offs and other places where schools of white bass will be found at night. Gasoline lanterns or floating electric spotlights are positioned directly above the bottom structure. When baitfish begin to show up under the lights, he catches even more fish by vertically jigging $1/2$-ounce Hopkins spoons or blade-type lures like Heddon Sonar or a Silver Buddy.

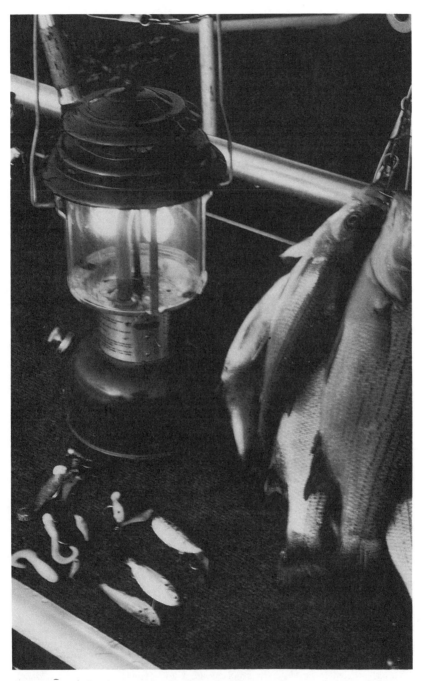

Anchoring over white bass in a shoreline area where they were last seen during surfacing can result in some great night fishing.

Spot And Chase Summer Schools

White bass are scrappy fighters and a day of catching 1- to 3-pound fish can exhaust a fisherman. When the bass are chasing shad, it is not uncommon for Charley Taylor and his clients to
catch 100 fish each in a day.

Live minnows are also highly effective for white bass at night.

A graph or LCR is a great aid for angling at night. When fishing without the aid of electronics, it is best to lower the bait down to about the 30-foot level, and raise it five feet at a time until bites occur. A bonus in this type of fishing may be had by casting floating Rapalas outside the perimeter of light. Walleyes are often found in the area where baitfish are collecting around the flickering light beams.

In addition to the dog-day period, white bass go on the jump again in late September and early October when the second-spawn shad reach desirable feeding size. Three-inch floating minnows such as Rapalas or A.C. Shiners with black backs and silver sides are deadly when jerked through the feeding fish. So are fly rod poppers and streamer flies presented from a good distance by expert long-line casters. Tiny tube jigs in white, yellow or chartreuse also work wonders for feeding whites during this season of intense feeding activity.

The Lake Erie rig that features three, or even four, $1/8$-ounce leadhead jigs dressed with 2-inch wiggletail grubs, is also productive, even in smaller lakes and rivers. The idea behind the multi-jig rigging is to simulate your own school of fleeing baitfish. Double and triple catches are frequent. Any bright colors seem to work well.

By following Charley Taylor's tips, even the casual angler can feel like an expert. It's easy to feel that way when you're fighting fish until your arms get sore—and the cooperative white bass provides that kind of action.

Catch And Release

32

The Future
Of Angling?

by John Daily

Most anglers think of fishing as a chain of events that starts with casting a lure or bait, includes catching some fish, and ends with a delicious golden brown fillet in a frying pan.

But these days the routine may go like this: An angler casts, hooks a fish, plays it, boats it and then releases it back to the lake to be caught again by someone else. Anglers are now finding they don't have to take home a limit of fish to be satisfied.

How did this new sportsman ethic come about?

A catch-and-release symposium in 1977 made the nation's fisheries managers aware of the concept as a possible management tool. At the time, this practice as a management tool was virtually untried. Most of the fisheries managers were using such tools as closed seasons and bag limits.

These management programs tried to increase the harvest of fish, while providing better growth and increased recruitment (successful spawning and survival). Fish stocking was emphasized. Creel censuses counted only fish caught, because harvest was the usual measure of fishing success. The idea that waters could be overharvested was new.

Once fisheries managers realized that overharvest can occur on intensively fished waters, they initiated many new regulations. Slot limits, size limits, further reductions in bag limits, and catch and release (voluntary or regulated) are improving the fishing in numerous waters where these practices are in place.

Anglers are now seeing that large, adult fish are more valuable in the water than on a stringer. The result is an increase in catch-and-release fishing.

The Future Of Angling?

Index

T

Tackle, 10-14
Tailbaits, 305, 310
Taylor, Charley, 336-343
Teddie Bait, 304
Telescopic rods, 96
Tench, 98
Tennessee River, 148, 154
Texas-style rigs, 37, 38, 56, 58
Thermal bars, 252
Thermoclines, 64, 265
Thermoshock, 350, 351
Thill, Mick, 98-107
Third Sister Lake, 112
Three-way rigs, 176, 178
Time of day, 21, 164, 308, 336, 340
Tippet, 241
Tip-ups, 292, 295-296
Tollett, Tim, 234-243
Topographical maps, 92, 142, 144, 147, 320
Topwater plugs, 316
Topwater techniques, 24-26
Treble hooks, 33, 152, 160, 249
Trolling, 90, 185-187, 187-189, 200, 253-255, 272-281, 331
Trolling spoons, 176
Trout, 98, 118, 234-243, 244, 252-253, 255
  brown, 118, 243
  lake, 118
  rainbow, 243
  Skamania steelhead, 253, 255
  steelhead, 118, 222-233, 244, 252-253
Tube-jigs, 337
Tuck cast, 234, 239
Twist-ons, 240
Two-hook snells, 184

U

Ultra-light tackle, 98, 100, 154, 352

V

Vegetation, 38, 40

W

Walking sinker, 163, 183

Walleye weed, 192
Walleyes, 168-179, 190-199, 253-255
Water cabbage, 14
Water clarity, 30, 36, 46, 68, 111, 153, 160, 265, 319, 337, 339-340
Water conditions, 17
Water depth, 14, 15, 17, 21, 68, 80, 89, 93, 164, 249-250, 278, 306
Water hyacinths, 14
Water levels, 228-230, 306
Water temperature, 47-48, 70, 72, 73, 87, 164, 89, 144, 148, 158, 319-320
Waterweed, 192
Wax worm, 134-135
Weather conditions, 24, 46, 231-233, 262, 265, 289-290, 308, 328
Weedbeds, 71, 73, 82, 84, 190-199
Weedless hooks, 12
Weedlines, 306-309
Wee Steelie Wart, 224
Wee Wart, 224
West Point Lake, 326
White bass, 326, 334-343
Whitefish, 286
Wigglers, 120
Wiggle Wart, 224
Wilkins, Greg, 116-125
Williams, Larry, 44-53
Wilson, Dave, 314-325
Wind, 46, 51
Windels Muskie Hunter, 304
Windels Whaletail, 304
Wire line, 168-179
World Northern Pike Championship, 302
Worms, 40-43, 58
Worm jerking, 34, 40-43

Y

Yakima Hawg Boss, 249
Yellow perch, 116

Z

Zara Spook, 29
Zoom Bait Company, 34, 36
Zooplankton, 336